Items s...
sho...
b...
t...
b...
Th...
H...
Fir...
inc...
be

L...

Born to Ride

Stephen Roche
with Peter Cossins

Born to Ride

YELLOW JERSEY PRESS

LONDON

Published by Yellow Jersey Press 2012

2 4 6 8 10 9 7 5 3 1

First published in Great Britain in 2012 by
Yellow Jersey Press
Random House, 20 Vauxhall Bridge Road,
London SW1V 2SA

www.vintage-books.co.uk

Addresses for companies within The Random House Group Limited can be found at:
www.randomhouse.co.uk/offices.htm

The Random House Group Limited Reg. No. 954009

A CIP catalogue record for this book
is available from the British Library

ISBN 9780224091909

The Random House Group Limited supports The Forest Stewardship Council
(FSC®), the leading international forest certification organisation. Our books
carrying the FSC label are printed on FSC® certified paper. FSC is the only forest
certification scheme endorsed by the leading environmental organisations,
including Greenpeace. Our paper procurement policy can be found at:
www.randomhouse.co.uk/environment

Printed and bound by CPI Group (UK) Ltd, Croydon, CR0 4YY

To my mother and father.
None of this would have happened without you.

CONTENTS

LIST OF ILLUSTRATIONS

AUSTRIA: 6 SEPTEMBER 1987

Lying in my bed in the hotel room I can hear the rain hammering down outside. Yesterday the temperature had been well over 30 degrees, but it feels an awful lot cooler now. I smile, and guess that Sean Kelly, lying in bed across our shared room, is probably smiling too.

I don't suppose either of us really fancies the prospect of spending up to seven hours enduring lashing rain and muscle-numbing cold in one of the toughest and most important races of the season, but if you're an Irish cyclist you're not going to be unfamiliar with those conditions. I won't say I like the bad weather, but it suits me better than the heat. Although I like the sun on my back as much as anyone when racing, I know the heat doesn't entirely agree with me.

It isn't the rain that has got me smiling, though. Hearing the growing buzz of activity in the building around us and imagining the same kind of activity in hotels throughout Villach, the Austrian ski resort hosting the 1987 World Championships, I can picture my 160-odd opponents gathering their thoughts ahead of the biggest one-day race of the season.

I'm sure half of them are thinking: 'Oh shit, it's raining.' That will immediately ensure they are below their normal level, so I can count them out as realistic rivals. Then there are another few per cent who don't ride well in the wet. I can count them out too. Then there are the guys who think they're in form but aren't. I can strike them off the list as well.

Then there are the guys who are going to crash. They're gone too.

Consequently, among my 167 opponents who will be racing for the honour of wearing the rainbow bands of the world champion, there are just a few who are realistically in contention. I don't know whether others count me among them, but I do know that if I can keep my nose clean and stay clear of trouble, there is a good chance I am going to be in the final shake-up. It's been that kind of season: everything has gone my way and the sudden arrival of the rain fires my optimism, which had dimmed in recent weeks.

Just a couple of weeks earlier I wouldn't have even entertained the slightest thought of victory at the Worlds. After the Tour, I had ridden some very lucrative criteriums in Belgium, Holland and France. One of them was on a circuit over the cobbled climb of the Oude Kwaremont, one of the key sections in the Tour of Flanders. We had to go over it 16 times – a crazy test for a criterium. It was wet too, making it even tougher. At one point my rear wheel slipped on the cobbles and I hurt my thigh muscle. I thought I'd torn something. I realised the injury was probably due to fatigue. I had to ease off.

Although the money was good, I cancelled my remaining criterium commitments and went to join my wife Lydia and young children, Nicolas and Christel, at my in-laws' holiday home on the Ile d'Oléron, near La Rochelle. I rested for a week, before starting to train again for the Worlds, getting up every day at six in the morning to avoid the heat. Next up, I rode in a series of three pre-Worlds preparation races in Italy with my Carrera team. I was in good form, but still kind of sluggish.

From Italy I had ridden across into Austria with my Irish teammates, Sean Kelly, Martin Earley and Paul Kimmage. We had arrived in Villach a couple of days before the road race, where, in theory, I had the chance to become just the second rider in history, after Eddy Merckx, to win the Giro, Tour and Worlds in the same season. But Merckx was a rider apart, untouchable, a phenomenon. His achievement could not be repeated. Besides, everyone – the great Merckx included – insisted that the course in Villach would suit a rider with a strong finishing sprint, which counted me out. Defending champion Moreno Argentin was most people's favourite, but our own Sean Kelly was getting good reviews as well. For the whole year, my objective for the Worlds had been to do what I could to help Sean take the rainbow jersey. The so-called Triple Crown hadn't entered my thoughts.

That suited me because it removed a lot of expectation. I'd been riding very hard and leading a team since February. I didn't need any more pressure. I didn't have it in my head that I could be world champion because everyone was saying it's a flat race. I was there to make up the numbers, to help Sean, the one Irish pro with a fearsome finishing sprint. That was it.

However, when I rode the circuit myself, I re-evaluated. I went out with Sean, Martin, Kimmage and our final teammate, Alan McCormack, in the 30+ degree heat, rode a lap and said to myself: 'This circuit ain't for no sprinter.' It was easy for one lap, not too tough at all, but we were set to do 23. I didn't tell anyone else, but I was sure it wasn't going to be a course for a sprinter. There were two climbs on it for starters. Going up past the start/finish line there was a climb of maybe 3 or 4km – a long drag really – but we would be going up it 23 times, so it would get increasingly difficult. There was another hill on the far side of the circuit. This one was much steeper. It was this second hill that got me thinking for the first time that, given good form and good luck, I might have a chance.

I still felt it was just a small chance, though. My season had been injury-free, but in the days leading up to the Worlds the knee problems that had all but wiped out the previous season for me had returned. I'd had pain in my left knee since those post-Tour criteriums and it was getting worse. Even the friction of my legwarmers over my knee made riding agony. I could only deal with it by cutting a hole in them around the sore point.

The heat, though, was beyond my control. The day before the race it had been 35, 36 degrees. I'd been saying to myself: 'Jeez, if it's going to be as hot as this, I'm going to suffer tomorrow.' I'd met up with Carrera directeur Davide Boifava and his assistant, Sandro Quintarelli, and bought us all an ice cream. They couldn't believe I was having an ice cream, consuming all of those calories the day before the Worlds. They told me the Italian riders would never consider doing such a thing, but I felt it would have done me more harm not having it and wanting it, than actually having it. Besides, the Worlds wasn't my race to win, was it?

But, lying in bed, hearing the rain slapping the window, I'm thinking: 'This will make it interesting.' Perhaps things might go my way.

I get dressed and join my teammates for breakfast. In the middle of it I am called across to the reception desk to take a phone call. It's my friend Angelo ringing me from Paris. He tells me I can achieve what Merckx has done. I'm listening to him, not really believing him, saying: 'Yeah, yeah, yeah, yeah! OK, OK. I'll talk to you later.' I put the phone down and notice I've been fiddling with something. It's the key to room 13 that someone has left on the desk. I'm a bit taken aback. I'm not overly super-stitious, but the number 13 seems to have some significance for me. It feels a bit strange, but it's nothing. Just a coincidence.

When the race gets under way I have three raincoats on – two light ones and a heavy plastic one over the top. Ahead of us lie 23 laps of the 12km circuit – 276km in total. I decide to keep the heavy raincoat on for the first hour or so. The rain continues to pour down, but after a couple of hours it starts to ease off and it's a relief to get rid of my top layer when it does. During these early laps I am just staying in the wheels, sheltering from the wind behind other riders, freewheeling almost. That's obviously an exaggeration, but that's how easy I want it to feel, so that I can save everything I can for the end.

As usual, I've given a lot of thought to my choice of gearing over the last couple of days leading into the race. Almost everyone else has selected a straight-through 12–18 block, the seven sprockets on the rear wheel providing a uniform range of gears. However, my thinking is that I want to be able to use the 18 as my last sprocket if it comes down to the crunch on the final climb during the last lap. When you have a 12–18 block and select the 18 to make an attack, the rear mech can easily end up caught in the wheel because it is sitting so close to the spokes. So I've opted for a 12–20 block, which means that I can use my big chainring with the 18 because it will be my second-last sprocket. It should give me more leverage and therefore enable me to generate more power than someone who is riding the equivalent gear ratio on the small ring, which may prove significant at the end of 270-odd kilometres of racing.

As the laps tick by, I remain in the wheels, saving energy by letting others sit in the wind. Every time I hit the two hills, I put it in the small ring and pedal as easily as I can, using as little energy as possible. Three hours in and I take off another jacket. The race is starting to open up. From time to time groups of riders break away but Sean, Paul, Martin, Alan and I aren't worrying because so far there have always been others prepared to bring them back. Argentin's Italian team is 13-strong, while all of the major cycling powers including France, Holland, Belgium and Spain have teams of 12. Martin Earley and Paul Kimmage are also doing a good job in keeping the pack together, but it's complicated trying to know when to commit resources from a five-man team that's vastly underpowered compared to many others.

The wet conditions provide another complicating factor: crashes. There are plenty of them, especially on the descents, which are treacherous. Fortunately, the Irish lads are staying upright.

With five laps to go the speed increases significantly. Italian leader Argentin goes clear with Holland's Teun van Vliet, Spain's Juan Fernández and Belgium's Jan Nevens. We sit tight for a while as the French organise the chase behind. The four leaders open a gap of almost a minute. The French are struggling to get it back. Martin joins them in driving the pursuit. The gap is coming down as we hurtle through the start/finish line to complete the fastest lap of the race. With less than four laps to the finish, I come out of the wheels for the first time, driving on the front of the bunch with Martin. We're bringing everyone back up to Argentin's group, but we know there's sure to be an attack when it comes back together.

With three laps to go the speed is relentlessly fast. Riders are consistently going out of the back now, their hopes of victory gone as the main pack leaves them. Belgium's Claude Criquielion attacks. France's Gilbert Duclos-Lassalle and Italy's new young star, Maurizio Fondriest, jump across to join him. I need to keep the race together for Sean, so that he has a shot at the sprint finish, but also keep the pace high enough that riders continue to drop out of contention. My acceleration splits the peloton for a while, taking 20-odd riders across to join the three leaders. The bigger group behind soon comes back up to us again, though.

On the penultimate lap, Holland's Erik Breukink, who had pushed me hard at the Giro, goes off solo. But there's no chance of one man staying clear with everyone this committed. The USA's Andy Hampsten tries his luck, and I chase him down.

Coming into the final lap and going into the first climb for the last time, another small group goes clear. I jump to the front of the peloton with Sean on my wheel and we ride away across to them. I go straight to the front and lead up the climb in my big ring.

It is almost the first time I've gone up this climb in the big ring and for most of the next 3km I am out of the saddle, winding it up as we go over the top. We've got a gap. I look around and see we've got a nice bunch of lads with us. Argentin is there, as are Criquielion, Germany's Rolf Gölz, Holland's Breukink, van Vliet and Steven Rooks, France's Marc Madiot, Denmark's Rolf Sørensen, Canada's Steve Bauer, Spain's Fernández and Switzerland's Guido Winterberg. There are 13 of us, and Switzerland's Jogi Müller joins us to make it 14 before the final climb.

I keep riding hard at the front to make sure the main bunch can't close the gap. Every time the pace decreases, I go to the front again. It's not just a case of going to the back, coming through and doing my turn. I am doing more than my turn to ensure the peloton remains out of range.

We drop down the descent and head around to the steeper climb for the final time. There is a flurry of attacks but Sean and I chase them down. One guy does get dropped, though. Madiot falls out of contention. We're back to 13 again. That number.

We hammer up the climb. I've still got Sean on my wheel. As we go over the top with about 4km remaining, I think to myself: 'If I keep riding like this, I'm not going to be able to lead Sean out for the sprint.' I drop towards the back of the line to get a bit of a breather.

A couple more attempts are neutralised, then van Vliet attacks and Gölz takes off after him. A gap starts to open so I accelerate away from the back of the line, jump onto Gölz's wheel and we join up with van Vliet. Winterberg and Sørensen are quick to follow, making it five at the front.

I'm expecting more riders to respond, but guess that everyone is waiting for Argentin to commit himself. He's the favourite, he's the only rider from the race's strongest team and he's defending the title. But the gap widens and I start wondering: 'What am I going to do?' I know I'm not going to beat these guys in a straight-up sprint: Gölz and van Vliet are much, much faster than me. I decide I'd better hold fire until the group comes back together again.

It soon becomes clear, though, that Sean's group isn't going to get back to us. 'OK, I've got to do something myself now because I don't want to finish fifth out of five,' I think to myself. My brain is ticking over rapidly, sizing up the situation. We drop down the descent into the final corner and up to the left I can see the finishing line, 400 metres away. The approach to it is flattish to start with, then rears up a bit underneath a bridge 150 metres short of the line.

In a few split seconds, I analyse everything. I know there is going to be some tension between Gölz and van Vliet as they are equally good in the sprint. If I surprise them by attacking, van Vliet knows that if he responds Gölz will chase him and will win because he'll be sprinting from a better position. If Gölz goes after me, he knows that van Vliet will chase him down and win for the same reason. Neither man will want the other to win having coming off their wheel. 'OK, that's those two covered,' I think. Sørensen is currently on the front, the worst position to be in as he won't see the attacks coming, so that's him covered as well.

I'm fourth in line but I have Winterberg on my wheel. If I'm right, he represents my biggest threat. How am I going to work this out? We swing in a wide arc around the corner into the finishing straight. The wind is coming off the right, so automatically we are hugging the left-hand side of the road. I wait, and wait, and wait.

I know that if I go on the right, I'll be heading into the wind with Winterberg on my wheel. Ultimately, he will come off my wheel and beat me. That's not the solution. I want to go and take no prisoners.

I keep waiting, noticing the gap against the left-hand barriers starting to narrow as Sørensen drifts left in the wind. It is beginning to disappear altogether when I accelerate, the instant zip provided by the 18 sprocket immediately putting some vital distance between Winterberg and me. I shoot down the blind side, past Sørensen's left shoulder just as he's about to shut the gap along the barriers. I'm out into the open and can sense that there's no one on my wheel. I guess that Winterberg has tried to follow my line of attack but has been baulked by Sørensen, who in turn is waiting for Gölz and van Vliet to react.

I get 10 metres clear, pumping the pedals as hard and as fast as I can. I take a quick look under my arm and can't quite believe it. 'Where are they? I'm going to win this thing.' I've not won a championship since taking the Irish junior crown in 1977. I never lead out and win sprints.

Then it's over. I throw both arms in the air, coast across the line. I've won the World Championship. I look back and see Sean sprinting for second place, but Argentin, the man everyone had to beat, is too quick and claims silver. Juan Fernández takes the bronze. But even as they are finishing, Sean has his arms in the air, an instinctive, heartfelt act from a genuine friend. He rides alongside me and, for a moment, we have our arms around each other. Then the press descend on us. There are microphones and mayhem.

'Stephen Roche, world champion, you've won the Triple Crown. How did you do it?'

CHAPTER 1

FROM PINCUSHIONS TO PEUGEOT

Although there was no racing history in my family at all, cycling did play a vital part in bringing my parents together. My father, Larry Roche, rode everywhere on his bike and often went out touring in the countryside around Dublin. My mother, Bunny Samson, was one of a group of girls who wanted to form a touring club but didn't know where to start. Larry offered his services and organised rides around Dublin for the group. The two of them started as friends and their relationship developed from there.

I was born on 28 November 1959, the second of six children. My elder sister Maria is 11 months older than me, then I came along, and eighteen months later came Carol. My brother Jude's about a year younger than her, then Laurence and finally Pamela. It's a large family by today's standards.

Like most kids I must have been three or four when my parents got me my first bike. It was a small blue children's bike that they bought at a second-hand shop down in Ranelagh where my mother was brought up. I never really had any big interest in cycling as a young kid. Like everyone else I played a bit of football, went swimming and just knocked around. I also worked with my dad on his milk round.

Later on I had a Chopper, which I used to deliver papers with a friend of mine, Derek Doyle. We delivered all around my estate and his. We used to earn one penny per paper, which wasn't much, but I would ask people to keep the papers for me and at the end of the week I'd go around and collect them and sell them back to the paper mill.

I guess seeing me delivering papers on my bike planted a seed in the head of Pat Flynn, one of my parents' neighbours. It was she who first thought that cycling might be the sport for me. Our estate was U-shaped and in the middle of that U was a playing field where the neighbourhood kids used to meet to play football. One day, I would have been thirteen years old, I was playing in goal when Pat walked off the usual path across the field to talk to me.

Pat knew everything that went on in the neighbourhood and said she had seen me out on my bike and seemed to like it. She explained that a new cycling club would be meeting outside the H. Williams supermarket the following Wednesday night and that if I was interested in riding a bit more I should go along. I said OK. That was my first step towards a bike-racing career and Pat's husband Steve would soon help me take many more. A good rider and one of the best wheelbuilders I've ever met, Steve quickly became a very good friend and mentor, taking me out on training rides and showing me not so much how to ride a bike, but how to enjoy the bike.

The club that met that Wednesday outside the local super-market was a section of the Orwell Wheelers, a Dublin bike club that had just re-formed. Three guys ran it – Paddy Doran, Noel O'Neill and the late Noel Hammond. Noel O'Neill had become the club coach after finishing his own racing career, which had reached international level, while Paddy was still racing at that time. Noel Hammond was one of the mainstays of the club and later took me on one of my first international trips to Junior Week in Harrogate. Every Wednesday night we'd meet up and ride in the countryside surrounding Dublin.

Encouraged by Noel, Paddy and Steve, I started to get a taste for riding and, not before too long, for racing as well. My first victory came in a slow bicycle race. The idea was to take as long as you possibly could to cover a short course. My victory prize was a pincushion, which my parents still have at home now.

I can just about remember my first road race victory as a 13-year-old. I was away in a break with a friend of mind called Paul Tansey, whose dad used to run Joe Daly Cycles in Dundrum. It was Joe who organised the charity race every year from Dundrum to Enniskerry and back that would, many years later, see my son Nicolas make his first competitive racing appearance. Anyway, this circuit we were on featured a very steep descent down from the Golden Ball bar, then a sharp left-hand turn into a long finishing straight on Ballyogan Road. We were going so quick down the hill that Paul missed the left turn and I only just managed to make it. I veered left onto a false flat that was perhaps a mile long and gave it all I had, my legs poking out all over the place. But I managed to hold on and win.

I liked the atmosphere of racing straight off. It also appealed because you could just turn up at an event and race. You didn't need to get picked like you did in football, where you'd play with your mates from Monday to Saturday then on Sunday end up sitting on the bench watching them play because you weren't good enough. With cycling, I would ride with my friends all week and then race with them on the weekend. It didn't matter whether you won, lost or even finished. The important thing was that we were able to compete together.

That winter Paddy Doran gave me an old frame and Steve Flynn gave me a pair of wheels to go with it. I've still got the front wheel from that set now, more than 30 years on, and it's still dead straight. Someone else got me a pair of brakes and I built the bike up, sprayed the frame blue and raced on it the following season. It was a 23-inch frame and I ended up riding a 22, so it was a bit big for me, but that bike gave me a few good runs until the frame broke a week before the National Championships. The timing of that wasn't great, but luckily my grandfather gave me the money to buy my first bike, which was a Mercian. To repay his generosity, I did some maintenance work on his caravan and his blue Fiat 124, which he later sold to me when I got my driving licence. I still have that bike at home in Ireland now and plan to get it renovated.

My parents very rarely came to see me racing because of family and work commitments. The important thing for my parents was that I was riding my bike in the fresh air and that I was enjoying it. They never thought, and no one else did either, that cycling could become a way of life. They were more concerned that I get my schooling done and get started with an apprenticeship.

In fact, my dad didn't use to hide the fact that he was against me getting heavily involved in racing because it might interfere with my schooling. He was also worried about me getting injured. Consequently, the first time I won a prize in a road race I hid my success from him. I say 'success', but I didn't actually win the race in question. I was the first finisher on high-pressure tyres – in fact, I was the only rider on high-pressure tyres. I won a set of draughts and chess in a box. I brought it home and had to hide it in the house. One day somebody found it and the question was asked of us where it had come from. I admitted, 'Er, well, I kind of won a prize in a race, you know . . .'

I'm sure my parents knew full well what I was up to. In fact, I used to talk about my cycling with Dad when I'd go out on the milk round with him. I had been helping him out there since I was five years old. Even when I went back home at the weekends or in the winter when I was racing I'd still go out and deliver the milk with him. I didn't need to, but I used to love the contact. I'd get up at three or four in the morning, go out on the rounds with Dad and be back home by nine or ten, feeling really happy that I'd done a day's work.

A large part of the enjoyment came from being with him. He liked having me along and I learned so much from him. He was so pleasant and polite to people, so professional in his job. He would do everything to the letter and his service was always 100 per cent for the client. I think that definitely rubbed off on me and subsequently on my son, Nicolas, in terms of our interaction with people and with the media. It's something that you either have or haven't got.

Even now, it's incredible going out with my dad because everyone remembers him. He used to be a milkman in Dun Laoghaire 50 years ago, a milkman in Dollymount 20 years ago, and he was a security officer at the Superquinn store in Blackrock 10 years ago. I've met people from all those different decades today who recognise him and all have a great word to say about the man. That's incredible in its own way. My mum and dad were my role models. It wasn't as if they hammered into me that you had to be nice to people; it was more a case of good manners starting at home.

I was never really one for school. In fact, I was considered a bit of a write-off, but I got my Junior Certificate and at the age of 15 or 16 I started my apprenticeship to be a fitter at Hughes Dairy, where my dad worked. The one thing that Dad always insisted on when us kids started working was that we had to give Mum our wages. We would come in from work on payday, hand over our pay packets and Mum would take out what she needed and give us something back. Us six kids all had to contribute to the household when we could.

I guess my dad's view was quite traditional, in as much as he felt that he was preparing us kids for later in life when we were working. In those days you would give your money to your wife, as she'd be the one looking after the house. I didn't mind that at all and never thought to question it, mainly because I really enjoyed the work I was doing. I used to love going to work in the mornings. I always used to clock in at 8.23 for an 8.30 start and was very proud of being so punctual. I'm not quite the same now, though . . .

I learned so much from the guys I used to work with and became particularly skilful with my hands. Even now I can do almost anything with them. I've built houses, refitted apartments and done renovations. I've also taken apart and rebuilt more cars than I can remember. When it comes to things like that I'm not afraid of anything, which is thanks to my dad and to the people I used to work with. In fact, those skills enabled me to earn some decent money from odd-jobs that went straight into my pocket.

One of my friends from school, David Kneeshaw, who had also been told that he wasn't likely to get anywhere, had gone into carpentry and the two of us started a bit of a business on the side. My maintenance work gave me experience in plumbing, central heating, refrigeration, welding and the mechanical side of things, so if neighbours or friends wanted a kitchen fitted David would put it in and I'd do the plumbing. David left Ireland for the USA in 1987 and he now has 30-odd guys working for him, fitting libraries and bars with high-quality furniture. We're still friends and we often laugh about those early days.

If I'm asked what I would have done if racing hadn't turned out how it did for me, I look back on those days and think I would have probably done OK. Certainly I was doing well enough by the time I was 18 to be able to buy my own car, a Ford Cortina 1600E, replacing the Fiat 124 that my granddad had sold to me. I kept the Cortina for 20 more years, restoring it two or three times over that period.

My racing career was advancing steadily, but was set back in 1977 because I had ingrowing toenails on both big toes. The pain got so bad I couldn't put a bike shoe on my foot. One evening I went up to Phoenix Park to watch the Tuesday night racing and was pumping up some tyres for a friend of mine behind a car. On the other side of this car, two guys were talking about a rider they knew, saying that he had been a flash in the pan but was now nowhere to be seen. He had been good, they said, but then the pressure had apparently got to him and he'd disappeared. One of them mentioned my name, but even before then I knew they were talking about me, and that lit a fuse.

The very next day I went into the Mater Hospital and had my two big toenails removed. I had no idea what the procedure was going to entail or the pain that was going to result. The memory of the pain gives me goose bumps even now when I think about it. They pulled them off and sent me straight out. Of course, I didn't think to take in sandals. So I had to press my bandaged toes into my normal shoes. Leaving the hospital I had to hold on to the fence as I walked up the road because I was in agony every time I put pressure on my feet. But having that procedure gave me a real spur, because before too long I was pain-free again.

I made the Irish Junior Championship my goal that season. I ended up in the front group with Lenny Kirk, who was a strong rider and very quick in a sprint. I realised that I had to wear him down because I knew he would beat me in a sprint. I would ride fast as I went by him, then ease up, then ride fast again, forcing him to push hard to stay with me, deliberately breaking up his rhythm. Finally, I got away from him and took the title.

I would never win the senior Irish title. In fact, the next time I tasted success in a major championship was when I won the Worlds in 1987. I had a good chance in the 1980 National Cyclo-Cross Championship, having won a cross event the week before. It was just before I went to France and going off there as a national champion would have been nice. But I skidded on black ice in the car on the way to the race and I took that as a sign to head back home.

I already felt pretty confident about my ability by that point, though. In 1979, aged just 19, I'd become the youngest rider ever to win the Health Race, previously known as the Rás Tailteann. That year was the first time the Irish Health Board had sponsored the race and the first time that the three federations in Ireland had come together to support the event. Up against me there was the great Billy Kerr, who was part of the Northern Ireland Cycling Federation, and John Mangan, from the National Cycling Association, who was racing at the time in France. I was the young kid from the big city, riding against these guys from the country who were thought to be much, much harder than city boys, so I was going to have my work cut out.

On my team I had Alan McCormack and Oliver McQuaid, and I ended up in the same kind of situation with Alan that I would revisit a few years later with Roberto Visentini at the Giro d'Italia. We both wanted to win, only one of us could, and neither of us would give the other any leeway. I was in great form that summer to the point where I even won a very fast uphill sprint on the stage into Westport – and I never really won sprints, ever. On one stage Alan McCormack got three minutes up on me in the break and I took off from the bunch and got across to him. I believed I was the strongest rider in that race and was determined to show it.

I was leading the race going into the time trial on the penultimate day, but shortly after the start I broke a spoke. There was no way I was going to jeopardise my chance of overall victory by stopping and changing a wheel, so I carried on with the brake rubbing slightly and won the time trial. On the final day we rode into Dublin to finish in Phoenix Park. I've got some footage of that stage and in it I'm on the front heading into Dublin and everyone is lined out behind me. Occasionally, you can see me waving to people that I recognise at the roadside. Eventually I got away with two other guys and left them to fight it out in the sprint knowing I had the overall sewn up. That was my first major stage race victory and also the first time I realised I got better and better as races went on.

I'd also been competing against Robert Millar, Phil Anderson and other top amateurs at the Tour of Ireland. I was riding on the Irish team there and I remember having a number of run-ins with both of those two. Coming into Dublin on the last day, I was in a breakaway with Millar, who was riding for a composite British Airways team, and I was threatening the race lead held by one of his teammates, John Shortt. Millar was trying everything to unsettle me. He wouldn't allow my team manager, Peter Crinnion, to come up in the car alongside us to give me time checks. Every time Peter came up in the car, Millar would get in between us, so Peter couldn't talk to me. Years later, I remember Millar saying that he and Phil had seen something in me because it had taken both of them to keep me in check and they were the best amateurs in France at that time.

It was extremely useful for me to have someone like Peter Crinnion around as a mentor during that time. Peter had raced as an amateur on the Continent, spoke French and still had lots of friends over there. He knew how the system worked in France, and I'd pick his brain all the time to hear about his experiences and get his advice. I really valued his opinion. For me, when Crinnion spoke it was like God had spoken, because he'd been there and done it. Peter was always very positive about things and when I eventually went to France I still talked to him every week on the phone, giving him updates on my training and my condition. He'd won races like the Route de France, which for many years was regarded as the amateur Tour de France, so he was well aware of the kind of pitfalls to avoid.

As far as racing went, during my early years in Ireland I never thought of it offering me a career. It was something that I was good at, but I wasn't overenthusiastic about my chances of making it, because the only Irishman who had in those years was Sean Kelly. But Kelly came from the countryside and everyone knew he had nails for breakfast. I was only a Dub, a guy from the big city, and I was in awe of Sean's achievements even at that stage. I'm not just saying that either. Last winter my parents were clearing out some stuff from their attic and found an old scrapbook in which I'd carefully stuck clippings about Sean's exploits.

It was only when I got onto the Olympic team that things started snowballing and a career in cycling began to look like a possibility. At that point, Lucien Bailly, who was the technical director of the French national team, came over to Ireland at the request of the Irish federation for a weekend of cycling with the national squad. We rode from Dublin down to Birr, about 60 miles away. That night he gave a presentation and the next day we rode back. The weather was awful and I was riding in the yellow oilskin that my dad had given me for delivering the milk, but I remember I rode pretty well going out to Birr and on the way back.

During the weekend Lucien Bailly took me aside and told me that I was wasting my time in Ireland, that I should be in Europe preparing for the Moscow Olympics. I told him I'd love to go, but didn't know anybody over in Europe. He said he knew of a club and that he could have a chat with them. When he got back to France he spoke to Mickey Wiegant and Claude Escalon at the Athlétic Club de Boulogne-Billancourt (ACBB). They wrote to me and said they could find a place for me for the following season, the year of the Moscow Olympics.

When ACBB's offer came through, I got six months' leave of absence from the dairy and they very generously gave me £500 as a send-off. My workmates at the dairy had a collection that raised another £500. Joe Daly Cycles had a collection as well, and they also got 500 quid for me. With a similar amount of my own saved, I left work on 10 February 1980 and the next day took a flight to Paris to join my new club. I had £2,000 in my pocket, a saddle, a set of handlebars in my suitcase, and hardly a word of French.

I felt nervous about leaving. It was going to be the first occasion I'd spent any significant time away from home and my parents. However, I was determined to make the step. I knew I had to prove myself on the Continent and was also well aware of ACBB's reputation. In recent seasons, Paul Sherwen, Robert Millar and Phil Anderson had ridden in their colours and had then stepped up into the pro ranks. Going further back, the great Irish rider Shay Elliott had been with them in the mid-1950s. So I was sure I was doing the right thing.

There was a lot of fog in Paris that day, so my flight was very late. Claude was supposed to be collecting me, but he'd gone. So I got a taxi to the address I'd been writing to for the previous few months. When I got there, it was closed up and empty. I hadn't eaten all day so I jumped over the fence, hid my bags in the porch and went to a local restaurant. I ordered what I thought was something nice, but which turned out to be green pasta. It was the first time I'd ever seen green pasta. Back home I was used to eating meat, potatoes and cabbage, but here I was with broccoli and olives. Usually this would have been a big turnoff, but I was so hungry I nibbled at it until finally it got cold and was totally inedible. The waiter asked me if it had been OK, then only charged me ten francs because they were a bit embarrassed as I hadn't eaten very much of it.

I went back to where I'd left my bags, bundled myself into the warmest clothes in my case and settled into the corner of the entrance of what I later found out was the ACBB's *service course*, where the team's equipment was kept. At about five in the morning, a car pulled up. I remember it was a small Peugeot 104. Two guys were in it: Pascal Cuvelier and Jean-Louis Barrot, two of my new teammates who had come down from northern France and were heading to the south of France to join the rest of the club for a training camp. They'd been told to stop off and pick up Roche. One of them said: 'Are you Roche?' I said I was and climbed into the back of the car. I didn't say much as we drove for 16 hours to the team's training camp base, where I was glad to meet another English-speaker, a British rider called John Parker. I picked up French very quickly, which helped no end, and I could also mix well with everybody. Later, I was able to grasp Italian in much the same way. I had little formal training.

Before I'd gone I had thought that I might end up racing at the ACBB with Neil Martin, who was going out with my eldest sister Maria. Later on, they married, and their son Dan has become one of cycling's very best climbers in the current era. Neil had been out with the ACBB in the autumn of 1979 but, as it turned out, didn't get an invite back for the following year. He was pretty upset about it and I think he may have felt a bit aggrieved at me for a while because just as he was let go I was taken on.

I'd first met Neil at the British Schoolboy ESCA Trials at a Butlin's holiday camp in England. Although he was a few months younger than me, he'd beaten me. We remained friends and, although we didn't race a lot against each other, we'd spend a week or two together at my home in Dublin or his in Birmingham. During one of those visits he met my sister and they settled in England, where he rode for many domestic teams but never really got the break his talent deserved. I don't know why the ACBB didn't keep him on. I can only guess that they thought Neil was already a very professional amateur and perhaps didn't offer the same potential for improvement that I did, given that I'd been in full-time work until the day I left Ireland.

Mickey Wiegant was the team boss, but he was getting on a bit by that stage and lived most of the time in the south of France, leaving Claude Escalon to look after things at the ACBB's Paris base. Wiegant always kept his relationship with riders at a very proper level. Whenever you spoke to Mr Wiegant you always had to address him using the more formal 'vous' rather than the more familiar 'tu'. During one of my first discussions with Wiegant I spoke to him using '*tu*'. Wiegant quickly pulled me up: 'Monsieur Roche, Monsieur Wiegant is not a friend, he is your elder. You must always use "*vous*".'

I learned a lot from Wiegant and Claude, and the ACBB was one of the best schools I could have ever gone to. Wiegant provided all our equipment, but he insisted that we had to appear in the correct kit at all times. For instance, we all had to come down to the dinner table wearing our orange Simplex-ACBB top. Never the black one, never the white one, always the orange one, and it was your job to make sure that it was clean. If you came down with something else on, you were told to go back upstairs and change straight away.

Always doing what Wiegant said extended to tactics on the road. I remember a race in the south during my first few weeks when I was in a break with a guy called Loubé Blagojevic, who should have turned pro in 1979 but had remained an amateur in order to ride at the 1980 Olympics. He was the star of the team and in great form at the start of that season. As the bunch started to close on the break, he jumped clear on his own. I thought maybe I could get across to him, so I jumped away as well. I was riding across the gap when a car came up. It was Wiegant. He shouted at me: 'Roche, what are you doing?' I told him I was trying to get across. 'No, no, no,' he said. 'Blagojevic is in front, you go back.' But I insisted I was going to keep on riding. So, bump! He put me straight in the ditch. Then I understood. That was one of the lessons I had to learn: to be aware of the hierarchy within the team and to respect team orders.

I won Wiegant over quite quickly, though, as he had a preference for time triallists and racing against the clock was one of my strengths. When we were preparing for the Grand Prix de France or any special time trial he would bring us down to his house and we would live in his basement. We would eat dinner with him and his wife. Then he'd take us into the back room with all these wheels and tubular tyres he had been keeping for years. Tubulars are stitched closed around an inner tube, making them very light, and the theory is that they improve with age, becoming more durable and resistant to punctures. Some of Wiegant's were 25 years old and positively vintage. He had Jacques Anquetil's wheels, Bernard Thévenet's wheels and he'd tell you that if you were doing well you'd be able to use a set of these special wheels in the event.

Training and racing in this environment meant I was changing very quickly. There were developments away from cycling too. One day I was racing at Longjumeau and saw a girl I liked the look of sitting with a young guy watching the racing. Pascal Cuvelier was also on the team that day and he happened to know she was called Lydia Arnaud and that the young guy with her was her brother, Thierry, who was on ACBB's 'B' squad. I found out that Thierry was racing in Mantes-la-Jolie the next evening and that Lydia would probably be there watching him.

Pascal drove me over there and we saw her again, this time walking around with Thierry's girlfriend of the time. Pascal got talking and I noticed that Lydia was wearing an ACBB top. That gave me a conversational opening, although my French was still far from fluent. We chatted haltingly and she asked me how many laps were left. I told her there were *quinze tours*, 15 laps. But with my Irish accent she thought I was saying *casse-toi*, which means 'fuck off'. I was mortified and said I hadn't known what I'd been saying.

When we were driving away we ended up stuck in traffic next to Thierry's car. Lydia was in there as well so I asked Pascal to invite them for a drink. We stopped, went to a local bar and chatted a bit more. Then I realised that I had no money so Pascal ended up paying for it. We got home pretty late that night and the next morning Pascal paid again as he had to race and spent the entire time on his knees.

I didn't see Lydia again until after the Olympics. We met at another race and organised our first date, which was a disaster for me as I got lost on my way to her house and arrived hours late. It wasn't the most auspicious start, but the relationship soon started to blossom.

At that stage I still didn't know how professional teams were set up, but looking back now I think the ACBB was better than most, primarily because of the education they gave you. We may not have had pro-standard equipment, but the ACBB was definitely run on very professional lines. Although Claude was more relaxed than Mickey Wiegant, he knew when to be serious and he wouldn't be messed around either. He was always very good at identifying talented young riders and was very strong and alert tactically.

However, to an extent the foreign riders were the whipping boys for the French guys. I think they despised us to a degree because they knew from past history that foreign riders were likely to get a place on a professional team the following year and they regarded that as us taking their bread and butter. Most of us moved on to the Peugeot squad, for which the ACBB was effectively the feeder team. But there might only be two places available for new pros at Peugeot each year. I think the English-speaking riders had an advantage when it came to nailing down those places because we were stronger both mentally and physically. We had to push harder to prove ourselves because we were foreigners coming into a sport dominated by the French and their way of doing things.

I think I was very lucky, though, because I got along with most of the French riders very well. But even then you'd be in a race and find that they'd been told one tactic and you'd been told another, usually to their benefit. They would form combines among themselves, which meant your own teammates sometimes ended up riding against you. But being tested in that way toughened up us foreign guys and perhaps made it more likely that we would step up to the next level.

I remember that I thought I was doing pretty well during the early part of that season, but I didn't know what might happen next. At the same time, I had to let the dairy know by June if I was going to come back to my job. With this in mind, as we were heading back to Paris after I'd finished second in the Route de France I asked Mickey Wiegant: 'Monsieur Wiegant, can you please tell me what my chances are of getting a professional contract because my employers are asking me now if I'm going to be coming back or not?'

He turned slowly to me and said: 'Monsieur Roche, how do you expect to get a professional contract? You got third in Paris–Ezy, second in the Route de France . . . You don't get professional contracts with a bunch of second places.' He wanted to see me winning.

Paris–Roubaix took place a couple of days later and I managed just that, beating a Belgian guy called Dirk Demol – who went on to win the senior version of the same race a few years later – by half a wheel in a two-up sprint on the famous velodrome. The very next day I called my boss at the dairy, told him that I had won the biggest amateur event in France and thought I would do well at the Olympics and get a professional contract. Consequently, I would not be going back to the dairy. The following week I won Paris–Reims and then I really should have won Tour de Liège, just before the Olympics. It was all falling perfectly into place. Then I went to Moscow and flopped.

Leading up to the Olympic road race, I felt I was doing really well and that it was going to be my day. But when we got there and went to look at the circuit, I started to have some doubts. It was man-made, quite artificial with banked corners – not my kind of circuit at all. There was a lot of tension around the Games because of the boycott by so many countries. But the worst thing for me was that it was very hot and humid. Unfortunately, I didn't go well at all and finished well down on the winner, Russia's Sergei Sukhoruchenkov.

I did make the front page of the papers locally, although not for my cycling achievements. One day we were heading from the Olympic Village to the restaurant where all the athletes used to eat. In the middle of a big square we were crossing, some girls were doing traditional Russian dances and myself and another guy were dragged in and we started doing some Irish dancing with them. Someone took some photos and we ended up on the front of a Moscow paper the next day with a caption saying something like: 'Athletes enjoying the friendly atmosphere at the Olympics.' That was certainly my biggest claim to fame in Moscow.

One afternoon after my poor showing in the road race I sat down with the Irish boxer Barry McGuigan next to a little river in the Olympic Village. We were both wondering what we were going to do next as the Olympics hadn't gone as well as either of us had hoped. I told him my sad story about giving up my job because I was sure I was going to get an Olympic medal. He told me that he had given up everything outside boxing in his quest for an Olympic medal and hadn't ended up with one either. We both faced the prospect of going home with nothing to show for our efforts and no work. Neither of us would have guessed that in the not-too-distant future we would both be world champions, Barry beating me to that accolade by a couple of years.

In fact, after he won his world title, Barry invited me onto the edition of *Saturday Live* he hosted on RTÉ as one of his special guests. The programme had a different presenter each week, and they could pick the artists who performed and the special guests who appeared. At the end of 1987, I returned that honour, inviting Barry onto the show I was hosting, seven years from us sitting down next to that river in Moscow. Unfortunately, at the very last minute, I couldn't host my show as I needed to have an operation on my knee, so the broadcaster Pat Kenny stepped in for me and did a great job. On the back of that he got his own show, *Kenny Live*, before later taking over from Gay Byrne as presenter of *The Late Late Show*.

However, when I left Moscow after the Olympics, I had no idea what my future in cycling was going to hold. Still feeling pretty downcast, I decided to go back to France to give it a final go that year. Claude Escalon had organised a racing-based holiday for himself, his family and some of the riders he got on well with in the French Basque Country. I drove down there with Pascal Cuvelier and Jean-Louis Barrot again.

We all rode really well together for those three weeks and earned a lot of money. Even better was the fact that I could feel my form coming again for the end-of-season Classics in northern France. Over the following few weeks I managed to raise my victory total for the season to 19 and during that period I got an offer from Peugeot to turn professional for 5,000 francs a month net. I was certainly going to take it. It matched the sum that I would have been getting if I'd stayed on at the dairy, which was important to me as it confirmed that I was moving in the right direction. Surprisingly, they agreed to that.

I went back to Ireland that winter with a dozen bikes I'd bought from the team and made enough re-selling them to give me a few bob to get me through to the new season. I trained as normal through that winter, doing some weight and circuit training, riding a fixed-wheel bike. Very early on in the New Year I was told to join Robert Millar for a ten-day training camp at Narbonne-Plage. From there we went to join up with the rest of the Peugeot guys at the team's training camp in Seillans in the south of France.

When we got to the hotel, Peugeot's team directeur Maurice De Muer was sitting in the lobby playing cards – *bulotte* was always his game. Millar chatted to him for a while and finally

Maurice turned to him and said: 'Is your driver staying with us for dinner or is he going now?'

Millar looked bemused for a moment, then said: 'This is Roche.'

'Roche the cyclist?' Maurice replied.

Millar nodded, and Maurice said: 'Huh, maybe in the amateur ranks he can win races carrying that much weight but now he's in the pro ranks he won't be able to.'

That was my welcome to the pro ranks from my new team boss.

CHAPTER 2

'THE ONLY BIKE RIDER WHO MADE ME SHIT MY PANTS'

In the 1970s and '80s, the ACBB provided the stepping-stone into the pro ranks for a lot of the English-speaking riders. Robert Millar, Graham Jones, Paul Sherwen, Allan Peiper and Sean Yates all came through with them. The ACBB's relationship with Peugeot meant most of us made the natural move from the former to the latter.

The two teams had a very similar philosophy. Maurice De Muer, who was in charge at Peugeot, was very much a traditionalist like Wiegant at the ACBB. When I was promoted into Peugeot's ranks, he must have been about 65 years old. He was a wise man and still very sound tactically and technically. He was also very strong on discipline. Even though De Muer's career was, unfortunately, almost over when I arrived, I learned an awful lot from him and built up a huge admiration for the man. Looking back, it feels like I spent more than the two years with De Muer, such was his influence on me.

The fact that I was the new guy coming into the Peugeot team wasn't easy for me as the new pros were always treated as cannon fodder. To some extent, first-year pros had to go out and earn the respect of the team managers and their new teammates. Once you had that, they would look at you differently. I was quickly made aware of my place in the team hierarchy at the GP de Monaco, which was just my third or fourth race. Peugeot had two guys up the road, Jean-René Bernaudeau and Bernard Bourreau. We kept on going over the same climb and as I was riding really strongly I made an attack and got across to my two teammates. I still felt very strong and thought I might have a chance of winning the race until De Muer came up to three of us in the team car.

Bernaudeau dropped back to him first, then I went back and De Muer said to me: 'Roche, Bernaudeau wins.'

I said: 'Maybe, but if I'm stronger perhaps I can win.'

'No, no, no, Roche, you don't understand. Bernaudeau wins,' De Muer insisted, making it quite clear what he wanted to happen.

I was OK with that and kept working to keep our advantage. After a few minutes though, Bourreau came to me and said: 'I'm going to be second.'

I wasn't having that. Bernaudeau was the leader and had been told he could win, but I felt second place could be decided on the line. We tore down the fast descent into the port of Monaco, where I led out Bernaudeau down the barriers for the sprint. I opened the door a little bit to let him sneak through, then closed it again as Bourreau tried to follow and nearly hung him out on the barriers. Peugeot still finished first, second and third, with me splitting the two French riders.

That night De Muer took me aside and said: 'Do you know why I said Bernaudeau was to win? If Bernaudeau wins then tomorrow we'll have headlines in the paper saying that Jean-René Bernaudeau, the leader of Peugeot, has won. If Roche wins, we might get headlines in Ireland, but that doesn't interest us. Roche is nobody. We're looking after the commercial interests of the team and for us it had to be Bernaudeau who won. That's the way it is.' That was my first run-in with De Muer. We had quite a few more interesting ones still to come.

The fact that I had started the season well and was getting results helped me, as did my determination to be up at the front as often as possible. Every blow I took, I would give one back. After second place in Monaco, I went on to the Tour of Corsica. We fancied our chances, but there was a strong Renault-Gitane team there led by Bernard Hinault and another new pro called Greg LeMond. Laurent Fignon was there too, riding his first big race against the pros with the French amateur team.

Peugeot won both of the split stages on day one, Phil Anderson taking the opening road stage and Jacques Bossis the very short time trial. On the second day, Bossis had got a few hundred metres off the front, but couldn't break the elastic pull back to the bunch. Seeing his attack, Renault had upped the pace and were leaving him out there to die. I understood what was going on and thought if I could get across to him Peugeot would then have two men at the front and Renault might have a harder job chasing us. So I made my move and hared across to Bossis. He didn't seem too keen to see me initially. 'What the hell are you doing here?' he asked me. I told him I'd come across to give him a hand. He shrugged and we got stuck in together.

Before too long we were in a groove. He set the pace down the twisting descents, we worked together on the flat, and I did most of the work on the climbs. Renault kept our lead down but weren't catching us, and coming towards the finish we thought we might stay clear. By now I'd been riding with Bossis for more than a couple of hours and Jacques was encouraging me, telling me I could win the stage, at the same time knowing he was about to inherit the leader's jersey from Phil Anderson. He had just about convinced me I could do it when, 300 metres from the line, the road turned sharp left up a very steep climb. I was almost spent, but Jacques somehow nursed me up it. When we dropped down the final 100 metres into the finish, he let me win. It was my first victory as a pro.

The race ended the next afternoon with a time trial and I'm sure he was thinking that he would beat me there and win overall.

I'm sure everyone else was thinking the same too. Before that, though, there was a road stage on the final morning, but it wasn't very difficult and Peugeot protected us both, assuming that an advantage of a minute over everyone bar me would enable Bossis to win the title. But the time trial was by no means a straight-forward test. It climbed for 10km up the Col de Téghime. Peugeot did win it, thanks to Michel Laurent, but I finished third behind him and Hinault, beating Bossis by 40 seconds to take my first stage race win just a month into my professional career.

The clearest memory I have of that win is not of the racing at all, but of an incident that had happened after I'd won that mid-race stage thanks to Bossis' generosity. That evening, three or four riders were invited to a supermarket to sign autographs by the event's organiser, Francis Ducreux. I remember Raymond Martin was there. He'd been the best climber at the Tour the year before. Two-time Tour winner Bernard Thévenet was there too, and Ducreux wanted Bossis as well, but Jacques couldn't go for some reason, so he told me to go along in his place. I was to get 5,000 francs for it, which was about a month's wages.

The only thing anyone knew about me was that I was the young kid who'd won the stage that day, but they were pleased to have me there. We did the signing and went back to our hotels, but I didn't see any of the money. I won the overall title the next day, but there was still no money for the supermarket appearance. I met Ducreux on a number of occasions during that year and he kept telling me the money was coming, but I still never saw it. Eventually, I asked Thévenet if he'd got his money and he told me he'd had it the following day. Martin said the same. It rumbled on until the following year when I was back on the start line of the Tour of Corsica. I asked Ducreux once again whether he had the money and he promised me he'd come to my hotel that night and pay me. But I'd had enough.

I went onto the start podium and said to him: 'Francis, you

either pay me or I'm not starting. And if you don't pay me I'll make a fuss and tell people why I'm not riding.' He wasn't happy but he gave me his word that he would pay me. Some of the race commissaires were standing nearby and could hear what was going on. I turned and said to them: 'You heard what he said, that he'd pay me when the stage had finished.' That seemed to seal the deal. I went back to him at the finish and he gave me a cheque for 5,000 francs. Years later he used to stay at a house near my hotel in the south of France and he'd come in for a cup of coffee every once in a while and we'd joke about it. He'd say: 'This guy here is the only bike rider who made me shit my pants.'

From Corsica we moved on to Paris–Nice, where my job was to work for Michel Laurent. We had a fabulous team. Laurent had won the race in 1979, Gilbert Duclos-Lassalle had won it in 1980, and we also had Phil Anderson and Graham Jones. The team time trial on the third day was in a small place called Bourbon-Lancy, which just happened to be Laurent's home town, so we were all particularly fired up. We won it convincingly, even though Graham, I think it was, punctured just before the bottom of the climb and we waited for him. Fittingly, that victory put Laurent into the leader's jersey. I felt I'd worked especially hard, particularly on the climb. But at the end, when everyone else was getting a hug and a kiss from him, I was pretty much forgotten, which didn't impress me at all.

The next day was a tough stage through the Massif Central to St-Étienne. Lots of riders were attempting to get away and I was policing these breaks. Then Laurent punctured and I dropped back to wait for him. There was no sign of the guys he'd been hugging and kissing the night before. They were all up the road in the peloton. Laurent got a new wheel and I paced him back up to the bunch, then led him towards the front of the pack. As we got there Serge Beucherie, Fons de Wolf, Adrie van der Poel and a few others clipped away. I checked to see that Laurent was

OK in the bunch, jumped up a gear and shot across to the breakaway.

I thought I was just policing another break that would come to nothing, but far from it. We ended up finishing with a lead of almost nine minutes and that night I found myself in the race leader's white jersey. There were now just eight riders effectively in contention for the title and as the only Peugeot rider among them I had a lot of weight on my shoulders. To add to that pressure, that evening our team doctor came into my room and told me Laurent was devastated by what had happened that day and asked me to go to his room to console him.

I went along, said I was sorry he'd lost the jersey and explained that it wasn't my fault, that I'd simply been acting in the team's interest by getting into the break. I didn't exactly cheer him up, but Michel did tell me: 'Stephen, you did a very good job today. You waited for me when I punctured and you still managed to get in that break in the end. I've got no complaints at all. I'm just disappointed for myself because I wanted to win Paris–Nice and now I won't. But I'm delighted for you and you can count upon my support right through to the end of the race. I'm happy you came to see me and I want to tell you that there are no hard feelings at all.'

I really appreciated his words, but what he had said didn't calm my nerves. There I was, just 21 years of age, the white jersey on my shoulders, with all of these experienced guys who'd been in that day's break to deal with, and the next day we were going up Mont Ventoux. It's a climb everyone fears, but I'd never ridden anything much tougher than the Sugarloaf in Ireland. Where I rode in the Wicklow Mountains, there was nothing like the Ventoux. I became so nervous that I could hardly sleep.

Once the stage got under way, I felt more relaxed and I rode OK to start with, calmed to a degree by the thought we were only climbing to Chalet Reynard, 7km short of Ventoux's summit, which is still snow-capped and closed off in early March. It was a lovely spring day when we set off and it was still sunny when we reached the foot of the Ventoux, so I took off my over-jersey and arm-warmers and passed them into the team car.

When we started climbing I was riding pretty well, but I was acutely aware that there was a time bonus for the first rider to Chalet Reynard, 11km up the climb, and that we had to tackle the steepest ramps of the Ventoux before we got there. As we climbed it started to rain. We climbed a bit higher and the rain turned to sleet and as we went higher still it turned to snow. The Peugeot car behind the lead group couldn't get up to me to hand back some clothing, and I began to freeze. Seeing me struggling, van der Poel attacked and got away to take the bonus on the top of the climb. But my problems were only just beginning.

When we started to descend it was snowing so heavily that we had to ride in the tracks left by the lead cars. I signalled for the Peugeot car to come up and asked De Muer for a jersey. He very politely told me: 'Catch the guys in front first. That'll get you warm.' I went down the descent like a madman and caught the first group, but once again the car couldn't get across to give me my top. By the time it did I was totally frozen and couldn't warm up at all. Although the bunch had largely re-formed and I had a lot of teammates with me, every time there was an acceleration I was yo-yoing off the back of the bunch. They managed to nurse me through to the finish, but I lost my jersey to van der Poel because of that lost bonus. I was so cold that I didn't really care at that point, but when I had warmed up I felt pretty glum. The only positives I could take out of the day were that I was still very much in contention and I no longer had the pressure of leading.

That night we looked at the race roadbook and decided the key stage came two days later, when the route went up the Tanneron and down its hair-raising descent into Mandelieu-La Napoule. We tried to attack on the climb, but that didn't work out. However, Duclos-Lassalle and Michel Laurent led me over the top as fast as they could, then Duclos-Lassalle pulled over and Phil Anderson went through. I was right on Phil's wheel with van der Poel stuck on mine – for a short while anyway. Afterwards van der Poel was sounding off about Phil being crazy on the descent, but it was van der Poel who got into trouble. He went off the road between a wall and a pole, rode down the other side of the wall until he came to the next gap, then rejoined the road again. He didn't fall, but he did lose some time. I had a few near-ones myself but it was one of those days when everything goes right. Phil won the stage and I finished just behind, gaining 30 seconds on van der Poel, which was enough to put me back in the lead.

The next day was the last one and featured a split stage. The key test was the final time trial up the Col d'Eze above Nice. I figured that everyone would be expecting me to hold fire until the time trial, so I suggested in the team meeting that morning that we should attack from the foot of the Tanneron on the road stage into Nice. De Muer wasn't completely convinced, but I persuaded him that because it was a short stage I'd be well recovered for the afternoon time trial if things didn't go our way. But I thought there was a good chance van der Poel could be dropped again.

As planned, we rode hard into the Tanneron and I got away at the bottom with Michel Laurent, Régis Clère and Jean-Luc Vandenbroucke. Coming down the far side I fell off on a corner, but Michel paced me back up to the other two. The whole of van der Poel's DAF Trucks team got organised behind us, but they couldn't reel us back in and we finished half a minute up, which gave me a more comfortable margin before the time trial. I was elated with how well our tactics had worked and fed on that emotion in the time trial. I won it by a couple of seconds, making me the Paris–Nice champion by a convincing margin as well as the first – and still the only – new pro to win 'the race to the sun'.

I had also firmly consolidated my place in the Peugeot team.

Looking back, one of the things that stands out about that victory is the way I created an opportunity for myself on a descent. That tactic would serve me very well on several other key occasions later in my career. I think I was lucky in that I was a very good descender, but not a dangerous descender. I did it when I had to do it and I did it right, but I wasn't one of those guys who 'cut the cables' on every descent. There were some guys who really impressed me on descents, though. Sean Yates was one of them. He was absolutely fearless. I saw him crash in a tunnel on the Giro one year. He was all cut up with gravel in his wounds and he just dusted himself down and carried on. It was unbelievable to see what he could do on descents. Sean Kelly was very good as well. Less well known but definitely one of the best was Frédéric Vichot, who had it down to an art. He was a fantastic skier and that made him very fluid and smooth. His style was slalom-like and was incredible to watch.

My first season was going better than I could have imagined, but so much had happened so quickly that I was desperate for a break. Lydia's parents had a holiday home on the Ile d'Oléron, and the two of us headed off there for a few days prior to the Classics. I rode the bike easy and relaxed as much as I could, but when I returned to the team for Paris–Roubaix, De Muer wasn't impressed. The night before the race he told me that I was a 'tourist' because I had taken a break and eased off on the bike. He made it very clear he wanted things done his way. He was even less happy when I finished ten minutes down the next day, suggesting it was the result of me 'going off on holiday halfway through the season'. He wasn't bothered about all of the work I'd done trying to keep our designated leader, Duclos-Lassalle, in contention.

There was a row brewing between us and it blew up at the team meeting the night before Flèche Wallonne. We'd had dinner in the cellar restaurant of our hotel and after we'd eaten De Muer started going around the table, asking each of us, 'How are you feeling for tomorrow?'

Duclos-Lassalle was first and he said, 'Yes, I'm OK.' Then he turned to Michel Laurent and got the same answer, then to Jean-René Bernaudeau and got the same again. Then he asked me: 'And you, Roche, what are you going to do?'

I was still smarting from his pre-Roubaix comment and from what I felt was his unjust criticism about my performance in that race. I said: 'I'm going to be a tourist. I'm going to take my camera with me and take photos.' I knew I had provoked him, but felt that his needling of me had justified that.

There was complete silence in the room. Nobody ever spoke back to Monsieur De Muer. He stood up on his Cuban heels, which he always wore to give him a bit of height, and said: 'Roche, don't you ever talk to me like that again. You're a young kid in this game. Monsieur De Muer knows what's right and wrong. You don't take holidays when you're racing. You're a pro cyclist now, you only rest when I tell you.'

But I wasn't prepared to back down. The argument raged between us for a while. I told him that I knew best when it was time for me to rest, but he made it clear he was in charge and would decide on issues like that. In the end, I said to him: 'Monsieur De Muer, I understand everything that you say but next time you want to talk to me like that, do it in your room and not in front of everyone else.'

There was silence for a few moments, then the hotel staff, who had heard raised voices and had wisely stayed out of the way for a few minutes, started to bring in coffee. After a while, we started heading back up to our rooms. When I was on the stairs Jacques Bossis pulled me aside and said: 'Stephen, you're going to be fired. Nobody talks to Maurice like that. Nobody! You showed complete disrespect to the man.'

I said to him: 'He shouldn't have spoken to me like that. If he had something against me he should have come and talked to me, but he shouldn't have talked to me in front of everybody like that.'

In the end it all blew over. In fact, it even seemed to help my relationship with Maurice. Years later he told me: 'Stephen, the main thing I liked about you was that you had character. Nobody ever spoke to me like you did that evening. But you were right. You were the only one who had the balls to tell me that I was wrong. I'm sure everybody else in that room would have loved to have spoken to me like that, but no one had the balls to do it. But I appreciated the stance you took and we both knew then where we stood.'

Maurice is 90 now and lives not too far away from me in the south of France. Every now and then I head over to see him. I knock on his door and say: '*C'est un Irlandais perdu à Seillans . . .*' – there's an Irishman lost in Seillans, can you help me? He always has a bottle of champagne ready in the fridge. He's an incredible man. I got a great education in the sport from him. My only regret is that he wasn't around for a bigger part of my career.

Our fall-out at Flèche didn't seem to impact on my opportunities at all. In fact, Peugeot's management were keen for me to ride the Tour de France in my debut season. But by the time we got to the Dauphiné Libéré, which takes place in early June and is one of the key build-up races for the Tour, I was exhausted. I was OK for the first few days, but when we got to the high mountains I ended up losing 45 minutes over a couple of stages. I know Graham Jones has said that he felt he was over-raced at Peugeot, and I think that may have been the case for me that year, given that I was only 21. But Graham raced a lot more than me. He clocked up 130 days in the saddle one year, about 80 more than some riders do these days.

I knew I wasn't ready for the Tour and wasn't too disappointed when I was passed over for selection. De Muer allowed me to ease off during July, which enabled me to come back strongly later that season, winning the Étoile des Espoirs stage race and working with Robert Millar and Graham to help Pascal Simon score a convincing win in the Tour de l'Avenir. I was feeling good, but as the season ended what I needed was rest. Unfortunately, my lack of experience meant that I didn't get it. Although at the time I didn't realise it, I was living the life of a star and letting the adulation I was receiving go to my head. I was being pulled here, there and everywhere, to receptions, to presentations, to dinners. All of a sudden the 1982 season was on me and I felt like I hadn't really closed the door on 1981.

I went into the new season with high hopes and with people expecting a lot from me, but the simple fact was that I hadn't really recovered physically. I'd made a huge step up from riding a normal amateur season to being a well-raced professional, which meant more events, longer distances and, therefore, extra physical and mental demands. I'd won nine races in my first year and most of those wins were overall successes in stage races. That meant I'd been under additional pressure, because I'd often had to defend my position for several days, usually against many of the top guys in the sport. It had put a lot of strain on me, but I didn't realise it. I hadn't switched off at all.

I ended up playing catch-up all year. The crunch came at the Dauphiné once again. I didn't finish the race, but Peugeot still wanted me to ride the Tour. I told them I couldn't do that because I was totally wasted. Instead of pushing me further, they did some blood tests and other investigations. The doctors told me I had chronic fatigue and a problem with my heart. In fact, they shocked me by revealing that I'd always had the heart problem, but hadn't known about it. I still have it now.

It's a syndrome called Wolff-Parkinson-White and it's rare for athletes to have it. You have an extra electrical pathway in the heart that may cause a very rapid heart rate, a condition known as supraventricular tachycardia. It's not dangerous in my case and only comes on when I am under pressure, but it shows up clearly when I do an electrocardiogram test. Late on in my career, I would do the pre-Tour de France medical check with Dr Gérard Porte and he'd always gather his medical team around me and tell them: 'Look at this, I'm going to show you something that you've never seen before.' He'd do the ECG and always said that I was the only athlete he knew competing at the top level who had Wolff-Parkinson-White. I still do a medical test with Gérard every year and he always looks for it. 'Yes, it's still there,' he always says. It gives him a kick seeing it, even now.

The upside of my struggles during 1982 was that I learned from my mistakes. I rested a lot more that winter, putting the bike aside altogether in October, when Lydia and I got married. The service took place in Paris and we had some friends staying with us for a few days afterwards. Then we got in the car and drove down to Lourdes for our honeymoon. Over the weeks that followed, I continued to take things easy, although the fact that I hadn't won much all year meant I wasn't getting many invites anyway, which was a bit of a rude awakening. However, this proved to be a real benefit when I got into 1983.

That year there were plenty of changes at Peugeot too, and not all for the good. Maurice De Muer had been eased out and replaced by Roland Berland, a two-time French champion who'd retired from racing a couple of years before. He started out as De Muer's assistant, but constantly questioned the older man's decisions and eventually got his job. But in my opinion he was a bit out of his depth. When he took it over, I think Peugeot was the best team on the Continent, the Team Sky of the 1980s to some extent. But it all went sour, leading to many of the English-speaking riders leaving in fairly controversial circumstances.

Graham Jones was the first to leave at the end of 1982. I was disappointed that they hadn't kept him on and I know others were too. Graham was a great guy to have on your team. He was a strong climber, a good time triallist and a very good captain on the road. He was brilliant tactically and good at staying cool. Graham didn't speak a lot but when he did what he said was gospel. Classy riders like Duclos-Lassalle and Michel Laurent were important, but teams need riders like Graham, guys who know the right thing to do and never have a problem riding for their leader. He was one of those riders who would always be there when you needed him, almost like a shadow for his team leader. In crosswinds, on the climbs, Graham was always there.

While De Muer had kept all of the riders focused and aiming at specific goals, it soon became clear that Berland had a different vision for the team, centred more on the French riders, as I was to find out to my cost towards the end of that season. My year started slowly enough, but victory at the Tour of Romandy in early May provided me with a huge lift as I prepared to make my Tour debut.

My first Tour de France turned out to be a race of great highs and lows for Peugeot, as Pascal Simon took the yellow jersey at Bagnères-de-Luchon in the Pyrenees, but fell the day after, sustaining a suspected broken shoulder. Because there were a few transition stages before the Alps, the team doctors bandaged him up and hoped that with a bit of time the injury might get better. So for the next few days our job was simply to stay close to him and get him to the Alps.

Every day we dragged Simon along, but nobody was really interested in attacking because they knew that once they got to the mountains they would be able to get rid of him. I commented at the time that the French riders were all going so easy on him that they were doing everything but holding his dick when he was pissing. Pascal's rivals were happy to sit back, let him have the lead and let us, his Peugeot teammates, shoulder most of the workload. But there was never any question within the team of anyone else being given a freer role. There were good commercial reasons for keeping Simon in yellow for as long as possible. Quite simply it came down to the fact that another day for Pascal in yellow meant another day on the front page of *L'Équipe* for Peugeot.

Laurent Fignon was the automatic beneficiary if Simon did fall away, and I always remember his directeur sportif at Renault, Cyrille Guimard, telling Fignon: 'Keep calm, keep calm, it's going to come. It's going to come.' Fignon didn't even need to fight for the jersey, because it was almost certain he was going to inherit it without needing to attack. Sure enough, on the first day in the Alps, Simon finally quit on the road to Alpe d'Huez and Fignon, who, like me, was a Tour debutant, took the yellow jersey and held it into Paris.

My clearest memories of that race come from the days after Simon quit. Heading for Alpe d'Huez, I learned an important lesson the hard way. I was riding with all of the top guys going over the Glandon, but I'd got so carried away with how well I was riding that I forgot to eat. I managed to get some food inside me on the way down from there to the foot of Alpe d'Huez, but it was too little too late. I blew up massively and lost 15 minutes.

The next stage went to Morzine and I spent most of it with Robert Millar, Jacques Michaud, Edgar Corredor, Lucien van Impe and a couple of others. Michaud and Corredor ended up out in front, while I stuck very closely to Millar. It was an education watching how he rode in the mountains. I learned how to ride the climbs from Robert that day. He never panicked. Going into corners he'd drop down a gear and was always prepared to lose a metre in the corner, then he'd smoothly bring it back coming out of the corner. There was no acceleration. He was totally smooth in his pedalling.

Of course, when he attacked he was very lively and could get away extremely quickly, but when he was making tempo he played a lot with the gears, just like you would in a car, changing down as you go into a corner on a hill in order to keep your momentum coming out of it. I sat on his wheel for a lot of that stage and climbed in much the same way as him after that. I felt it was the best way for me to climb. I wasn't a pure climber. I didn't have the zip that Robert had. Nevertheless, I could set a fast tempo on a climb and could hang on to him the best because I was able to judge my effort so well.

On the mountain time trial up to Avoriaz I had my best result of the race, finishing second to van Impe and pushing myself up towards the top ten. Two days on from that was the race's final long time trial in Dijon, where I finished third, just 37 seconds down on Fignon after 50km of racing. One experienced observer thought I could have performed even better. At the finish in Dijon, five-time Tour winner Jacques Anquetil took me aside and bluntly told me: 'Stephen, you lost the time trial before you'd even got under way.'

I was a bit taken aback, feeling that I'd ridden very well. 'What do you mean, Jacques?' I asked him.

'I saw you talking to an old lady before the start.'

I told him that it was Lydia's grandmother who lived in Dijon and that I didn't see her very often.

'That doesn't matter,' he said. 'You can see her whenever you want to. You're in your office here and you don't see anybody. You don't see your family, friends, neighbours, anybody. You see nobody when you're preparing for time trials, especially when you're so close to the off.' When a five-time Tour winner gives you advice, you listen, and I took that on board.

I finished the Tour in thirteenth place, which I was pretty pleased with. The team made it clear they were happy as well. Berland said he wanted me to re-sign for the following year, but I told him I didn't want to finalise anything at that point because the Worlds were still to come and, frankly, I didn't feel he was offering me a great deal. We did a lot of bargaining and in the end he came to me and said: 'Here's an option for you. We can agree the figures and the other aspects of the contract and then, depending on how you do at the Worlds, we can thrash out the final details. But I would like to have the basis of an agreement in place with you because I want to keep you for next year.' And I said OK to that.

So I signed part of the agreement on the understanding that if I got a good result at the Worlds we would renegotiate my salary with a view to me staying with Peugeot in 1984. That was fine until I finished third in the Worlds. Suddenly, other teams became more interested in me. So I went back to Berland to renegotiate. He said he still wanted to keep me. But every time I tried to talk to him to discuss the deal something came up.

Eventually we made an appointment to meet at Peugeot's *service course* in Paris to sign my contract, but when I turned up at the team's base Berland wasn't there. Instead, a secretary met me and told me that Berland had left a contract and all I had to do was sign it. I opened the envelope, took out the contract and saw right away that he hadn't improved his offer. That simply wasn't on, as we hadn't negotiated a price. I kept ringing him. He kept putting me off until finally I insisted we had to get it sorted out. I eventually got him on the phone and he told me any debate was effectively over because, he claimed, I had actually signed the contract already. He said he was sticking to his price, agreeing that I'd had a good result at the Worlds but that Peugeot couldn't exploit it.

But all I had signed was an agreement that I would stay with the team in 1984. The paper I had signed also included details of endorsements that I could look for in my own right – a shoe contract, for example – and also the car I would get for the following year. I told him that I wasn't happy at all; that he'd basically screwed me. I added that if he was going to hold that line I was going to leave. I said: 'Look at the contract. I haven't signed the page that stipulates my payment. Only you've signed it.'

In the end, I got an offer from La Redoute that was almost twice what Berland was offering, and I accepted it. I showed La Redoute the contract I had with Peugeot and they told me that there was no way that Peugeot could make it binding. They even agreed to defend me if Peugeot came after me and they stood by that. However, when the case finally went to court, we lost.

I still felt hard done by, so we appealed the verdict.By this point the case had been running for two years and I was negotiating to join Carrera. I told them that I was ready to move but still had this legal issue with Peugeot hanging over me. Because I'd already lost once, they decided that they would prefer to work something out with Peugeot, so their team manager, Davide Boifava, negotiated a deal to avoid any further legal problems down the line. They agreed that, in return for Peugeot agreeing to drop the case, all of the Carrera riders would have Peugeot's name on their shorts for the next two years.

Everyone was happy, except me because I felt I'd done no wrong. So I paid a lawyer myself to take on the case. For me it was a matter of principle. Finally, about 18 months later, we went to court and I won the case, and that was the end of it.

Ultimately, I was glad to move on from Peugeot. They had given me a fantastic grounding but the shenanigans with Berland left a bitter taste. I was looking forward to moving on.

CHAPTER 3

MINCEMEAT, MOUSE TAILS AND MR MOTIVATOR

I thought I had put team management problems behind me when I signed with La Redoute, particularly as moving there meant a reunion with Maurice De Muer, who was the team's general manager. In fact, working with him again was one of my principal reasons for going there. Two-time Tour de France winner Bernard Thévenet was there as well as directeur sportif, but it soon became clear that he didn't have the same class behind the wheel of a team car as he'd so often shown on the bike. To a degree, this was De Muer's fault, because rather than providing overall organisation of the team and advising Thévenet, as his title suggested, he tended to undermine him.

Thévenet is one of the nicest guys you could meet, perhaps too nice for that kind of role. I got an early indication of his greenness early on in the season. Riding Nice–Alassio, I was away on my own on the finishing circuit, which we covered two or three times. Robert Millar was attacking behind in an attempt to catch me on a long climb. Thévenet came up to me in the team car and told me: 'Stephen, keep it going. Millar's not far behind, keep it going. If you can keep it going over the top, you never know . . .' And he put his hand out of the window and onto my saddle and my butt to push me along. I swung my arm round and caught him right in the face with my fist. I could never have someone touching me from a car like that. It just wasn't on. I didn't have a moment's hesitation. My fist went out and I hit him: 'Boom!' A moment later he was gone. I managed to get over the top and down the other side without being caught by Millar and won the race, but I still wasn't happy.

I carried that form into Paris–Nice, winning a stage and finishing second to Sean Kelly, who won for the third year in a row. Sean beat me by just a second in the deciding time trial on the Col d'Eze to win by a dozen seconds overall, with Hinault almost two minutes back in third. But, as was often the case, it was Hinault who took the headlines.

Robert Millar had been leading after a very good ride to finish second behind Eric Caritoux at Chalet Reynard on Mont Ventoux. We knew Bob wasn't a great descender and the drop off the Col de l'Espigoulier a couple of days later was very dangerous with lots of gravelly corners. Closing on the summit everyone started to move towards the front and you could read what was going to happen. We attacked the descent like crazy. As the pace got faster and faster, the lead group split, with Millar in the second group.

We got onto the flat and all of us in front were very anxious to keep the pressure on Millar. We weren't too far away from the finish when we got news via race radio that the local dockers were on strike and were barricading the road. We started muttering to each other but didn't really know what was going on. All of a sudden, we came around this corner and there were dockers right across the road. All of us but one pulled hard on the brakes. The one who didn't was Hinault. He kept going full throttle and threw his bike forward into the midst of the dockers. Even before he'd jumped off his bike and got his feet on the ground, he was throwing punches. It was crazy. The funny thing was he had aluminium cleats on his shoes so he was slipping everywhere but still swinging as people tried to pull him away and avoid his punches at the same time. He was totally out of it. He'd lost it.

There are lots of pictures of the incident and in one you can see me looking at Hinault in astonishment as he's punching one of these dockers. It was incredible what he did. He could have smashed himself up really badly and injured other people as well, so he was very lucky. But that was Hinault. He didn't take any prisoners. No one was going to stop him racing.

Like almost every other pro, I was in awe of Hinault when I first came into the sport. Within a few weeks, though, I was being compared to him after I'd beaten him at the Tour of Corsica and Paris–Nice. The press branded me 'the new Hinault'. Rather than see that as an overblown compliment, the comparison raised my blood pressure. I famously said that: 'Hinault has two legs and two arms and so have I.' I'm sure it seemed pretentious as I'd been a pro for only two months and won only two races, but I never actually felt there was a guy I couldn't beat or a race I couldn't win. I always aimed high. Suggesting I was on a par with Hinault was part of that. Maybe I could beat him, maybe I couldn't, but the only way to test it out was to give it my best against him and see where that took me. However, three years on, I'd come to realise that Hinault was quite extraordinary in all kinds of ways. The encounter with the dockers only underlined that.

He had missed the Tour the previous year due to injury, but had made it his principal target in 1984 as leader of the new La Vie Claire team. As a team leader myself now at La Redoute, I was looking forward to taking him on at the Tour, and my confidence increased as my form built through the first half of the season and into July. However, my chances of doing anything at the Tour disappeared when I crashed at the end of the first week of racing on a very long stage to Bordeaux.

It was one of those crashes where you don't have to be going fast for it to hurt a lot. We were dollying along and chatting away when all of a sudden there was a big pile-up. About 25–30 guys came down and I felt a chainring cut into the back of my calf, leaving it open and very badly bruised. It developed into a huge haematoma. I thought about quitting but kept going as the team's doctors felt the pain might ease as the days passed. But it didn't. I struggled through the Pyrenees and then through the Alps. In the end, the injury only got better once the Tour was over. After Bordeaux, I spent the rest of the race basically riding on one leg.

When you get an injury like that, you do whatever you can to get to the finish knowing that anything can happen overnight, that it might not be as bad as you think it is. Even though you know deep down it's going to be difficult, you always have a go. I was never one to abandon a race, because I always felt that once you've done it the first time it gets easier to do it the next. It wasn't a habit I wanted to develop. You have to be prepared to suffer, especially if you want to reach the very top. It's no good having the option of quitting in the back of your mind.

The shame was that I felt like I was going pretty well up to then. I'd finished fourth in a long time trial at Le Mans after leading three-quarters of the way in. Riding stages like that was a big part of the learning process for me because the time trials at the Tour were so long. That one was 67km and as it came in the first week of a three-week race it was always difficult to know how to pace yourself. In my early Tours I wasn't very consistent. If my form wasn't so good on a flat stage it didn't really matter as you didn't tend to lose any time, but when it was down in a time trial or during a hilly stage, then I paid cash.

But that July did have a silver lining. My first child, Nicolas, was born during the opening week. Going into the race I was feeling under a lot of pressure. I was leading a team for the first time, having come thirteenth the year before, but mostly it was because Lydia was heavily pregnant. By coincidence, the race was due to stop overnight in Cergy, near Paris, where we lived, and Lydia thought it would be a nice surprise for me if I was able to see the baby that night. So, without saying a word to me, Lydia went to the hospital, where she was due to have a Caesarean section, and asked if it could be brought a few days forward.

Generally I called Lydia in the evening just before dinner, but the evening before the Cergy stage she called me and told me she was tired and going to bed. I didn't know she was already calling from the hospital. She knew that if I called her later she wouldn't be at home and I would worry. The next day the Tour raced into town and when I got over the line my mother was waiting for me. She had come over to help Lydia after the birth and I was a bit taken aback to see her, even more so when she exclaimed: 'You've got a son! You've got a son!'

'What do you mean I've got a son? I spoke to Lydia last night and there was nothing happening,' I said to her. I showered and changed and went off to the hospital and Lydia was there with Nicolas in her arms. It was a very courageous act on her part and absolutely wonderful to see them both. It struck me later on in my career that one of the major drawbacks about being on the road so much was I missed many of these milestone moments. In 1987 I was away from home almost every day between the start of Romandy in May and the end of the Tour at the end of July. When I left for Romandy, my daughter Christel was still crawling but when I got back from the Tour she was walking around.

One year, when my eldest two were still very young, I remember going on to the Tour's post-stage television programme on Europe 1, which was hosted by Jean-René Godart. I was asked to pick out some music and I chose a song by Claude François called 'When the Telephone Cries'. It's about a daddy who's away a lot and he's talking to his wife on the phone and asks to speak to his young daughter. She asks him: 'Who are you?' And at the end of the conversation, she says: 'But do you know my mammy?' The lyrics are a bit corny perhaps, but apparently I had half of France in tears that evening.

Throughout my career, Lydia was always determined to keep

quiet about anything that could distract me from racing. I remember during another Tour she fell down the stairs and broke her coccyx, but when I called her she didn't mention it and I didn't know anything about it until two weeks later. Generally couples go through these things together, and I'm not saying that I didn't want her to share them with me, but she chose not to, because of the importance of my career, not only to me, but to our whole family.

I always said that 'you don't bring your wife to the office'. I wasn't being nasty about Lydia when I said that. When I was on the road I had to focus on myself, and I couldn't be worrying about her. I know it sounds selfish, but it was never an issue for Lydia. She knew that being on the road with me was just too complicated. But we were a team as well, in as much as I was out working and looking after that side of things and she had the house and the kids to look after.

She used to come to the big tours on the rest day, but my feeling was that I had to be with my teammates in the evenings. My team was nine riders, not eight riders and one guy with his wife in the corner. I always felt that the riders had to stick together during the day, but when we were riding we didn't have much time to talk. So, after the evening meal, it was more important to have a chat with the other lads than having our wives there. We were a team on the road and we had to stay a team off the road as well. That was one of the strong points of most of the teams I rode for and I felt it helped to improve performance. I was groomed in that traditional way, but things have changed since, and not always for the best.

The management issues at La Redoute that had rumbled on since the start of the season came to a head at the end of the Tour. We found out the news from *L'Équipe*, rather than from the team. De Muer and Thévenet were out and Raphaël Géminiani was being brought in to replace them. 'Gem' was another one of the golden oldies of team management. He'd been a great rider in his time and was the man behind many of Jacques Anquetil's greatest victories. I was suspicious of him at first, particularly after he announced at the presentation of the 1985 Tour route that I was going to win the stage to the summit of the Aubisque. Not only that, he said I would win that afternoon's stage back over the Aubisque as well. It was a bold statement, delivered in Gem's typically booming fashion, which was hard to ignore.

That claim showed how impulsive Gem was. He was a very strong personality, who liked to be the centre of attention and could be explosive. And he drove the team car like Lewis Hamilton. He did go on a lot about the old times, but when he needed to be focused he was totally with you and I really appreciated that. He won me over very quickly, largely because he was brilliant at motivating his riders, particularly his leaders, and I reaped the benefit of that from the very first weeks of 1985.

I finished third in the Tour of the Med, second in Paris–Nice, and then went on to Antibes, where I live now, to ride the Criterium International. I was fighting with Sean Kelly for the overall lead, which would be decided in the final time trial. Some time before the race, a guy from Alstom Atlantique, who manufactured the TGV trains and later built the Eurostar equivalents, had come to us as they'd just invented what they said was a revolutionary disc wheel. He'd been to most of the big teams, but nobody would take it on. Géminiani, though, said we'd give it a go and that I'd ride it in that time trial. My bike was fitted with the new wheel at the back and I won it.

Francesco Moser had been the first top road pro to use a disc wheel, but that had been when he broke the world hour record on the track in Mexico City in 1984. I think I was just about the first rider to use one on the road in Europe. There was a lot of fuss over it that day. I remember a TV journalist suggesting that the wheel had won the time trial for me. I pointed out that it may have helped, but my legs had done most of the work. They were looking for a name for it and Gem suggested Discjet. I used it later that year in the prologue and time trial at the Dauphiné and won on both occasions.

Later on in the evening after that first win using the new wheel, Gem came up to my hotel room and told me: 'Get dressed, you're coming out with me tonight.'

'Where are we going?' I asked him.

'Don't ask questions, just come.'

It was about half past ten, a very strange time for a directeur to be taking one of his riders out. We got in the car and went up to this nightclub in the back end of Nice somewhere. There were only a few people in there because it was still very early. A girl wandered over to us and sat down, and Géminiani said to her: 'The other day you showed me a mouse and told me that if I pulled its tail and it squealed, whatever I was thinking at that moment would happen. When I pulled the mouse's tail, it squeaked and I was thinking of Roche winning the Criterium International on Sunday. And I told you that if he did win I would bring him here to meet you and here he is.'

This kind of thing was typical of Géminiani. He was incredibly superstitious. He had it all calculated. I finished third in the Tour of the Med, second in Paris–Nice, so it followed I'd be first in the Criterium International. I was number 21 in the race, and two minus one is one. All the signs were there that I was going to win. He sounds odd and perhaps he was, but his school, like Maurice De Muer's, was a very good one to be in.

Even though he was comparatively old, he was well up on diet and equipment. For example, before big time trials he would go out and buy mincemeat for me and would soak it with lemon juice. He'd spread the meat out, squeezing lemon over it as he did so. He'd leave it for a few minutes, then add more lemon, until eventually it had completely permeated the meat. There was no oil, no fat, no cooking. He was very thorough when it came to preparation for time trials. He'd always be with me on the day of a time trial, too. Someone else would look after the rest of the guys. He'd be overseeing my meals, my warm-up, my recce of the course in the morning, my choice of bike, wheels, gears. I'd always had a bit of a routine right from the early stages of my career, but I was learning things as I went along and my preparation got better thanks to his influence.

For instance, he had noticed that I had struggled on the climb to Guzet-Neige during the 1984 Tour and that the same climb would decide the Tour of the Midi-Pyrénées (now the Route du Sud) in 1985. Building up to that race, he coached me into doing a great ride to win that stage and the overall title. He saw it almost as an act of revenge for what had happened to me on the same mountain before. I think that my positive approach chimed with his and that provided a feeling of affirmation, that I was doing the right thing.

Gem had spent a lot of years working with Jacques Anquetil and always said that I was the closest cyclist to Anquetil that he'd ever seen in terms of my pedalling style and tactical ability. Jacques wanted to win and he wasn't interested in anything else. I wanted to win as well, but I was a different kind of an athlete. But when it came to time trialling, Gem said we were very similar. I paid so much attention to detail and Anquetil had been the same.

He used to call me his TGV. Because I had a smooth and rapid cadence, I could set a fast tempo, and he would tell me that if I got a gap on my rivals at the right moment in races they wouldn't catch me. It was as a result of that theory that I won the stage on the Aubisque in 1985. On the morning of the stage he presented me with a special silk skinsuit that he had had handmade for me. My first reaction was to tell him that I wouldn't be turning up at the start wearing a kit like that, that I'd be a laughing stock. But he insisted. 'The stage is only 40 kilometres. You don't need food, you're going to get clear on the Aubisque and they won't be able to catch you. You're going to ride it like a time trial.'

I was still embarrassed about lining up in the skinsuit, so I put a jersey over it. For the initial fast stretch to the foot of the Aubisque I kept the jersey on, then tossed it away just before we started climbing. There were lots of attacks, notably from Lucho Herrera. He went off early on the climb and got a decent gap. Then I made my move from the group behind, caught Herrera and went straight past him. I was thinking all the time about what Géminiani had said about my fast tempo, that no one would catch me if I got clear. Of course, Gem had also been telling everyone for the last nine months that I was going to win this stage, so I couldn't let him down. Thankfully, I didn't. His strategy was spot on. Kelly was second, a little over a minute back, with LeMond another few seconds back and Hinault about 1 minute 30 back. Unfortunately, I couldn't complete the double that day, but no one minded all that much as my La Redoute teammate Régis Simon won the afternoon stage into Pau.

Although that Aubisque win is my favourite memory of the '85 Tour, most fans probably remember the Luz-Ardiden stage prior to that more clearly. Hinault had been fighting the effects of the crash he'd had in St-Étienne for a few days and could definitely have lost the yellow jersey to his La Vie Claire teammate LeMond that day.

It all started when I attacked on the Tourmalet and got away with Pedro Delgado and LeMond. We went over the Tourmalet, down the other side into the valley and started up towards Luz-Ardiden. The problem then for LeMond was that he couldn't ride with me because Hinault, his teammate and the race leader, was some distance behind us and I was the closest rider to them both in the overall classification. He knew that if he did attack he might be able to take the lead and win the Tour, which he wanted to do, but he couldn't be sure that I wouldn't beat him. He didn't know what to do really.

LeMond wasn't fully committed and I was a bit concerned that he might just be setting up to attack me. He kept jumping away, but he wasn't going full on. He'd attack, get a gap, then let me get back up to him again and ride, then he'd attack again. I wouldn't let him get away, but I wasn't committing fully either. He was peed off with that, and I was peed off with him because he wouldn't ride. It was a stalemate.

In the end, Delgado went clear to win the stage and I finished a couple of seconds down on LeMond, with Hinault another minute or so back and still in the yellow jersey. There's no doubt, though, that LeMond could have won the Tour that day and I could have finished second in Paris. Even though La Vie Claire would probably have kept the yellow jersey if LeMond had worked with me, he couldn't know for sure what would have happened and that frustrated him. He felt he could have beaten me, but his team wasn't sure.

But I wasn't the slightest bit disappointed with finishing third. One of the key points for me was getting away with the likes of Delgado and LeMond on the Tourmalet and leaving Hinault behind. Add to that the way that I performed on the Aubisque stage, the way I was riding in time trials, the fact that I didn't have a bad day, and my third place that year was definitely a positive sign. It proved to me that I was going in the right direction.

We knew by that point, however, that La Redoute were pulling out of the sport, having achieved their promotional goals. I didn't have a deal set up coming out of the Tour, but back in 1983 I'd spoken to Davide Boifava, the manager of the Italian Carrera team. We picked up those conversations again at the Worlds, which were held near Venice that year. I met up with Boifava the night before the World Championship and signed with Carrera that evening.

I was keen to take Géminiani with me. He'd helped me a lot in '85. I felt he knew me properly and thought he could be of benefit to me, but Carrera weren't having any of it, even though Gem spoke Italian. I think perhaps Boifava felt that if he had Géminiani on the team he would lose his power to him. In addition, Carrera are a very discreet company, whereas Gem wasn't like that at all. He'd be getting attention from every direction and that didn't fit with their philosophy. Gem didn't really like the fact that we separated, but we still get on well now. I see him every year at the Tour of the Med, and even though he's in his mid-80s, he's still as loud as he always was.

The key thing for me, though, in signing for Carrera was that I had joined another team built in a traditional mould around stage race leaders. They had a lot of strong riders on their roster and with that podium place at the Tour behind me I felt that something big was just around the corner.

CHAPTER 4

'WHAT ARE YOU DOING? YOU'VE GOT TO GO ON'

With the Carrera deal sorted, I planned to see out the 1985 season in what was by now my usual way with appearances in two or three six-day races. Raphaël Géminiani was always keen for me to ride on the track because he was sure that one day I'd make an attempt on the hour record. But I'd competed in track events even before I came under Gem's influence.

In 1983 I went to Ghent to get a feel for riding on the boards and then partnered Tony Doyle in the Dortmund Six that we were using as preparation for the Paris Six, which was the first event to take place at the new Bercy indoor arena early in 1984. Six-days could hardly be more different from road racing. Taking place on wooden tracks, the idea is straightforward enough with up to a dozen teams of two attempting to complete the greatest number of laps.

However, a huge variety of skills are required as racing comprises several different formats, including time trials, paced racing behind specially designed motorbikes, sprints and Madisons. The name derives from New York's Madison Square Garden, where all of the riders were on the track at the same time, one team member racing, then sending his partner into the action with a hand-sling. I found the format extremely complicated, but having a teacher like Tony to keep me straight made it an awful lot easier. He knew the ropes and was hugely respected on the six-day circuit.

I was coming in as a name from the road and I remember that they called me 'the pursuiter' because I was always three yards off the back of the group. I couldn't stay on the wheels. Tony used to curse me in the Madisons because I'd go to sling him in, but panic and miss him. Or I'd be waiting up the banking for him to sling me in and I wasn't going fast enough and he'd end up doing another lap. But he was very calm and we got on very well together.

By the winter of 1985 I was much more confident and absolutely loved the racing and the atmosphere in the arenas. We finished a good third in Dortmund, then moved on to Paris, where we would almost certainly have won if it hadn't been for me crashing in the penultimate Madison of the event. The idea was that I would throw Tony in for the final sprint in that Madison, but as I threw him in my rear wheel blew out and I went down most of the back straight on my back. A load of guys crashed into me as well. Daniel Gisiger, who was leading the event at the time, ended up with eight or nine stitches in his head. There was a bit of a pause while we were all patched up.

I felt very sore on my left side, which had taken all of the impact, and was pretty shaken, but not as much as Gisiger who wasn't able to continue. When we got on the track again for the final Madison, I wasn't really aware of what was going on. Etienne De Wilde and Stan Tourné attacked straight away and got a lap. After that they combined cleverly with other riders, particularly Eric Vanderaerden. Every time I'd go to throw Tony in they'd come in between us. It got very dirty. The crowd was going crazy because they could see what was going on. Finally, the judges disqualified Vanderaerden, but by that time it was too late for us to get any laps back and we ended up finishing second, which was still a great performance.

As we left Bercy that evening I had no idea of the extent of the damage I'd done to my knee. I had some pain, but it wasn't too bad. With hindsight, the error I made was putting my bike away for a month or so, during which time I didn't feel the injury at all. However, when I got back on the bike again in January to start preparing for the new season it hurt straight away. At the time, I didn't think it was from the crash. I tried changing shoe plates, shoes, pedals, bike sizes, saddle height, everything. I'd signed for a new team as well so I was extremely anxious to get some form and a result. I went to the training camp and saw the team doctor. They looked at everything and couldn't find any reason for the problem, and it wasn't until I went to see their specialist in Italy, Dr Capuzzo, that he diagnosed a crushed knee cartilage. He operated on me in April 1986, but when I got back on the bike again it was still sore.

He had diagnosed the injury correctly and shaved the cartilage where it was damaged, but the injury had had a knock-on effect. I'd been off the bike for so long that I'd lost some of the muscle around my knee, which meant that my kneecap wasn't being held precisely in place. It was slightly off to one side. Consequently, when I got back on the bike, bone was rubbing against bone. It wasn't until I got treatment two years later from Dr Hans-Wilhelm Müller-Wohlfahrt, a world leader in the treatment of sports injuries, that I found out what the underlying problem was. By then I'd been pushing and pushing, had had lots of cortisone injections into my knee and taken loads of anti-inflammatories.

After I had that first operation in April 1986, we were told that the injury had been corrected, so I was put into the Carrera team for the Tour of Romandy. I started OK but it swelled up again. The team decided that racing rather than resting was the best solution, so put me into their team for the Giro, which provided me with my first taste of riding with Roberto Visentini, who was Carrera's big Italian star.

I didn't have much training behind me but I did all I could to help him win the title, which wasn't as much as I'd have been able to do when fully fit. I probably had my biggest impact in the team time trial, when our main rivals were Del Tongo. It was that day that I discovered that Visentini had this tendency of riding three yards off the front of the line, not understanding that he had innate power and why that meant no one else could push as hard as him. He didn't compromise at all. I tried to keep the rest of the team working together. In the final couple of kilometres, which rose steeply to the line, Visentini was up in front shouting at everybody: 'Come on! Come on! Come on!' I was behind him controlling the line, making sure that we still had at least the five riders we needed to stop the clock on the line. We finished two minutes down in fourth place.

I pulled out a couple of days before the end with the intention of going back to the doctor in order to get myself sorted out in time for the Tour. I felt like I needed to rest, that I'd done too much too soon, but I was determined to ride the Tour to repay Carrera for their investment. So, it was my fault as much as anyone's that I headed to the start in Boulogne-Billancourt, home of my former club, the ACBB. I thought I needed the miles, that I'd recover and get back to my physical peak again, but racing there was like trying to get onto a travelling TGV from a standing start. It was impossible to get up to full racing speed.

It really hit me when we got to the Pyrenees. Lying third overall, I fell back on the Col de Marie-Blanque and was never in contention after that, losing 20 minutes that day. On the stage up to Superbagnères I actually got off my bike and sat down on the parapet of a bridge with my head in my hands. An old man came over and said to me: 'Roche, what are you doing? You've got to go on. This is the Tour de France. You can't quit like this.' I seem to remember that I gave him my hat, got back on and rode to the finish, where I was half an hour behind the winner. I remember at the Tour the following year – it was in Dijon, I think – the crowd parted as I moved through it and the same old man was there. 'Do you remember me, Stephen?' he asked. 'You gave me your hat when you stopped.' It was an emotional moment because he'd seen me at my lowest point and then at my highest.

My problems opened the door to my teammate Urs Zimmermann, who ended up finishing third behind LeMond and Hinault. I tried to do what I could but I wasn't a lot of help to him or anyone else. On the flat I was still useful, tactically I could help, but on the climbs I was no good at all. In fact, the team did pretty well in the race as Jørgen Pedersen was in yellow for a few days, Erich Maechler won a stage and Guido Bontempi won three bunch sprints. But I was the leader and I was nowhere.

One of the few good aspects of the year was the friendship that I developed with Eddy Schepers. He'd ridden with Eddy Merckx late on in his career so he knew what it was to ride for an out-and-out leader. I'd seen the hard work Eddy Schepers had put in riding for Visentini at the Giro and then for Zimmermann at the Tour. Despite his efforts, at the end of that year Carrera were letting Eddy go and Visentini wasn't making any attempt to persuade them to keep him. In the end, I said to Boifava: 'We need the Bontempis, we need the Lealis, we need Ghirotto, Giancarlo Perini, Pedersen, but we also need guys like Eddy who can climb. If myself or Roberto are going well, we'll need riders who can support us in the mountains.' In the end, Boifava decided to keep Eddy.

Eddy appreciated what I'd done for him. He also realised that although he'd helped Visentini win the Giro in 1986, Visentini hadn't returned the favour that winter. Eddy remembered that. He was a simple guy, had a good amount of class, but not enough to be a leader. He was very courageous. Above all, he knew that he had the ability to help other riders win big races and that was his value to the team. Other teams recognised that value as well, which was why he had such a long career. You never had to put your hand up and call Eddy. He was always there when you needed him.

The other thing that I discussed with Boifava was my contract. He wanted to reduce my salary but I refused. I said to him: 'If I'd won the Tour and the Worlds you wouldn't be coming along to me and saying: "Stephen, look, here's some more money." You'd be saying: "We've got a contract, I'm not paying you any more." I'll admit to you now that I know I haven't done much this season, but I'm confident that I can be OK in 1987. I know you're under pressure from Carrera and the other sponsors, but what I'd like you to do is to leave my contract as it is until next April, and if I haven't performed by then, then we can sit down and you can call the shots. But I think you have to be fair. I've a knee injury, a bad year and that's the way it goes.'

My season ended with a painfully disheartening appearance in the Baracchi Trophy time trial. Teams of two covered a 97km course and I was paired with Visentini. After we started, it soon became clear to me that he wasn't going to make any allowances for my knee injury. He was riding flat out. Everyone knew about the problems I'd had, especially within the team. While I had very little form and was suffering, he'd won the Giro and was still in good form. He kept surging past me so hard that there'd be a gap between us, then as soon as I got back up to his wheel he'd pull over and drop back again, gathering himself for his next effort. After a while, though, I was so angry I almost couldn't feel the pain and was able to hand out some punishment of my own. But I wasn't giving him what I'd taken from him. I simply didn't have the ability to do that.

Two weeks after the Baracchi, I was back on the operating table. This time a surgeon I'd consulted with before in Paris, Dr Jean-Baptiste Courroy, diagnosed fibrosis of the tendon. He opened my knee up, removed part of the meniscus and closed it up again.

My routine changed that winter. I'd not had a consistent run of races all year and I knew I needed to put in a lot of graft once I got the OK from Dr Courroy to start riding again. That came in mid-November. I began very tentatively, doing perhaps just half an hour a day. But for the first time in almost a year there was no reaction – no swelling, no pain. This meant I was able to build up the length of my rides very steadily.

In the back of my mind was the commitment I'd made to Boifava about my contract, that we would talk again in April if I was still not producing any results. But it never came to that. Instead I had a great start to the 1987 season, winning the Tour of Valencia in February. Continuing the upward trend, I then performed very well at Paris–Nice, although I left the race with mixed emotions, knowing that I could have won and unhappy because I hadn't.

The race could hardly have started better for me. I was third in the prologue and Carrera won the team time trial the next day to put me in the lead. I hung on to the leader's white jersey on Mont Ventoux, finishing just behind Sean Kelly as he won the stage at Chalet Reynard. After that, it got more complicated.

The next stage was to Mont Faron. Late on that day, Jean-François Bernard, who was the big upcoming French hope, went off the front of the bunch to have a pee. In situations like this, the rider concerned would ride off ahead of everyone, find a place to stop where there were no spectators around, then wait for the bunch to come up to him again. Consequently, we were all riding along behind, not really paying much attention. But after a while someone noticed that Bernard hadn't been brought back. The guy with the blackboard who provided time gaps dropped back and we saw that Bernard was several minutes up on us. We called up Paul Koechli, Bernard's directeur sportif at Toshiba, and asked him what was going on. Koechli told us that Bernard had gone for a pee and that because we hadn't been going hard he just kept going. We reacted then, but it was too late. Bernard was a powerhouse on the flat and climbs, and he won the stage, taking the jersey from me.

I was furious and didn't wait long the next morning before launching an attack as the stage headed towards St Tropez. A few other guys came across and we kept riding and riding, but they eventually caught us on the Col de la Garde-Freinet, just before St Tropez. Going over the top, I hung on as Laurent Fignon attacked and went away with Sean Kelly, Charly Mottet and half a dozen other guys. Crucially, Bernard did not make the cut. We flew down the descent, riding eyeballs out into the finish, where Fignon won the stage and I took the lead again.

After that it seemed likely that the race would be decided in the time trial on the Col d'Eze on the final afternoon. I safely negotiated the stage into Mandelieu on the penultimate day. The final day started with a shortish stage through the hills inland from the coast and down the Col de Vence into Nice, with the time trial to follow. Normally I'd have had nothing to worry about on that morning stage, but I punctured just before we reached the descent off the Col de Vence. Because the tempo had been quick from the start, the only teammates I had with me were Bruno Leali and Eddy, who was shadowing me closely. When I punctured, I jumped off my bike and took Eddy's wheel, which was a big mistake, as that meant I'd lost him as well.

I thought I would get back on easily enough, but Sean's Kas team, who had already been setting the pace, upped it even more when I fell back. Instead of waiting for some of my teammates to come back up to me and then close down the gap to my rivals, I panicked on the way down the descent, chased across to the lead group and picked my way back towards the front. Only then did I realise that a group containing Kelly, Fignon, Bernard and a few others was another 50 yards up the road. I started to chase with Leali, but as there were only two of us we couldn't close the gap.

At one point, as Bruno and I rode full throttle behind Sean's group, a motorbike photographer came alongside us to take pictures of me battling to hang on to the lead. A moment later,

Kelly's directeur sportif at Kas, Christian Rumeau, came up as well. All I could see was the nose of this Citroën CX right up under my handlebars and then, bump! He went right into the back of the motorbike. He was driving him off the road to prevent him giving me some shelter and, therefore, a means of cutting the gap. I was never one to get in behind a motorbike, but Rumeau wasn't going to give me the opportunity anyway. Eventually the bunch caught Bruno and me, but by then it was too late to react. We lost two minutes and I lost the lead.

I wasn't happy about it, but it was one of those things that can happen in bike races. There are unwritten rules about incidents like this – not attacking when someone falls in the feed zone, for instance. But on that occasion no one actually attacked, they simply didn't ease off after I had punctured, which was fair enough. You could compare it with the incident in the Pyrenees at the 2010 Tour when Alberto Contador attacked Andy Schleck after his chain came off. Contador was getting it in the neck from everyone. People, including Schleck, were saying he hadn't acted in a sporting manner. But I think saying that was totally ridiculous. They were in a bike race, for heaven's sake.

My view was that when Schleck attacked he was in the small chainring. That meant that the chain was very floppy and, in that situation when he's suddenly making a full-on attack, you'd almost expect the chain not to catch or to jump. You can't blame Contador for that. He responded to Schleck's attack and just kept going. I don't see why people said he should have stopped. These things happen in bike racing, as I found out to my cost that day.

A peculiarity of Paris–Nice back then was that the start times for the time trial were set out first thing on the final morning. Consequently, as the leader going into the final day, I was supposed to be the last man off. The organiser came to me before the time trial and said: 'Stephen, you're the moral victor and I'd like you to stay in the leader's jersey for the time trial.' I said I couldn't do that as Sean had earned the right to wear the jersey, but I was determined to win the stage. I did beat Sean that afternoon by ten seconds, but it wasn't enough. I finished fourth in the General Classification. The time-trial win was no consolation for losing the overall as I was riding very, very strongly.

I wasn't happy about it for a few days, but it didn't affect the relationship between me and Sean. After Paris–Nice we had a training camp and he turned to me during a ride one day and said he was sorry about what had happened. 'It wasn't my fault. I had to follow the others,' he said. I knew he was right about that, that he had to go with that final attack, and I wasn't one to moan about it anyway. It was simply the way that racing went sometimes. Looking back now, it was just one of the many great battles the two of us had on that race. Every year that we won Paris–Nice – and we did so eight years in a row, with me starting the run and Sean taking the next seven – we won the time trial on the Col d'Eze. We were unbeatable there. Sean won it five times and I won three, and added another one in 1989. That famous climb truly was part of Ireland during the 1980s.

Carrera didn't have to wait too long for a big win, though, as Erich Maechler judged his effort perfectly at Milan–San Remo to win Italy's biggest one-day race. From there I moved on to the Criterium International in Antibes, where Sean and I went at each other again. He won the final time trial there to leave me second but I was very happy to have kept my run of form going.

We moved on to the Classics and I placed well again at Flèche Wallonne, crossing the line in fourth place, but Davide Boifava was getting concerned that the form I had wasn't producing the victories it merited. That evening he came to my room and said: 'Stephen, you're riding so, so well but you haven't won any big ones yet this year. You're knocking on the door, you're riding aggressively, you're in all the good moves, but you're just not quite pulling it off. You've got to be prepared to lose to win.' Initially, I thought that sounded very profound.

Riding Liège–Bastogne–Liège four days later, Claude Criquielion and I annihilated the field. As we were coming towards the finish Boifava's words were stuck in my mind: 'You've got to be prepared to lose to win.'

I thought that if I led Criquielion out in the sprint there was a good chance he'd beat me, but if he led me out there was a good chance I'd beat him. However, for some totally unfathomable reason, we both forgot that there were still other guys in the race, that the rest of the field hadn't all just climbed off.

I was so focused on what Boifava had told me that all I could do was think about Criquielion. Coming down the final section on the Boulevard de la Sauvenière, we went around a roundabout, and went back up the other side of the road we'd just come down. You would imagine that any rider in that position would have glanced across to check what was happening behind. Even now I still think: 'Why didn't I look back and see if the other guys were closing?' I can understand why some people don't believe that I didn't see Moreno Argentin coming before we started to sprint.

With 200 metres remaining, I started to come off Criquielion's wheel and 'whoosh!' Argentin came flying past me and beat me to the line by about half a bike-length with Criquielion third. Even 25 years on, the hairs still stand out on my arms when I think about that.

Usually after big races I'd get back in the car and put it in fifth gear all the way home. But that night's drive was the longest ever from Liège back to Paris because I couldn't get what had happened out of my mind. 'It's impossible,' I was thinking. 'Did I almost win Liège–Bastogne–Liège? Was I so stupid that I didn't see Argentin coming from behind? Why didn't I look across? Why was I being so stupid focusing completely on Criquielion? How has this happened? Is this a nightmare? Will I wake up and find it was a dream?' But when I woke the next morning, of course, I was still second and even to this day it haunts me. I think it was the only time after a race that I cried.

Eventually the wins did start to come. In early May I went to the Tour of Romandy, one of my favourite races, and convincingly won the split stages on the final day to take my third title there. That set me up perfectly for the Giro, where Carrera had two cards to play in me and Visentini. He was the defending champion so I understood that he had the right to be a leader, but I felt I had earned that status as well, thanks to my performances during the first part of that season. I wasn't expecting to be sole leader or thinking that I wanted to beat Visentini. My feeling was that I wanted to have the same status as Visentini on the road, and the road would decide which of us was the stronger.

Of course, it was never going to be as easy as that. Visentini was the local guy. He was from Brescia, where Carrera were based. He always rode well in the Giro, which made him very popular with Italian fans. In fact, he had a reputation as a guy who was only interested in riding the Giro. It was the only race all year that he really wanted to win. But I still thought that things would resolve themselves on the road. Unfortunately, when we got there, that wasn't how it worked out.

As usual, the Giro had attracted a good field. The Panasonic team was particularly strong with Erik Breukink, Robert Millar, Phil Anderson, Peter Winnen and Johan van der Velde in the line-up. Then there were guys like Flavio Giupponi, Moreno Argentin and Marino Lejarreta. But our team was extremely powerful as well, and I think Visentini would have beaten those guys because he was so strong in time trials.

The start of the race was a bit odd. The first two days comprised a short prologue, a short mountain stage and a short downhill time trial off the Poggio into San Remo. Visentini won the first, Breukink the second, taking the leader's *maglia rosa* in the process, leading us into the third of those tricky tests, the descent off the Poggio. Back then, the Poggio wasn't the same kind of descent on smooth roads that it is today. It's like a boulevard now compared to how it was then. It was rideable, but bumpy and by no means safe. So why ask us to ride it in that situation? The dangers we faced were very much in our minds at that time because an Italian rider, Emilio Ravasio, had died on the race the year before, and two more had died earlier in the season. Consequently, having a time trial on a descent on the second day was asking for trouble. I certainly questioned the wisdom of it when asked for my thoughts by a journalist.

Visentini thought he was going to win that stage because he was an extremely good descender. I remember before the stage he was on at me about how he was going to ride his special time-trial bike with a disc wheel and everything else. But I didn't see it the same way. When I did my recce with my mechanic, Patrick Valcke, we could see that the descent was very bumpy. The 8km test started 2km from the top of the hill, then it went sharp left downhill following the same road as Milan–San Remo.

Everyone was talking about using low-profile time-trial bikes with special wheels because it was 2km flattish, 4–5km downhill, then another 2km flat into the finish. I said to Patrick that that was one option, but my concern was that you could lose a lot more time on the descent if you weren't comfortable that you'd ever gain on a time-trial bike on the two bits of flat road. So we decided that I'd ride a normal bike with 28-spoked wheels.

Everyone was talking about disc wheels or special time-trial wheels being more responsive. In my opinion, that was true on the flat, but when the bike was jumping around they weren't as responsive as a springy 28-spoked wheel. You get far more grip with spoked wheels on corners. They track around corners much more smoothly and safely. In addition, when you come out of corners and start to push on the pedals again, the bike responds very quickly because spoked wheels hold better, which boosts power transference.

When I went to the start with Patrick everyone, including Visentini, still thought that we were going to change the bike. They thought we were bluffing. Even Boifava came to see me in my room and asked if I was sure it was the right decision to ride a normal bike. But, once I'd consulted with Patrick and made my decision, there was never any going back on it. Even when I went to the start and could see guys like Urs Freuler, van der Velde and Argentin, who were all very good descenders and were all on low-profile bikes, I still wasn't tempted to change. But the tactic paid off. I beat Lech Piasecki by three seconds, with Breukink another three back in third. Visentini was fifth and that made things a little more difficult for him. I'd beaten him at his own game and he wasn't very happy with that.

The next big test was a 43km team time trial on the fourth day. There weren't a lot of hills but it was pretty tricky. Carrera were lucky that we had some fabulous team time-trial riders like Guido Bontempi, Bruno Leali, Massimo Ghirotto and Erich Maechler. They were all monumental to sit behind when riding a team time trial. And there was Visentini, of course. He was a fabulous time triallist, but he was what the French call an '*électron libre*' – a free electron. He did his own thing and was completely in his own world. He couldn't understand why the rest of us couldn't follow him. So it was quite complicated doing team time trials with Roberto. But, at the same time, he was a great guy to have in a test like that because he was very, very strong and when he went to the front he would produce a really powerful turn. It was just a matter of controlling what was going on behind him.

I know that if I hadn't been there to keep things together, it would have been much more difficult for the team. Time trialling was my thing. I really loved it. I had to make sure Visentini's powerful turns didn't disrupt our rhythm too much. If you tried to stay on his wheel as he went to the front the whole line would break up. But we kept it together so well that we won by almost a minute, giving me my first pink jersey as I was Carrera's highest-placed rider thanks to that victory on the Poggio.

Although I was now the race leader, Visentini was the reigning champion and he wasn't going to let go easily. As the opening week continued, it became increasingly clear that Visentini was doing no more than follow me about wherever I went. If a move went and I wasn't there, he didn't go either. If he had wanted to be a good teammate, he'd have been making the most of those groups that I wasn't in. He would have been joining them and hoping that something would work out. Instead, he was waiting for me to chase behind any groups and then shadowing me again.

The funny thing was that we were still talking to each other. Things were grand between us. I can't say we were particularly close, but we did get on well together. However, he was a guy who never spoke a lot to anybody. He would come down early for breakfast, grab a coffee, take a newspaper and disappear. Then we'd see him on the race, then after racing he'd be one of the first guys to the dinner table. He'd be shouting for service, basically saying: 'I'm here!' He'd eat and then he was gone. But he was a nice guy. We both shared a passion for cars. In 1986 he had a Mercedes 190E, one of the nice souped-up versions – it was very, very fast. He brought it along to the training camp and he was quite happy for me to have a go in it, which was good fun.

Then things started to go wrong. On one stage there was a hairpin bend into a 2km uphill climb to the line – a typical finish for the Giro. A couple of guys fell on the hairpin and I went down with them. As I was lying on the ground, I looked up and I could see Visentini coming around me and scarpering off up the hill. I was shouting, 'Roberto, Roberto!' But he didn't even look at me. He just kept on going. I got back on my bike and chased and chased and chased and just barely got onto the back of the group as they crossed the finishing line.

I lost no time that day, but it was a bit of a shock to see my teammate going off up the road. I said something to him about it, but he played it down and said there was no problem at all, but I was a bit taken aback by his attitude. It seemed he was more interested in me than in our rivals, and acted as if he wanted to maintain his leadership of the team, and the only way for him to do that was to be in front of me. The problem was that at that particular time I was ahead of him. It wasn't a great situation for either of us, to be honest.

I know some of our challengers thought they might be able to take advantage of our rivalry at the first major summit finish on the Terminillo, which came a week into the race. But I was covered in more ways than one by some canny manoeuvring by my roommate Eddy Schepers. That stage demonstrated perfectly why it's important to have very loyal teammates, riders who don't think only of themselves.

Eddy was away with Fagor's Jean-Claude Bagot. Fagor didn't have any riders capable of challenging for high overall honours, so their focus was on making the most of stage-winning opportunities. But Eddy, who was up there cleverly defending my interests as race leader, had a legitimate reason not to ride. There was no reason for him to cooperate with Bagot, which meant that Eddy was fresher and would almost certainly have beaten Bagot in the sprint because Eddy was pretty quick.

However, during the course of the day, he said to Bagot: 'Jean-Claude, if you want to win the stage, then I'm prepared to help you. But, as you've got a very strong team of climbers at Fagor, it would be good for Stephen to be able to call on their help if he needs it at any point in the next few days in the mountains. It would be appropriate for you to give him a hand in return for the win today.'

Jean-Claude Bagot said: 'Yes, OK. It's a done deal.'

So Eddy led out the sprint at the end of the stage and Bagot went by him to take the win. I had no idea how useful that deal was to be to me later in the race, when I would end up getting very isolated on the Carrera team with nobody but Eddy to help me.

That stage was a good one for me as I managed to put some distance between myself and a couple of my rivals, including Moreno Argentin. Visentini was in the group with me at the finish, but didn't do any work to increase the advantage we had on riders we had dropped. It was in his interests as well as mine for him to cooperate, but he was clearly saving everything that he had. Once again, other teams noticed that.

His watch-and-wait strategy began to pay off when I got caught up in the aftermath of a big pile-up on the road to Termoli, halfway through the race. About half the bunch went down coming towards the finish. I didn't actually crash, but as I braked someone's handlebar went into my buttock and bruised me really badly. On the days that followed, when the road went uphill and I tried to push down on the pedals, I had no power in my left leg. Well, there was power there, but it was extremely painful delivering it because of the belt that I'd got.

There were some suggestions that I might abandon, but there was never really a question of me quitting the race. I just wanted an easy day or two in order to recover. In the big tours you can have form, lose it and then get it back again because they are three weeks long, so abandoning wasn't something that I was considering. I just wanted to try to keep Visentini at bay while I got my form back and had treatment for the injury. The likes of Breukink, Giupponi and Argentin were still watching the battle going on between Roberto and me, laughing at us, and hoping that they could piggyback on it.

What had only been an undercurrent of tension became much

more obvious on the day of the crucial San Marino time trial almost two weeks into the race. Up to then there had been a bit of friction, but the race was going well for Carrera. Visentini had won the prologue, I'd won the time trial down the Poggio, we'd won the team time trial, Bontempi had taken a bunch sprint and I had the pink jersey.

I felt all right about Visentini ghosting around behind me because I felt like I had his card marked. But where things started to get dusty, before they got dirty, was with that time trial into San Marino.

To help prepare before a time trial I always tried to ride the whole stage in advance, and I did so that morning despite the fact it was raining. My problem wasn't the rain, but having Roberto sitting in the team car behind me. He kept coming up alongside me and asking: 'Stefano, which direction is the wind coming from?' 'Stefano, what gear are you using?' 'Stefano, is it raining?'

He was pestering me all the time. When I'm doing this kind of thing, I'm in my own world, my little bubble. I don't want anybody talking to me. I especially don't want anybody asking me questions. I could feel the frustration building inside me. I wanted to tell him where to go and to leave me alone, that if he wanted to find out which way the wind was coming from he should get on his bike and ride it himself.

When we had finished the recce we went back down to our hotel for lunch. On days like that I would have everything set up just as I wanted. My whole day was planned around my time trial. Three hours before my start, my lunch was prepared. I came down to the table that had been set for me and all of a sudden Roberto sat down too and started eating. And he just kept on talking and talking and talking and talking. He asked me the same things all over again: 'Stefano, after 5k there's a little climb, what gear did you go over on?' He never stopped.

Those moments were very precious to me. I was in my own world, going over the course in my mind, sitting lost within myself. Tension would be building up inside me – lots of nervous energy. When I started to ride, I would feed off that, use it to help me get a good result. But on this particular day I was so wound up that when I got to the start line I had no energy left. Everything was gone. I was totally wasted.

I ended up riding a really poor time trial. I couldn't lift the pace at all and Visentini put almost three minutes into me, which was a huge gain for him. But what made it difficult to take for me was getting across the finish line and seeing everyone hugging and kissing Visentini, telling him how great he was, that he was going to win the Giro now.

I couldn't believe it. I was devastated after flopping and losing my jersey, and no one could give two hoots. I'd been putting money in the pockets of these guys with all the races that I'd won over the previous six months, I'd been keeping the jersey afloat for the last ten days in the Giro and now everyone was basically saying: 'Visentini is our man!' I was disappointed to say the least with that reaction. But that was nothing compared to how I felt when I got the hotel and started watching the television.

Visentini was having a conversation with a journalist, who was saying to him: 'Any rivalry in the team is now over. Roche is now two minutes back. That means that Roche is going to ride for you, Roberto. And I suppose that you're going to be quite content to return the favour and ride for Roche at the Tour de France . . .'

And Roberto turned to the journalist and said: 'No, no, no! Stephen is going to ride for me here, that's true. But I'm not going to be riding the Tour de France. I'm going to the beach!'

Now, that might well be your plan, but a wise man would know that you don't bloody well say it because that's really asking for trouble. I was sitting on my bed, with Eddy next to me on his, watching Visentini and saying to Eddy: 'This guy is saying bluntly that I'm going to ride for him and he isn't going to pay me back. That's just not on.'

Eddy started looking at the roadbook. Visentini had taken all the chances he'd had to attack me up to that point, but because he was Italian he could get away with a lot. However, being Irish, a foreigner, I knew all too well that I had to be very careful how I managed myself. I couldn't do anything that could be seen as attacking the local hero, so I sat down with Eddy and looked at the stages still to come.

We decided it was going to be difficult to do something to get rid of Visentini on the high mountain stages because he was climbing as well as I was. Also, he'd be expecting me to respond there. But the real problem for me was that I couldn't be seen to be attacking him. So how could I get around that?

We debated this for a while, looked at the mountain stages, and then at the medium mountain stage that preceded them up to a town called Sappada. Although there was one flat stage before that, we knew that Roberto would still be very tired going into the Sappada stage due to the huge effort he'd made in his time trial. Posting the time he had, it was clear he hadn't kept anything in reserve. His strategy was clearly to give it 110 per cent in the time trial, knowing that the days that followed weren't particularly hard and that he would be able to recover and be ready for the key mountain stages.

We assumed that Roberto wouldn't be expecting me to attack or be in a breakaway group on that stage into Sappada. But we were still stuck with this dilemma of how to attack without being seen as doing so. We decided the only way around that was to wait until some other guy went away and then I could maybe try to follow. It wasn't a great plan, but it was the only hope I had.

CHAPTER 5

'ROCHE VA A CASA'

The stage to Sappada had been designed as a warm-up for the bigger days in the mountains that lay beyond it. Starting down on the coast near Venice, the first 100km, almost half that day's total, were basically flat as we headed north. The first of three main climbs, the Forcella di Monte Rest, came at about two-thirds of the distance, followed by the Valcalda and then the Cima Sappada, from where there was a short drop down into the finish. None of the climbs were that big or tough. The final one was the highest of the trio but rose to less than 1,300 metres.

The day's main action began when Jean-Claude Bagot jumped clear on the Forcella di Monte Rest. Soon after, there was a flurry of attacks as Robert Millar and Roberto Conti duelled for points in the mountains competition and I tracked them.

Strategically, if there's a group away and your team doesn't have someone in it, somebody should try to get across to it. OK, it wasn't my job as one of the leaders to try to get in that group, but at the same time if we had a rider in that break then our team wouldn't have to set the pace behind it. So Eddy and I decided this was the moment to move, but Visentini was quick to follow. Just before the summit, however, Ennio Salvador, an Italian rider a long way down the overall standings, attacked. Soon after Salvador went over the top of the Monte Rest, I strolled over the top behind him, but once the road started going down I 'cut the brake cables'.

I went down without looking to see who was following, hoping of course that no one was very close behind and thinking I would decide what to do when I got to the bottom. It was one of those days when everything went right for me going down that descent. I closed a gap of 1 minute 15 or 1 minute 20 to Bagot and Salvador, looked round and realised I was on my own with them. I thought: 'I'm with two nobodies as far as the overall is concerned. I can just ride along with these guys, but at the same time are Panasonic and Bianchi just going to let me ride away off the front?'

I guessed that those two teams would start chasing after me – in fact, Erik Breukink and Robert Millar both later confirmed that the Dutch team were about to do that – but I knew I couldn't be seen to be riding very hard. Plus, there were still two climbs ahead, including a final ascent to the finish, so riding hard would have been tactical suicide.

I was happy to sit in behind Bagot and Salvador for a while. Remembering the deal he'd done with Eddy back on the Terminillo, Bagot certainly didn't object. But after a while I thought I might as well ride with them as they weren't in contention on GC and by doing so I would be making things more difficult for the Bianchi and Panasonic teams, who were sure to be chasing behind. We lost Bagot when he punctured and fell back to the bunch, but I still wasn't too concerned about what was happening back there until the Carrera team manager Davide Boifava came up alongside me in the team car.

'Stephen, what are you doing?' he asked me.

'I'm defending the jersey. Roberto has the jersey – there were two guys off the front. We had nobody there, now we have somebody, so it means that the team can relax now and let the Panasonics and the Bianchis do the riding.'

'But Stephen, the problem is that there are riders hanging in trees and all over the place because you went down the descent so fast. The whole race is disorganised. And now your Carrera teammates are riding on the front of the bunch.'

'Tell the lads to stop and let the Bianchis and the Panasonics ride.'

'I can't. Roberto's riding.'

'Well, tell Roberto to stop.'

'No, he won't stop.'

'Well, tell him to keep something under the pedal because when he catches me he's going to need it.'

The car went away, then a few minutes later the second team car came up with my mechanic, Patrick Valcke, in it. He held out the radio and on it I could hear Boifava telling me once again to stop riding. Boifava said all the other teams were laughing at Carrera, that if I didn't stop he would come up and drive me off the road. But I told him I wasn't going to stop unless the Carrera boys stopped chasing me.

I said to Patrick, 'What do you reckon?'

'Stephen,' he replied, 'if you've got any balls now is the time to show them.'

So I put the gear lever down and went for it. I remember we were on a dead flat road that was so straight that I could see the bunch way back about a minute and a half behind. I was riding eyeballs out, so pumped up with anger by the fact that my team was riding behind me that I didn't feel any fatigue at all. Rage drove me on for almost 40 kilometres. The bunch was almost on me approaching the foot of the second climb, the Valcalda. Just when it seemed my chance had gone, Jean-François Bernard attacked off the front of the bunch and Phil Anderson, Conti, Millar, Pedro Muñoz, Marino Lejarreta, Johan van der Velde and a couple of others joined him. As they pushed on past me, I got on the back of the line and this group started to move clear of the bunch again.

The poor tactical sense that Visentini and Boifava had shown in getting the Carrera team to chase me between the two climbs then rebounded on them. Seeing me edging away again, Visentini looked around for his teammates, but found he was isolated. He called in some favours and, thanks to the work of some other Italian teams, the bunch brought our group back before the final climb, which didn't suit me.

The good thing was that when the peloton came up to me Eddy Schepers was there as well. As we went onto the final climb, he started riding shotgun for me, encouraging me along, trying to keep me in contact. Visentini was also in the group, but near the back and steadily falling further back having given far too much in the chase. One report the next day colourfully described him as not even having enough strength to work the muscles in his face, let alone turn a gear that would keep him in contention.

After a while the team car came alongside Eddy and me and Boifava said to him: 'Eddy, you've got to work for Roberto now.' Boifava told Eddy that Visentini was struggling and ordered him back. But Eddy said: 'Stephen is the guy who looks after me, not Roberto. Stephen's been up at the front for a long time, he needs more help than Roberto. Roberto shouldn't have been riding behind Stephen.'

Then Eddy turned to me and said: 'Stephen, I'm your man, but I hope you'll cover me.' From that point he rode tempo on the front for me, coaching me along, until we were almost at the top of the climb. About a kilometre from the top he told me he couldn't do any more. 'You've got to go for it now, Stephen. This is the day you win the Giro. Go for it!'

I gave it everything for the last few hundred metres over the top of the climb and then on the shallow drop into the finish. Panasonic's van der Velde won the stage, but the key thing was that I finished just ten seconds down on the group led in by Tony Rominger. He gained a bonus of five seconds for finishing second on the stage, but he needed an additional five seconds to jump ahead of me in the overall classification. Six minutes later,

Visentini crossed the line, putting me back in the pink jersey, but with the narrowest of leads over Rominger. As Roberto finished, he pointed up at the podium where I was just getting the pink jersey and said: 'Tonight somebody's going home.'

Given events that day, if Rominger's group had finished another five seconds ahead of me and given him the pink jersey, Carrera's big boss would probably have said, 'Right, Stephen, you'd better go home.' History could have been very different. But because I had the pink jersey, because Roberto had lost more than six minutes on the stage and it was now highly unlikely that he was going to win the Giro, Carrera needed me.

There was mayhem after the stage. Even the police officers were jostling me when I finished. I was all but locked away in my room and told not to talk to the press. I didn't say anything to them – for a while. But then I realised that if I didn't talk to the press then everybody else's story would be heard apart from mine – and it wasn't a bad story.

Our hotel was very close to the finish line and I could hear there was a big buzz with all the frantic activity down there. I wondered what they were all talking about. So I went out onto my terrace and right under my window I could see Angelo Zomegnan, who was then working as a reporter for *Gazzetta dello Sport* and would later become the Giro director. I shouted down to him: 'Angelo, come here. I want you to be my spokesman. I want to tell you my story.' I gave him my side and he was happy to hear it. But when I'd finished he told me there was a bit of a problem. The following day's paper had already been sent to print, so my story would only come out the day after. 'So, whatever happens tomorrow,' he said, 'you're just going to have to get on with it . . .'

That evening Carrera's two bosses, the Tacchella brothers, arrived at the race. They'd come to sign my new contract for the following year, but we never got around to that. In fact, I didn't even end up seeing them that evening. Instead, there was a partial team meeting. All of the team bosses were in there with the Tacchellas. Roberto was so far back on GC that they had to bite the bullet and keep me on board. They talked about how to deal with Visentini and what events might arise given what had already gone on.

The next morning the papers were full of it. That day must have been like Christmas for them. Tino Tacchella tried to calm things by telling the press that the team had drawn a line under what had happened. 'The sixth of June never existed,' he told them. What happened was just an accident. The Giro is compromised but not lost. We've cleared the air.'

It sounded good, but I don't think anyone was listening. In some ways, events over the following few days reminded me of some of the stories I read about the shenanigans that had gone on in the '40s and '50s, the era of Fausto Coppi and Gino Bartali. I had often wondered exactly how things had been back then. Well, the '87 Giro provided a good insight, especially the four or five days after Sappada. I was made out to be a terribly bad guy, dubbed Judas by the press for taking the bread out of my teammate's mouth. Eddy was 'The Rebel'. Patrick was 'Satan'. It might have been funny if people hadn't taken it so seriously.

From that point on Visentini didn't talk to me at all. I felt it was quite stupid the extent he took it to at times. And he kept on attacking me – the day after Sappada, and the next day, and the next day. I remember seeing some footage of the race some time afterwards and on one of the climbs he's riding in the left gutter and I'm riding in the right. He has a line of riders on his wheel and I have a line on my wheel. We aren't really attacking each other, but at the same time he is trying to get away from me. I am on the opposite side of the road to him calling his bluff, basically saying to him: 'You can ride, but I can ride hard as well and you're not going to drop me.'

It was mayhem on the road that first day back in pink. Everybody wanted my blood. I would never in my wildest dreams have imagined it was going to be as difficult as it turned out to be with the fans. They had been whipped up into a frenzy because there was all this stuff in the press about me being a traitor, cheating on my teammate. People were waving banners daubed with images of raw meat dripping blood and saying, 'Roche Bastardo', 'Roche va a casa' – Roche go home – but seeing that hardened my determination. They got me thinking that there was no way I was going anywhere.

On the climbs, the fans were shouting all kinds of abuse and trying to punch me. Some had rice in their mouths and then, as I approached, they were taking a mouthful of red wine and spitting it all over me. At the finish line my pink jersey was spattered with red. I'd never been so afraid on the bike. It got so hostile that French television even came down to do a 20-minute programme on me. That hadn't happened even when a French star like Hinault was regularly winning the Giro.

Other riders were frightened as well, not because they might be attacked but because they were afraid of what might happen if a fan ran into the bunch to assault me. There could have been bodies everywhere. It was a very tough stage too, crossing five big peaks, including the famous Sella, Pordoi and Marmolada passes. The atmosphere was particularly hostile on the latter two as fans had been up there all day waiting for the race to arrive. Some were beside themselves with anger. The blackness of the weather that day made the atmosphere feel even more intimidating.

Thankfully, I had Eddy with me riding shotgun on one side and Robert Millar on the other. I was extremely grateful to Bob for giving me a dig out. I think he was pretty upset about the way people were treating me. That was the kind of guy Millar was. He had his own way of seeing things and would often go against the grain. We were friends, having spent a lot of time on the

Peugeot team together as well as doing our own training camps. Bob could see the way that the Italians were getting at me and took my side. The deal that Eddy had made with Jean-Claude Bagot on the Terminillo was also very useful that day. I called on one or two Fagor riders, and together they effectively acted as my armour, creating a protective shield around me.

I look back now and realise how resilient I was to get through the race. If someone had said to me before the Giro that this scenario would arise and had wondered what I would do, I'd have told them that I would be on the first plane out of there. But when it did happen there was no way that I was going to go home. I was virtually saying to these people: 'Do what you want, say what you want. I'm not going home.' I think I'd shown that kind of courage on a few occasions before: first of all when I'd had the operation on my ingrowing toenails, then when leaving home and going to France, then with my knee problem. I had had plenty of ups and downs, but every time I had fought back. And here I was down again and still fighting back. I drew on that willpower right the way through my career.

It wasn't only the fans that I had to deal with. Visentini did everything he could to get clear that day and that wasn't all he was up to. As we were coming over the top of one of the big climbs, Eddy and I had fallen back a bit and Roberto dropped back towards us. I thought for a moment he was coming back to help. But when we reached him he kind of swerved. We didn't know why, but we managed to avoid him. Then he veered again, as if to force me over the cliff. I avoided him again but he almost put Eddy right over the edge. I rode alongside him, put my hand on his bars and made it clear that if he tried that again he'd be coming over the edge with me. It was an unsettling moment, and I had another involving Visentini a few days later.

I was a good descender, but coming down the far side of a climb something didn't seem quite right. Was it me? Was it my

My time trialling ability meant that I was likely to be a contender
in just about any stage race even from my first days in the pro ranks.

(*Previous page*) A flurry of high finishes, wins and a gift for a quote meant I was quickly
in demand from the press soon after I joined Peugeot.

Posing with fellow
Irishman and close friend
Sean Kelly before the 1982
World Championships
at Goodwood, where
Sean finished third.

Teeth gritted, completely
focused and making things
very tough for a string of
riders trying to cope with
this acceleration.

Winner of the amateur version of Paris-Roubaix in 1980,
I got a proper introduction to 'the hell of the north' in 1983.

After three years at Peugeot,
I got the chance to lead a
team in my own right when I
joined La Redoute in 1984.

Heading for my first Tour de France stage victory on the Aubisque in 1985 wearing the one-piece silk skinsuit provided by team boss Raphaël Géminiani.

Géminiani had said months before I would win on the Aubisque, now here I am telling the press how I did it.

It looks like I'm giving Sean Kelly a tow at the Nissan Tour of Ireland in 1985.
Both of us won two stages, but Sean took the overall title as well.

Sitting pretty in the pink leader's jersey at the Giro d'Italia. I don't know whose wheel that is right behind mine but I would be willing to place money on it being Roberto Visentini's.

On the Giro podium with Robert Millar, who's wearing the green King of the Mountains jersey. Visentini was just below pointing at me and saying: 'Tonight, somebody's going home'. Who could he possibly have been talking about?!

bike? Something was wrong. Finally, I realised that my front fork was cracked. I could feel that there was a fracture below the crown of my fork and the bike wasn't taking the corners properly. In panic I shouted across to Visentini: 'Roberto, Roberto, my frame is broken,' not thinking of the consequences. And what did Roberto do? He attacked, of course – in a tunnel!

Because we were in a breakaway group and our team car wasn't right behind us I couldn't stop to get a spare bike. The bike on the neutral service car didn't suit me as it didn't have the right pedals. I had to go down the descent not knowing the extent of the damage to my fork. I just had to keep going and praying that nothing bad would happen. When I came into the finish I sprinted in a group of 11 or 12 because there were time bonuses available and I wanted to make sure that Visentini didn't get them. I came sixth or seventh, which was incredible given the state of my bike.

At the finish I told my mechanic Patrick that my front fork was broken. He released the skewer on the front wheel and the right blade of the fork fell out. All that was holding it in place was the central support within the fork. That was a very dramatic moment for me. Even though on the day I was happy to be there, to be in the break on the way down the mountain, in later years that episode has haunted me when I'm going down descents. On the day itself and those that followed, I never thought about it. I just got on with it. But now I have visions of that fork breaking and imagine what could have happened had it all gone wrong that day. If the fork had broken on a descent it's no exaggeration to say that my life would have been in jeopardy. It didn't bother me for a few years, but from 1992 on it really started to play on my mind.

When we got to the finish in Canazei after the stage over the Pordoi and Marmolada, I went up onto the podium to receive the pink jersey and was still getting abuse from the fans. The podium then wasn't the flash set-up they have today. It was on the back of a juggernaut with a divide halfway along. The podium was on one side and RAI's broadcasting area was on the other with the legendary Italian commentator Adriano De Zan presenting their live post-race coverage.

There were two heavies standing at the divide to dissuade anyone from going through into the broadcasting area. But I could see that I might just get a chance to give my side of the saga if I could get past them. I was waving my flowers on the podium, which wasn't going down well with some of the fans, and edging closer to these two guys. Then, as I threw my flowers to the crowd, distracting the two big monsters for a moment, I barged through the divide and into the show.

De Zan was clearly shocked to see me as I sat down in one of the chairs next to him. After a brief pause, he recovered his composure and said: 'And here we have a surprise visitor. Here is the pink jersey wearer, Stephen Roche. Stephen, do you have something to tell us?'

Up to that point I didn't think I could speak much Italian, but somehow it flowed as I told him: 'I want to give my side of the story. Roberto's given his side and so has everyone else except me. Everyone has portrayed me as the bad guy, but I don't think that's the case.' And I went on to give my point of view.

Things did calm down a little bit after that but there was still a good degree of hostility, particularly in certain places. It reached the point where I had to eat in my room for a few nights after Sappada. My masseur, Silvano Davo, was even making up food for me because they were afraid that someone might poison me. Patrick had my bike and only my bike to look after because they were afraid that someone might sabotage it. While it wasn't as bad as it had been in the '40s and '50s in Italy, they were still fairly chauvinist. They liked their own boys.

That said, I do think that journalists in Italy were by then more prepared to accept their riders being beaten on home ground by someone who was better than them as I did get quite a lot of support in the press, one prominent writer saying that 'if Roche gets punched, we feel those punches, we're with him'. But the general public weren't writing the papers, they just wanted to throw them.

I wasn't the only one in the line of fire either. Davide Boifava was also the target for a lot of anger. On one stage the cars all ground to a halt on a climb, people came into the road and someone tried to pull a bike off the roof-rack, shouting at Boifava: 'Hey, get out if you want to stop me.' But no way was he going to get out of the car. He drove on with the bike hanging half off the car and stopped in a quiet spot further up the road to fix it back onto the rack.

They thought Boifava was a traitor, that he should have put me in the ditch to stop me doing what I'd done. But Davide was still working with me. He was a good motivator. He would make sure I was OK, that I had what I wanted. He could see that he needed to support me, even if only behind the scenes, because I had the pink jersey and that was the most important thing of all. But he had to play his cards close to his chest because he also had to be seen to be behind Visentini.

It helped me that the weather turned wet for a day or two, as it took a lot of the heat out of the protests and allowed me two or three easier days. The last really serious incident happened a couple of days from the end of the Giro when we raced into Como, which wasn't too far from where Visentini was from. There was a very tight finishing circuit there. As we approached the finish there was a big crash, but as we were outside the final kilometre we were too far out for the commissaires to award us all the same finishing time. Our times would still be taken on the line. So I jumped back on the bike, zipped through seven or eight corners and just got onto the back of the front group as they crossed the line.

Generally when I finished, the police would surround me and whisk me off to the podium, then take me to Patrick, and then I'd be off with him to the hotel. However, on this particular day, because the peloton had split and riders were still coming across the line, the police couldn't get to me. There I was leaning over my bars with my heart in my mouth after frantically racing through these last few corners, and suddenly angry fans surrounded me. People were hitting me and shouting: '*Bastardo! Bastardo!*'

It was pretty frightening and not only for me. I didn't know it, but my friend Angelo from Paris, who had Irish radio reporter Des Cahill in his car for a day or two, had seen that I was ready to crack and had organised for Lydia to come down to the race, thinking she would be able to give me a boost. She was there in Como. As I fought my way out of the melee I saw Lydia standing there in a white dress, looking pretty horrified. I said to her: 'What are you doing here? Are you going to a wedding?' trying to make light of what was quite a frightening situation. She wasn't too impressed.

I was very upset because I thought I was producing something spectacular in this big event and this hostile crowd were all over me, and there was my wife watching it all. I'd have preferred for her to have seen me on the podium with everyone acclaiming me. But it did me a lot of good to see her. I had my dinner, then a coffee with Lydia and then started to prepare for the next day's stage up to the summit finish at Pila.

It is easy to forget that while all this was going on I also had to focus on the race, which was still far from won. Erik Breukink was very dangerous because he was a good time triallist and had several teammates riding strongly including Millar, Anderson and van der Velde. I'd also never led a major tour before the '87 Giro, so that was a new experience and I was worried about how I would hold up. There was so much pressure from the fans and I felt very vulnerable within my team. I didn't know whether I would be able to sustain my form.

Visentini wasn't out of it either. I knew that I couldn't leave everything hanging on the time trial on the last day as that could play into the hands of Breukink and Visentini. So I had to drive the final nail into Visentini's coffin on the final mountain stage to Pila. I had to show him that I wasn't weakening, that if he was going to attack me, then I was still feeling strong.

I worked out a plan with Eddy. We'd seen that there was a ramp about 7 or 8km from the finish where it got very, very steep, which would have been an ideal launchpad for Breukink or Visentini or anyone else who still had aspirations of winning the race. So we decided that when we got to that point Eddy was to make things very, very hard and then I would take over. Eddy did his part, riding eyeballs out for as long as he could, then I took over and rode faster and faster, and to my astonishment when I looked back I'd dropped everyone else apart from Millar and Marino Lejarreta.

I knew it wasn't down to them to ride, that it was up to me to keep the pace going. Robert and Lejarreta helped me a bit, but I did most of it because I wanted to distance the guys behind. I wasn't worried about Millar being there because he was a few minutes back on GC, but I was aware of the help that he'd given me during the race so I felt that if he did win the stage it wouldn't be a bad thing.

I knew that Robert was going to go for the win from a fair way out. There was no way he was going to wait for the sprint because Lejarreta might have been a danger to him. When he did attack, I could have got out of the saddle and gone after him, but I basically rode tempo to the finish and was happy to see Robert win the stage. I suppose if I'd been Lance Armstrong I'd have gone for the stage win and, if I had got it, it would have been another success to add to those I'd taken, but at the same time there's more to bike racing than going out and winning every stage. There's a human side.

It's been suggested that I gifted Robert the stage, but you have to remember that he was Breukink's teammate and so he couldn't work with me too much once we got away. That meant he was a touch fresher coming towards the finish. The other aspect to it is that once Millar had got into the move behind me he was a good bet to win the stage because he was such a good climber and very clever tactically. Those were his key weapons. So it was no surprise when he did win the stage. There was no need for me to give him a present. What really mattered to me was that I increased my lead over Breukink, Visentini and the other guys. It was a win-win situation.

In the end, though, I didn't need to worry about Visentini. While I was getting most of the bad press, Visentini wasn't exactly portrayed as a choirboy either. He was still doing a lot of talking whereas I wasn't saying anything at all. He was telling anyone who would listen that I should be sent home, that I shouldn't be in the race, shouldn't be in the team. He was going on and on and on, and soon the press started to turn on him, even though he had been the Italian favourite.

One paper called him 'a little rich boy with a short temper', but I think more than anything Roberto simply cracked. After losing the pink jersey that day at Sappada, he never challenged for a major title again. I had been expecting him to come back strongly in the final time trial to prove a point to everyone about his strength and endurance, but he didn't even make it to the finish at Pila. I don't know exactly what happened as I was up at the front of the group on that final climb, but it seems that he touched a wheel at the back of that group somewhere, crashed and broke his wrist.

He said later he was coming after me but you could see on the television that he was yo-yoing off the back. You couldn't actually see the incident that he was involved in, but when the camera cut back he was on the ground. He left the race with a plaster cast on his wrist, although he still managed to saw up his bike and present the pieces to Davide Boifava in several plastic bags before he left. He headed off saying that he hoped that I never crossed his path again because there'd be trouble. But he also wished me all the best for the Tour, which was nice.

After finishing second to Millar at Pila I knew I would go well in the final time trial at Saint-Vincent the next day. I just edged out Didi Thurau to win it, which was important because it showed that I was the strongest rider in the race, that there was absolutely no doubt about that. That victory put me almost four minutes clear of Robert Millar in second place, with his Panasonic teammate Breukink another 30 seconds or so back in third. It was a fairly emphatic success in the end.

In that Giro I rode well in the mountains, I rode well in the time trials, I was up there every day. You only have to look at the Pila stage where I finished second after basically annihilating the whole peloton to see that. There was no debate at all about who was the strongest rider. It made me very proud to have won in that particular manner.

Having gone through all I had done over the previous three weeks, I wasn't keen on hanging around too long in Italy. Almost as soon as I'd come down off the podium in Saint-Vincent after receiving the trophy as the Giro champion, I wanted to be on the road home. Two friends, Bruno and Laurent, who followed my whole career, had driven down from Paris that weekend to see me in that final time trial and were heading right back to Paris after the victory ceremony because they working work the following day.

I barely hesitated. I put my bags in the boot of their car, my bike in Angelo's car and we all piled in and drove back to Paris. Eddy was with us as well. We drove all night, got what passed for dinner from a petrol station somewhere en route, and arrived back home about five in the morning. My brother-in-law had come round with champagne and gateaux, and we had those and went to bed. The next morning I got up early, bought some croissants for breakfast, then said to Eddy, 'Let's get dressed, we'll go out for a ride.' My training for the Tour de France started that morning.

CHAPTER 6

TEN TOUR CONTENDERS, ONE YELLOW JERSEY

The 74th Tour de France was always going to be a bit special. For a start, it was the last of the old-style Tours that stretched to well over 4,000km in length – the 1988 race was a thousand kilometres shorter! Strung out over 26 days, it featured 59 categorised climbs and, with 23 teams and 207 riders, brought together the largest field in the race's history. It was also the final Tour overseen by Jacques Goddet. His career as Tour director stretched back to 1936, when he had succeeded the race's founder, Henri Desgrange.

That Tour also stood out because as many as ten riders went into the race with realistic hopes of victory. After winning the Giro, I definitely counted myself among the contenders, but, as the riders gathered for the opening stages in West Berlin, the quantity and quality of the opposition meant that picking a winner was by no means a straightforward call.

Two-time champion Laurent Fignon had shown signs that his best form was returning and formed a potent threat in conjunction with his Système U teammate Charly Mottet. Upcoming French hope Jean-François Bernard headed a strong Toshiba team, and Sean Kelly had something to prove after being forced out of the Vuelta a España by a saddle sore when on the verge of a first grand tour success. Spain's Pedro Delgado was bound to be a handful in the mountains, as would his compatriot Marino

Lejarreta and Colombia's Lucho Herrera. Phil Anderson and
Robert Millar could also be a threat, as could emerging stars such
as Erik Breukink and Andy Hampsten.

Two very big names were missing, though. Five-time winner
Bernard Hinault had retired at the end of the previous season and
had since anointed Jean-François Bernard his successor. Defending
champion Greg LeMond was absent too, after being accidently
shot by his brother-in-law while they were out turkey hunting.
That incident had taken place towards the end of April, and even
as the Tour got under way we didn't really know what was going
on with Greg. We were all shocked when we heard that he'd been
shot and, more than anything, we were simply hoping that he'd
pull through.

I have to admit, though, that I didn't really think about his
absence at all. I didn't think for a minute that the Tour would be
substantially different because the defending champion was not
on the start line. In fact, I would argue that rather than making
the '87 Tour easier, the absence of LeMond and Hinault made it
a more complicated race because no one was able to enforce the
same kind of control that their La Vie Claire team had imposed
in the two previous editions. But I wasn't thinking about any of
that. My priority was simply to win, as was the case with any race
I lined up in.

One of the best things I did as part of my preparation was to
tell Carrera team boss Davide Boifava to forget about me for the
18 days between the Giro and the Tour. I had to recuperate both
psychologically and physically. I knew that if I raced in between
the Giro and the Tour I might be able to maintain my physical
condition, but I'd struggle to stay fresh mentally. I also knew that
if I kept racing, every journalist I came across would be asking
me about stories from the Giro and getting me to look ahead to
the Tour. For that reason alone, I felt I would be better off
keeping away from competition altogether.

So I stayed at home and wound down a little bit. After a week or so I began to build up gradually. A few days before I travelled to West Berlin, I started training behind the motorbike with one objective in mind: making an impact in the prologue. Everybody was talking about how hard the Giro had been and wondering whether I'd recuperated. Consequently, I wanted to make a point about my physical and mental condition by finishing in the top five.

During those days at home, I also sketched out a plan for the race. Firstly, I considered the strengths and weaknesses of my rivals. I thought I'd be able to match riders such as Fignon and Kelly on the climbs and would gain time on Bernard and Mottet in the mountains. But I was also aware that climbing was my team's weakest point. So I assessed where I could gain time on the riders who were likely to be stronger than me in the mountains. With someone like Lucho Herrera that was easy to do, as I knew I would gain significant time on him in the time trials. But with Pedro Delgado it wasn't so clear-cut.

Delgado wasn't a great time triallist, but he was nowhere near as poor as Herrera. In fact, his PDM team had done a lot of work with him in this discipline and that had led to Delgado producing much better time-trial performances before the Tour. He also had some very good riders behind him, strong men who would make his team very competitive in the team time trial. As it was a very mountainous Tour, I felt right from the start that Delgado would be my main rival, that he was the man to beat if I wanted to win. Even at that very early point, I figured I could be no more than one minute behind him going into the final time trial in Dijon if I wanted to have any chance of winning the title.

The other aspect of my planning was to decide where the Tour was most likely to be won and lost. Due to the complicated nature of the race, the large number of riders likely to be in contention and the fact that my team wasn't strong on the climbs, I felt some days would be especially crucial. I looked at the route and decided that, rather than regarding the Tour as a 26-day race, there were six or seven stages that were crucial. These were my appointments. Those appointments were the days when I had to perform well if I wanted to be in with a chance of winning the Tour.

The first was the prologue, where I was determined to make a statement about my form. The next was the team time trial, a discipline where Carrera were very strong. We needed to do well there to make sure I was still in contention. Then the next big stage was the time trial at Futuroscope. In between, of course, I had to stay out of trouble and avoid any silly mistakes. The next key point was the first mountain-top finish at Luz-Ardiden. If I was still in contention coming out of the Pyrenees, where I had tended to struggle in the past, I would focus on the Ventoux time trial, then on the summit finishes at Alpe d'Huez and La Plagne. I even looked as far ahead as the final time trial in Dijon, assessing what would be the ideal scenario for me going into that crucial rendezvous. Of course, a lead of several minutes would have been the ideal, but I had to be realistic. When I reached Dijon I needed to be in a position where my time-trialling ability would either carry me into the yellow jersey or enable me to defend it, depending on who my closest rivals were.

That year the Tour was starting in West Berlin and we arrived two or three days before the start and took the opportunity to see the Wall. We went up one of the observation towers, from where you could look over the Wall into the no-man's-land that separated West from East. One of the guides told us that there were two lines of barbed wire and that anyone who tried to get across them would be shot before they reached the second line. Seeing it really brought home the awfulness of the situation. It was sobering to think that something like that could still happen in 1987.

My clearest memory of being in West Berlin, though, is the massive crowds that turned out to watch the Tour. The race had gone there because it was Berlin's 750th anniversary, and the support we got in Berlin and during the other stages in Germany was absolutely incredible. Apart from one or two appearances at the GP de Frankfurt, I hadn't ridden in Germany before and the crowds were the biggest I'd seen anywhere in my career up to that point. It definitely compared with the numbers that came out for the Tour starts in Dublin in 1998 and London in 2007. I guess that everyone who's even half-interested turns out when the Tour starts abroad – it's a one-off occasion and no one wants to miss out.

I achieved the strong start I wanted when I finished third in the prologue. The two riders ahead of me, Jelle Nijdam and Lech Piasecki, were both specialists in that kind of test. Consequently, I felt like I'd said to everyone: 'Look, I'm here. I'm ready.' Almost as good was the fact that Guido Bontempi finished just behind me in fourth, while Erich Maechler was 12th, indicating that I wasn't the only Carrera rider in great time-trialling form.

I was completely aware that my Carrera team was relatively weak in some areas, notably in the high mountains, but in flatter terrain and in tests such as the team time trial I knew I wasn't going to lack for support. With me I had guys like Bontempi, Ghirotto, Perini, Leali, Pedersen and Maechler, who all knew the value of the team as a unit and of acting in conjunction with each other. They knew that when riding a team time trial it wasn't simply a case of going as fast as you could whenever you hit the front. Instead, all nine riders have to be in harmony, which demands that you take your weakest riders into account. You want them to be able to contribute.

Having those guys together provided me and Carrera with a dream line-up. I witnessed a similar thing when I was at Peugeot and rode with the likes of Graham Jones, Gilbert Duclos-Lassalle,

Jacques Bossis and Phil Anderson. The Carrera riders were big guys, good team riders, all capable of winning races themselves. But there had to be some organisation too, and one of my strong points was not only being able to ride strongly in time trials, but being able to orchestrate a team time-trial performance. It was a discipline that I understood perfectly. As well as playing a huge part on the physical side, I was also able to get the guys to ride within themselves and judge the speed that we needed to maintain.

I used to look at the cyclists we had on the team, break up the route, and then set out the strategy. So I might decide that for the first 15–20km we couldn't afford to lose anybody, and that might mean us waiting if somebody punctured. Another key thing is that, although each team's time is taken when its fifth rider crosses the line, you don't want to drop any of your teammates so early that they might be in danger of finishing outside the time limit. You need to stay together as long as possible. In fact, I always felt that it was better to finish with a full complement of riders if you possibly could. This not only showed your strength and togetherness as a team, but also gave the whole team confidence because it meant each rider would have contributed.

Our performance was perfect. We not only won, but all nine Carrera riders crossed the line together, averaging almost 55km/h for the 44km test. Our closest rivals were another Italian team, Del Tongo, who finished eight seconds back and kept Piasecki in the yellow jersey he'd taken from Nijdam on the stage through West Berlin that fell between the two time trials. I gained 30-odd seconds on Bernard, Mottet and Fignon, a minute on Delgado and 90 seconds on Kelly. The stages in West Berlin had gone as well as I could have wished for.

Tactics were difficult to work out during the early part of the race because there were so many riders in contention. That meant it was a tough race to police and, consequently, the pace was phenomenally high for the first few days. I remember joking that if we kept going at that speed we'd all arrive on the Champs-Élysées a day ahead of schedule. It was frantic as the contenders tried to outsmart each other and a host of other riders vied for the yellow jersey.

Three different riders held the lead in the opening few days. The last of them was our own Erich Maechler, who took the lead at the end of a tough stage over very lumpy terrain into Stuttgart. It was Erich's role to keep an eye out for dangerous breaks, and he fulfilled it perfectly that day. It was just as well he did, because there were 21 other riders in the break, including Charly Mottet and one or two riders who might become a threat if they got a significant advantage. One was Sean Kelly's Kas teammate Acácio da Silva, who wasn't a contender at the start of the Tour but was a good climber and would certainly have come into the frame if he'd finished that stage ten minutes up.

The advantage of having Maechler up there in the break was that we didn't have to ride behind it. We could let those teams who had missed out set the pace alongside Del Tongo, who wanted to keep Piasecki in yellow. However, we did start setting a bit of a tempo late on in the stage to reduce the break's advantage a little because we were a bit worried about da Silva and Mottet. Near the finish, da Silva got away but Maechler stuck with him, the Portuguese winning the stage as Erich took the yellow jersey. They finished almost six minutes up on the bunch, which was not enough to make da Silva a threat. I was more concerned by Mottet gaining five minutes.

Riders like Mottet were incredibly tough opponents. They were always scheming. Anything could happen on any one day. At night you'd be going over the roadbook trying to imagine what might happen the next day, what they might be up to. You had to analyse your opponents very carefully and start each day with a strategy based on your knowledge of them. I don't think riders today analyse things in quite the same detail because they are waiting all the time to be told what to do over race radio.

On the other hand, it's probably more complicated today to know and analyse all of your opponents because there are so many more riders at the top level. I was speaking to Daniel Mangeas, the Tour's announcer, about this and he was saying that in our day he might have to know 300 names during a season, but now there are maybe 2,000 riders who might come onto his radar during a season as a result of the globalisation of the sport. There are so many Poles, Russians, Czechs, Australians, British, American and Asian riders in the sport now, lots of them doing very well.

I mentioned that one of the good things about the riders at Carrera was that they realised the importance of acting as a team and Erich Maechler demonstrated this over the week he spent in the yellow jersey. Even though he was the race leader, he didn't mind going to the front and closing down groups for me. He knew he wasn't going to hold on to the lead in the mountains, and that I was likely to challenge for it. I did feel, though, that we didn't get our tactics completely right during the time he was in yellow. On occasions, and particularly during tough stages like the one through the Vosges mountains to Épinal, we were doing too much chasing behind breaks. I felt that we should have had someone in some of those breaks and was a bit annoyed that we didn't. I was also concerned about the amount of work my team were doing in chasing breaks down. I wanted my teammates to save something for the mountains so that they could help keep me in a position to win.

At the same time, I couldn't begrudge Erich his moment in the spotlight. He was a good guy and very likeable, although he did unwittingly create some trouble for me during that week. In those days riders tended to sign contracts for the following season during the Tour, but in order to do that you had to be talking to interested parties well beforehand. Because I'd been going really well since February that year, people had been talking to me from very early on in that season, knowing that my contract was up. They were also aware of the problems I'd had with Visentini at the Giro and guessed there was no way I'd be able to stay at Carrera. Consequently, I was talking to several teams, including Fagor. Or, to be more precise, Patrick was talking to them on my behalf.

During the Tour's first week, it came out in the press that Patrick had sounded out some riders about the possibility of them joining Fagor with me in 1988. Maechler was one of them and he went to Boifava to see whether Carrera were prepared to offer him a contract extension, which led to a bit of a scene between Boifava and Patrick. The press made more of it than there was, saying Boifava had wanted to throw Patrick off the race and that I'd responded to that by threatening to go home. But all that happened was that Davide got pretty angry about Patrick talking to riders while he was still working for Carrera. It didn't amount to much. The thing is that the Tour is always a huge marketplace where everyone talks to everyone else. I'm sure Davide himself was sounding out potential recruits. In the end, the dispute didn't go as far as me threatening to go home. I just told Davide to back off a bit, that we all had to concentrate on the race and leave everything else until Paris.

With the Vosges behind us, the race settled down for a few days and I began to realise that riding and winning the Giro was helping me in other ways besides giving me a physical and motivational boost. It brought tactical and mental benefits as well. On more than one occasion, I used the fact that I was the Giro champion to my advantage. When groups got away I was able to bluff a little bit and say to my rivals: 'Look, I've won my grand tour this season, so there's no pressure on me. But if you want to win yours you'd better go . . .' I led them to believe that winning the Tour was important for me, but not as important as it was for them. Remember that I was riding for an Italian team and had just won Italy's biggest race, so to an extent the pressure was off me – or at least that's what I managed to get some of my rivals thinking.

As a result of some easier days, I went into my third 'appointment', the Futuroscope time trial, feeling strong and confident. Measuring 87.5km, the time trial was extremely long. In fact, I'd never ridden an individual time trial of that distance before, apart from the GP des Nations, which was usually 85 or 90km. But that was a one-off event at the end of the season when conditions tended to be a lot cooler. This test came after racing at the Tour for ten days and in very hot conditions. I felt that I measured my effort well, but sprinting up the final hill to the finish I wasn't exactly smiling. What was interesting, though, was how different the result would have been if you'd stopped the clock at 50km. A lot of guys blew after that point because they weren't used to riding such long time trials.

The only mistake I made was not having a bottle of water with me. I'd opted to carry a sugary drink called Perform because I wanted to keep my fuel levels topped up. But, because of the heat, I found it too sticky to get down late on in my ride and I finished a bit parched. This may have impacted on my performance slightly, but I was still extremely happy with my effort. I paced myself well over two hours in the saddle and won the stage by 42 seconds ahead of Mottet, who took the yellow jersey. Bernard wasn't too far behind and, surprisingly, Delgado edged into the top ten, losing 2 minutes 29 on me, which was an impressive performance by a climber. Several other leading contenders found it a lot harder, though. Fignon lost more than four minutes, Kelly more than five, Hampsten more than six and Herrera nine. For me, these gaps were a huge bonus on top of winning the stage.

The other incident that stands out from that day is a collision I had with a press guy as I came across the line. I was making a beeline for Patrick when the journalist walked across in between us. I had to pull hard on the brakes, which sent my back wheel shooting up into the air. I don't think my wheel had even regained contact with the ground before I'd taken a swing at him. I used to get so tense before a time trial, with all kinds of emotions building inside me, but usually these all came out on the road in an explosion of effort. Clearly, though, I had a little bit left at the end of that one. I don't know whether I made contact with the guy. I think I only caught him with a glancing blow to his shoulder. But he certainly didn't respond in any way. He also had the good sense not to ask me for a quote.

When I checked the results sheet after the time trial I wasn't surprised to see that Charly Mottet had taken the yellow jersey from Maechler. I knew that Mottet had hidden himself away in the bunch for most of the first week, just as Delgado had. I wasn't surprised by that either, as they were both very intelligent and tactically adept. However, even though Mottet had a good lead, I was sure I would gain significantly on him in the mountains. Delgado was the rider who worried me most. He was the man I had fingered as my main rival, especially after his strong ride at Futuroscope. His performance emphasised that I needed to be no more than a minute behind him going into the final time trial if I wanted to win in Paris.

I'm sure Delgado was making similar calculations, and his sums would have looked even better when he regained 17 seconds the very next day on an uphill finish at Chaumeil. Mottet lost the yellow jersey that day, but his Système U team kept it as Martial Gayant took the stage and became the fifth rider during that Tour to wear yellow.

Feeling the effects of the time trial and the tough seven-hour stage to Chaumeil that had followed, the bunch finally took it easier the next day to Bordeaux, to the extent that we were really only ambling along looking at the scenery when someone pulled hard on the brakes in front of Sean Kelly. Sean couldn't react fast enough to avoid a collision and went over his bars, landing on his shoulder. It may seem odd, but the worst crashes often happen when the racing is not eyeballs-out because you tend not to be paying full attention. If he'd been going faster Sean might have escaped unscathed, but sadly that wasn't the case. He had gone down hard and broken his collarbone.

I went back to see what had happened and tried talking to him, but he was in such great pain that he couldn't respond. Showing its respect for Sean, the bunch slowed up for a while and he did manage to get back on. But he couldn't hold the bars, so it was curtains for him, unfortunately. Although this meant I had one fewer rival, I was sad to see Sean leave the Tour. I was always pleased to be up against him on the big races. Even though we never raced on the same team, we'd talk with each other a lot. Sean opened the way for Irish riders to the Continent and once I turned pro we became good friends.

However, being in direct competition did lead to some fierce encounters between us, notably at Paris–Nice. I've mentioned the disappointment I felt in losing that race in 1987, but we'd already had a good few battles before that. In 1984, we were up against Bernard Hinault and we both knew that Hinault was the only guy likely to beat us in the Col d'Eze time trial on the final day. So, on one stage, we decided that if one of us got away, the other wouldn't chase but would stay in the bunch and mark Hinault.

Almost as soon as we had agreed this, Sean went away in a break that got a couple of minutes up. I was sitting back in the bunch saying to myself: 'Shit, here I am stuck in the bunch with Hinault and I can't ride because I told Sean I wouldn't.' But then someone did ride and we caught Sean's group, which was grand.

Just as we got up to them, I took my chance and accelerated away in a small group. We'd been riding for a while when I heard on the race radio that Sean Kelly's Skil-Sem team were riding. 'What's going on here?' I wondered. 'Why is Kelly riding after me?'

After a while, the group came up to me with Sean's team on the front. I said to him: 'What are you doing?' although my question wasn't phrased quite as politely as that. Sean said: 'If you'd have finished ahead, you'd have been first, but this guy would have been second, that guy would have been third, and the best I'd have got was fourth. If I don't win, I want to finish second.' When I'd let him go, I wasn't thinking about second. I was thinking that Kelly would win and I'd finish wherever. But Sean had made his calculations and he didn't want to lose out. I was a bit peed off, but he was right in what he did in the end as he took the title again.

Even though we only rode together on the Irish team at the Worlds, I did help Sean on occasions when it was clear to me I had no chance of winning myself. Let's face it, he was a great sprinter and I wasn't, and that was partly the reason I helped him win his first Classic at the Tour of Lombardy in 1983. He was also fighting for the Pernod SuperPrestige award for the best rider of the year with Greg LeMond. Lombardy finished in Como then and at the final climb Pedro Muñoz was off in front, with a good group of us chasing behind. Sean had just one teammate with him, Jean-Marie Grezet.

I told Sean to get Grezet to ride for him on the flat and that I would look after him on the climb, and that's what happened. I rode a tempo on the climb, which helped keep the chase group together and we caught Muñoz on the descent into Como. I thought I was going to be in the shit because everyone could see me riding and I had no reason to do so, although my Peugeot teammate Phil Anderson was in the chase group as well. I set the pace again coming into the finish, but with 300 or 400 metres left everyone started coming past me except Sean. I couldn't see it, but he was at the back of the group trying to lose LeMond in traffic because Sean had to finish ahead of LeMond to take the lead in the SuperPrestige. There was barely any time left when Sean finally shot past me, with LeMond still stuck on his wheel. Sean edged LeMond out on the line to win Lombardy, although LeMond's second place secured him the SuperPrestige title.

I helped Sean out like that because he was a friend of mine, we were Irish, we shared a lot of things together, and I preferred to see him winning when I couldn't win myself. I did him a lot of favours, although that was never an issue I thought about. If I helped Sean it was my problem. No one obliged me to do it. I always felt that he was loyal and you can see that in his reaction to my victory at the Worlds. He was absolutely delighted for me. He threw his arms in the air as he crossed the line, then threw them around me, which said more than words could.

When he was forced out of the '87 Tour, I knew that he was devastated. He'd been forced to quit the Vuelta when he was in a great position to win. Now, bad luck had hit him again at the biggest race of the year. I was sad to see him go. But I couldn't dwell on Sean's misfortune for long. The race was half over, but just about to start.

CHAPTER 7

WRONG TIME FOR A RAINCOAT

I expected that the next key stage would be the race's first summit finish at Luz-Ardiden. However, the two days we spent in the Pyrenees showed that even the best-constructed plans can go wrong. Experience, common sense and the roadbook suggested that the first Pyrenean stage over the tricky Burdincurutcheta, Bagargui, Soudet and Marie-Blanque climbs would be testing. But there was a long run-in to Pau off the final climb, and I expected my rivals to hold fire until the following day when the road to Luz-Ardiden led over the Marie-Blanque, Aubisque and the Bordères passes before the climb up to the final summit finish. However, those two days underlined how much of an impact the weather can have at the Tour.

The stage from Bayonne to Pau was one of the hottest of the race so far, adding very significantly to its difficulty. The yellow jersey group stuck together over the first two climbs. On the Soudet, the status quo ended and, not surprisingly, it was Lucho Herrera who was at the centre of the action. The Colombian was more than 15 minutes back, but such was his ability in the mountains that you couldn't write him off. What was more surprising, though, was seeing Jean-François Bernard accelerate across to Herrera. There were still some 100km to the finish.

By that point, the heat had become so intense that the road surface was melting in places, as was the glue that attached the tubular tyres. A lot of riders crashed on the descent of the Bagargui. The effect of the heat and crashes led to a dozen riders quitting the race that day, among them Del Tongo leader Giuseppe Saronni.

Up ahead, Herrera and Bernard went past most of the riders who had been in the break early in the day, picking up Erik Breukink and another Colombian rider, Pablo Wilches. I suspected that they wouldn't be able to maintain their pace going up the steeper side of the Marie-Blanque and that Système U would start to chase, but I was wrong on both counts. Going over the summit of the Marie-Blanque, Bernard and Herrera were more than five minutes up on the chase group, where I was with Delgado, Andy Hampsten, Fabio Parra and just a few others.

We were trying to reduce the deficit on Bernard's group, but the heat had taken a considerable toll, particularly on Système U. Race leader Martial Gayant was long gone, but that wasn't really news as there was very little chance of him holding the jersey in the mountains. But Mottet and Fignon had slipped back too, and it was only when these two and a couple of their teammates got back up to us coming off the Marie-Blanque that our group really started to ride hard. Delgado had a number of teammates with him as well, and they helped drive us along, but Bernard still gained 3 minutes 39 on all of his rivals after Breukink had jumped him to take the stage win. Mottet was back in yellow, but must have been worried as that stage had under-lined his limitations in the high mountains.

I have to admit I was fairly worried too with Luz-Ardiden to follow the next day. It was Bastille Day as well, which meant the French riders and teams would be more fired up than ever. However, the weather took almost all of the heat out of the day. After the inferno of the day before, we woke up to low skies, rain and cold. That suited me a lot better.

You can talk about tactics, condition and teammates, but one of the main factors behind my extraordinary year in 1987 was the weather. In the Giro we went down to Bari in the far south, where we were expecting it to be blisteringly hot, but we had snow, hail and rain. The weather in the Dolomites wasn't very good either, which suited me down to the ground. At the Tour, every three or four days there would be a bad day. It would be incredibly hot, the weather would break, then it would be hot again. When we got to the Worlds later that season, the weather turned in my favour once more.

In order to help me deal with the heat at the Tour, I'd have an icebox back in the team car that contained sponges dipped in cologne. These were wrapped in plastic bags, which were kept in freezing water. I'd send Eddy Schepers back to the car and he'd bring back one of these plastic bags. I'd take the sponge out and wipe it all over my head and body, which freshened me up. I had a dozen of these in the icebox when it was hot because I really suffered in the heat. Delgado, of course, knew that I suffered in those conditions and was even counting on the heat helping him to get the better of me.

The night before the Luz-Ardiden stage, we were particularly concerned about someone launching a long-range attack on the Aubisque, especially having seen the amount of time Bernard had gained the previous day with just that kind of offensive. But when we reached the Aubisque it was so foggy that you couldn't see five metres in front of you. Bernard struggled badly there, dropping out of our group. Although he got back with us on the descent, he was clearly paying for his efforts the day before.

In fact, the only attack from the peloton before we got to the foot of Luz-Ardiden came from 7-Eleven's Dag-Otto Lauritzen. Although not among the best of climbers, Dag always rode well in poor conditions and he made the most of them that day, overhauling all of the breakaway riders on the final ascent to take the stage. As Dag was riding towards the win, back down the road in the main group, Herrera attacked on Luz-Ardiden's early ramps, but I managed to get up to him with half a dozen others, including Delgado and Robert Millar, who was also riding well.

Herrera went again a few kilometres from the top, cutting another minute or so off the losses he'd suffered before the mountains, but I was pleased to finish just six seconds down on Delgado and to gain significant time on Mottet and Bernard. Mottet still led, but by just 1 minute 13 on Bernard. I was another 13 seconds back in third with Delgado almost a full three minutes behind me in fourth. I felt that I was just about where I wanted to be. The two riders ahead of me had both shown signs of weakness in the mountains, while I still had a considerable buffer on Delgado.

As we headed away from the Pyrenees, I got some stick from the Spanish press because they claimed all I had been doing in the Pyrenees was sitting on Delgado's wheel. Yes, I was marking him because I viewed him as my main rival. We were the only two guys at that point who hadn't had a bad day and he was keeping a close check on me too. He knew he had to beat me in the mountains and I knew that if I let him beat me there the race was over for me. So I think that tactically it was quite a normal position for me to be – perhaps not right on his wheel all the time, but never too far from him. I wasn't a super climber. I could get over some of the big mountains with the top riders, but he was a pure climber and most of the climbing was still ahead of us.

The other advantage Delgado had over me was that his team was an awful lot stronger in the mountains. He had Steven Rooks and Gert-Jan Theunisse, who both won the King of the Mountains title at the Tour in subsequent years. He also had another Spanish climber with him who was very good, José Luis Laguia. Laguia had won the Vuelta's mountains title five times, a record that still stands.

The Spanish press also made a lot of the fact that Delgado was number 51, the number worn by Eddy Merckx, Luis Ocaña,

Bernard Thévenet and Bernard Hinault when they first won the Tour. They were convinced it was going to be his year because Federico Bahamontes had first won the title for Spain in 1959, Ocaña had taken a second Spanish victory in 1973 and we were now another 14 years on and a Spanish rider was in contention again. But I was number 11 – first in the Tour of Italy, first in the Tour de France! That's what my friends were saying anyway.

Normally, the Tour features two or three so-called 'transition' stages between the Pyrenees and the Alps. These tend to be days when the overall contenders can ease off and riders further down the classification get the chance of a moment in the spotlight. But, as I mentioned before, this was no ordinary Tour. Instead of allowing the overall contenders the chance to recuperate a bit, the next two days were extremely complicated.

The first of them was to Blagnac. It began straightforwardly enough. My fellow Irishman Martin Earley was one of three riders who broke clear soon after the start. Rolf Gölz jumped away a bit later to join them. Their advantage stretched out to 20 minutes at one point and that was the last we saw of them until after the finish. It was another wet day, but not too bad until, with about 50km remaining, a violent storm came over us and all of a sudden there was lashing rain. Within minutes the water was a foot deep on the road. Some riders said later we rode through raw sewage at one point, but I didn't notice that. I had other things on my mind.

For some strange reason I did something that wasn't normal at all for me. As the rain pelted down, I started dropping back to look for a raincoat. Clearly, I was becoming a real pro – it's raining, so I'd better put on a raincoat. I made that mistake just once in my life, but it was that day. I always remember saying to myself as I was doing it: 'Stephen, this is not good.' But the mistake had been made. I started to get this feeling that it could go sour.

Just as I was falling back, Mottet, Fignon and a bunch of other Système U riders went to the front of the bunch and, sure enough, they took off. The rain was so heavy that it was difficult to see who had got away to start with, but when I got back to the front of the bunch I realised soon enough. The Système U guys forced a gap, helped by Delgado and a number of his PDM teammates. Even Herrera was in there. It was usually the Colombians who got caught out in ambushes of that kind, but on this occasion the two major absentees were Jean-François Bernard and me. For the next 50km into the finish, Carrera and Toshiba drove the peloton along in pursuit, but we never managed to bring them back. I was lucky in the end that I only lost a minute. I already had some credit built up from earlier in the race, but it did close things up a little bit.

The following stage brought more change at the top of the classification. It took us to Millau, or to the Causse Noir climb on the edge of the town to be exact. Régis Clère won it by a distance – 14 minutes, no less. When the peloton reached the climb to the finish, which was only about three kilometres away, Andy Hampsten attacked and this time Bernard and I were ready. We weren't going to get caught out again. Delgado was with us too, but Mottet and Herrera missed the move. Mottet lost all of his gain from the day before, reducing his lead to little more than a minute.

That left just one stage to Avignon and a rest day before the time trial up Mont Ventoux. The latter part of the Avignon stage was flattish, but there were a couple of decent climbs in the Massif Central early on, including Mont Aigoual. With the road heading up, Herrera launched yet another attack. Hampsten went after him and I followed Hampsten. We all joined up and it worked for a while, but eventually we were brought back, so it came to nothing.

It may have looked like a kamikaze effort, but I was prepared to take a risk in following Herrera because there was a rest day before the Ventoux time trial. I figured there might be a chance of gaining some time without compromising my chances in the time trial if I got into the right break. It didn't work out in the end, but it showed once again how riders at that time tended to react if they saw an opportunity. I knew I couldn't win the race or even take the yellow jersey on stages like that, but there was always the chance I might gain a few seconds. It also kept my rivals on the back foot, worrying about what I might do and when.

Charly Mottet, in particular, was inclined to race in exactly that way. His greatest weapon as a rider was probably his tactical brilliance. He could time trial well, could climb well, but he knew, and so did everyone else, that in the big mountains he wasn't going to be good enough. So he was always on the look-out for the lucky break, the one that might enable him to gain some time.

That brought us to Mont Ventoux. The first time I had climbed it, during Paris–Nice back in 1981, I had got so cold I could barely use my brakes or gears, but in mid-July we were all worrying about the heat, about how bad it might be when we came out of the trees at Chalet Reynard for the final seven kilometres of the time trial to the summit. I did my recce that day and was pretty confident that I was going to do well and when I finished I felt I hadn't ridden a bad time trial at all, finishing fifth. The problem was that my time looked poor compared to Jean-François Bernard's, as he beat me by 2-19. The consolation was that nobody else's time looked good compared to Bernard's either. He had absolutely blitzed everyone as he took over the yellow jersey.

Bernard got his strategy spot on that day. It was a time trial of two halves, the first through rolling terrain to the foot of the Ventoux, followed by the long climb up the mountain itself. Bernard had opted to use a low-profile bike up to the foot of the climb, then switched to a normal road bike for the climb itself. He may have lost 15 seconds or so when making the switch, but it was a very clever thing to do. He still finished almost two minutes up on Herrera and Delgado, who were the pre-stage favourites. I was fairly consistent all the way and came in just about where I should have been, compared to climbers like Delgado and Herrera, or perhaps even a little better off than expected. But Bernard was in a class of his own. He rode incredibly well that day. The only mistake he made was on TV later that evening.

I was sitting in my room with my roommate Eddy Schepers and we were both amazed by Bernard's performance. We were equally surprised when we heard him on the TV saying: 'I've won the stage, I've shown everybody how strong I am. There's still some climbs and one more time trial to come in Dijon, but I've just shown everybody that I'm the strongest guy in the race.'

Eddy and me were looking at each other and saying: 'Has he seen the roadbook? We've still got a week to go.' We chatted about it and tried to gauge what might happen in the days to come. Bernard was two-and-a-half minutes up on me after storming the time trial, with Mottet a few seconds behind in third. Delgado was another minute back. We knew Bernard had a very good team, so we looked ahead and wondered which stages might offer some opportunities to get some time back. We took into account the effort he must have made to win the Ventoux TT by that margin and thought he might struggle a little bit the following day, especially given his reputation for being strong one day and faltering a bit the next. Bernard would have wanted a flattish day after making an effort like that, but the stage to Villard-de-Lans was anything but flat.

As well as having a lot of faith in Eddy's ability to read a race, I also trusted Davide Cassani, one of my Italian teammates. They were both very good at looking at the Michelin maps of the stages, seeing how the contour lines were arranged and assessing how the terrain might affect the racing. They'd pick out features on the map that suggested points where there could be problems or where we might be able to create problems. We took a closer look at the route of the Villard-de-Lans stage. Most of it was on the small and bumpy roads typical of the Vercors range. One point that jumped out at us was the feeding station, which came about two hours in, just after the first-category Tourniol climb. The feed was located on a very narrow back road, the ideal point for some kind of ambush. We decided we needed to be very careful there. There could be an attack and the resulting rush of action might lead to a crash. So, we had to be extremely watchful, ready for anything.

The strange thing is that I am sure that Delgado, Fignon and Mottet must all have been thinking the same thing at the same time. I bet we all heard what Bernard had to say, reeled a bit, then took out the roadbook and looked at the route of the very next stage with the idea of taking Bernard down a peg or two. Even at a glance you could see that it was going to be complicated, which underlined how much of a mistake he had made. It wasn't a good time to knock our pride by saying he had all but won the race, that he was strongest. I know my ego had been dented a bit because Bernard had put 2 minutes 19 into me on a stage that I had been expected to do well on given my good history in mountain time trials. I felt humiliated to a degree. But at the same time that made me think: 'I'm going to show this guy . . .'

In hindsight, it was clear that all of Jean-François Bernard's rivals came to the same conclusion as they sat in their rooms that night. There was no consultation between us at all. What happened next was uncanny.

CHAPTER 8

THE RELUCTANT RACE LEADER

When looking back at the 1987 Tour, most people tend to view the stage to La Plagne as the pivotal day. There is no doubt that it was a spectacular stage and incredibly important with regard to the final verdict, but I don't think the significance of the stage into Villard-de-Lans should be underestimated either. Going into it, Jean-François Bernard looked odds-on to be the Tour champion. Coming out of it, he wasn't even in a podium spot. The turnaround in fortunes from the previous day was that dramatic.

The stage start was in Valréas, just to the north of the Ventoux, where Jean-François Bernard had given us all such a hiding in the time trial the day before. That morning I chatted briefly with photographer Graham Watson and one or two others and bullishly told them that Bernard wouldn't be in yellow that evening. I knew there would be attacks coming because we'd all seen the effort he'd put in the day before and we all knew that he tended to be inconsistent. But there was also a good degree of bluster in my comments. While I wanted to show that I wasn't beaten, that I had plenty of fight left in me, I think as much as anything I was talking myself up in my own mind, trying to convince myself that Bernard was still beatable and that I was the man who could do it.

Word was also going around that riders who knew the roads in the Vercors very well were saying that the stage to Villard-de-Lans would be very difficult to control. There was some talk about the location of the feeding station that I'd discussed with Cassani and Eddy the night before. I spoke to Paul Kimmage, who was riding for RMO that year, and warned him to pay attention at that point.

There were also plenty of rumours that Système U were planning something. I heard later that a journalist had asked Laurent Fignon after the Ventoux time trial if he viewed Bernard as his successor. In typically prickly fashion, Fignon responded: 'Does that mean you've got me dead and buried already?' He said that he was ready to 'spring some surprises' and later confirmed that he, Charly Mottet and the rest of the Système U team had spent the previous evening poring over the roadbook, just as we had done. They had decided that the feeding station at Léoncel was the ideal place for an offensive of some kind.

When we got under way, the speed was very fast immediately. There were breaks going off left, right and centre. I even tried to get away once or twice myself, but Bernard marked me closely each time.

When you've got a good feel for race strategy, you know that something is happening when you see different teams sending riders up the road. You ask yourself: why are they doing that? One possible reason is to have someone ahead who can offer support to a leader later on. The other option is that teams are doing it to make their rivals ride behind, freeing them up from the responsibility of having to set the pace and allowing them to stay fresh.

That day we were all sending teammates up the road, me included. Jeff, as everyone called Bernard, was doing it as well. But it quickly became apparent that his team, Toshiba, were overdoing it. Every time there was an attack, a Toshiba rider was in it. In the end Bernard had three teammates up the road and found himself a little bit isolated. I half-joked with him at one point: 'Jeff, you'll soon have more riders up the road than you do back here.' He replied gruffly: 'Don't worry, it's OK.'

Bernard's three Toshiba teammates were in a break of about

20 guys that finally got away before the first of the day's four climbs, the Col de Tourniol. That did leave him a little isolated, but it was a good sign for us because if the shit did hit the fan then we suspected he might struggle to find support. I had Eddy Schepers up in that break too. He was just sitting in the wheels mostly, saving himself to help me later on in case I got across to him.

Although we didn't know it at the time, Bernard's problems increased when he punctured just before we passed over the summit of the Col de Tourniol. He quickly got a wheel from his teammate, Jean-Claude Leclercq, and returned to the back of the bunch as we descended into the feeding station at Léoncel. But taking Leclercq's wheel meant he was another rider down. Two more of the Toshiba riders had already fallen back, leaving him with just two teammates in the peloton coming into Léoncel.

Feeding stations can always be a bit dicey, and this one was a real mess because it was on such a small road. There were soigneurs and musettes everywhere. So it was an ideal place for something to go wrong. As we approached it, the speed was getting faster and faster. It was obvious something was going to happen.

There was no attack as such as we went through the feed, but there was no easing of the pace either. Fignon and Charly Mottet were on the front of the line with their Système U teammates Martial Gayant and Marc Madiot. I was up with them too, and so were some of the other big guns. The bunch got lined out, then someone let a wheel go, no doubt because they couldn't maintain the furious speed being set by so many big names. There was a split. Those of us at the front immediately saw that Bernard wasn't with us. In fact, he was the only top guy who missed the move.

There's no doubt he was unfortunate because his chain had unshipped at that key point. But the simple fact was that, after his puncture, he had been caught in the wrong place at the wrong time and didn't have the team support with him to help right things.

All of a sudden the top 15 riders or so in the Tour found themselves altogether – apart from Bernard, of course. Generally, the first thing you would do when you got into a break would be to look around and see who was with you. But what was strange about this break was that no one bothered to look and see who was and wasn't there. All that mattered was that Bernard was missing.

You would have expected some of the guys to have weighed up their prospects and decided: 'I've got no chance here so I'm not going to ride.' We all knew it was a tough stage and that before we dropped into Villard-de-Lans there was a tough first-category climb, the Côte de Chalimont. Most of the riders in the break would have been expecting Pedro Delgado to make a move there, a move they would probably be unable to follow. On that basis, you would expect them to hold a little back in order to avoid being blown out on the climb, not to commit themselves completely. But the strange thing was that everyone in that group actually rode. It was incredible.

We soon started to close down on the group at the head of the race. As we neared them, we passed Bernard's teammates, who had been instructed to drop back and wait for him. But the damage had been done. Even if Bernard had had those team-mates with him when he had started to chase after the feeding station, he still wouldn't have closed the gap on our group. As well as me being committed 100 per cent to working, the likes of Mottet, Delgado, Fignon, Herrera, Lejarreta and others were as well.

In my opinion everyone was determined to show him that the race was not over, that he still had opponents and he needed to have respect for them.

Jeff was a terribly nice guy, but I felt that he was not that mature at the time. It was only his second Tour, so perhaps he was a little bit inexperienced. There was also a lot of attention centred on him. In his first Tour in 1986, he had been the mascot of French TV's coverage. He was the guy they followed each day because Bernard Hinault had flagged him up as his most likely successor. He'd also been put on a pedestal by the French press, so he had a lot of pressure on him and maybe that went to his head. That attention certainly did him more harm than good because he hadn't really suffered until then. In telling people he was the strongest man in the race, intimating that he was going to win, he'd forgotten how hard the Tour really is and how much of it was left to run.

It's also been said that he may have been feeling the effects of his efforts in the time trial, but given the full-on way that he chased us after we'd gone clear I don't think that was the case. By all accounts he was like a man possessed, driving the pursuit himself over the Col de Lachau and through the Vercors forests. The mistake he made was being – to my mind – a bit too cocky and that rebounded on him when he ended up in the wrong place at the wrong time.

Over the 50km or so beyond the feed, the group containing Bernard's rivals continued to cooperate and we eventually joined up with what remained of the earlier break. Behind us, Bernard used up most of his teammates and then started to call in favours. Ultimately, though, he had to do most of the chasing himself, although by that point it was simply a case of damage limitation for him.

Up at the front we all continued to ride hard and the group was whittled down until there were just eight of us as we went onto the final climb, the Côte de Chalimont. Eddy was still there, doing all he could to keep the tempo high for me, together with Mottet, Delgado and Herrera. Finally, Delgado attacked and I was the only one able to go with him, but I was really suffering. I was right on the limit.

I know the Spanish press thought I'd been doing it earlier, but that was the one day I really did sit on Delgado, and I did it because I was bluffing. I had to make him think that I wasn't on the limit. If you look at photos or footage from that stage you can see that I'm riding on his bottom bracket. I was doing that because if I'd sat on his wheel he might have thought I was dying, which I was, and attacked me. If he'd attacked, I wouldn't have been able to hold him, so I stayed on his bottom bracket doing one or two short turns, bluffing him all the way up the climb, effectively saying: 'Do what you want, but you're not going to get rid of me.' He did try accelerating a few times, but I always managed to get back up to him. In the end, he settled for riding tempo with me. Going over the top, I rode the descent very fast but couldn't get rid of Delgado because the roads were too wide. Finally, coming into the finish, he did jump away to win the stage, and I took the yellow jersey.

In the end, I'd been right in saying that Bernard wouldn't be in yellow in Villard-de-Lans, but I hadn't expected that I'd be the one to take the jersey from him. In fact, leading the race at that point wasn't part of my plan at all because I knew that I didn't have many good climbers on my team and that the Tour was only really just starting in terms of its mountain tests. Putting the yellow jersey on my back gained me a lot of attention, but it left me open to attacks. It made me the target, the guy that everyone wanted to blow out.

That night, after Delgado had won the stage and I'd taken the jersey, I sat down with Eddy and said: 'Well, this is a fine mess I've got myself into.' There was a week to go, I was in yellow and the next day was to Alpe d'Huez, where I'd never finished in the front group. I wasn't at all convinced that having the yellow jersey was a good thing. For a start, having it meant that I had to defend it. My team wasn't strong in the mountains and even before we got to Alpe d'Huez we had to deal with the Col de Coq and the Col de Laffrey. I felt pretty uptight.

Memories of previous encounters with Alpe d'Huez didn't inspire much confidence either. My first encounter with it dated from the final week of the 1983 Tour. I had been riding in the front group with Lucien van Impe, Joop Zoetemelk, Fignon and all these other guys going over the Col du Glandon and thinking: 'This is OK. I can cope with this.' I was so happy to be in there that I wasn't thinking about eating. About a kilometre from the top of the Glandon there's a big granite wall and, with no warning at all, I ended up feeling my way around it. There was nothing in my legs.

I got a load of sugary drinks on the descent and caught the front group again on the long stretch of road along the valley into Bourg d'Oisans. I always remember hearing on the race radio that the green jersey group of Sean Kelly was something like five minutes back. When I hit the bottom of Alpe d'Huez, I went into a state of nothingness. There was no light, just a complete blackout. I got from the bottom to the top, but I've got no idea how I did it. In the end, Kelly finished ten minutes ahead of me. I'd lost more than 15 minutes on the climb. My early mentor, Peter Crinnion, had come over to watch a few stages and he later told me that he'd run beside me on Alpe d'Huez shouting encouragement, but I never saw him or heard anything.

Subsequent performances hadn't been a great deal better. They had ranged from me losing 3 minutes to losing 23. I knew that if I lost 3 minutes on this occasion my Tour hopes would be over. At the start of that day Charly Mottet was my closest rival, 41 seconds back, but I knew Delgado was the real threat. He had steadily trimmed back the 3-minute buffer that I'd built up on him during the first half of the race and was now just 1 minute 19 down. In addition, the forecast was for high temperatures, exactly the kind of conditions where he thrived and I tended to struggle.

My objective at the start of that day was to lose the jersey, but only by a handful of seconds, so that Delgado's team would have to defend the jersey on the following stage. Of course, Delgado might have the bad day that always tended to hit him when he rode grand tours, but I couldn't count on that. For all I knew, he might have had his bad day already on one of the flat stages and had battled through it without anyone realising.

There was a good deal of attacking on the Col de Laffrey, the last climb before Alpe d'Huez, and I was very interested to see whether Delgado would respond. I thought that if he did attack there I'd be able to go with him and that would suit me because he would have to eat into his reserves. On the other hand, if he held back until Alpe d'Huez, that climb would suit him.

As it turned out, he got his strategy spot on and didn't follow the attacks on the Laffrey. I knew the key for him on Alpe d'Huez was the first five kilometres of the climb because that is where the ramps are steepest and it was those ramps that offered his best chance of gaining time on me. Because he was a pure climber, he could accelerate any number of times on those steep sections, whereas I could only accelerate once. I knew that if I responded once and tried to accelerate again, my legs would just go.

There is no gentle build-up to Alpe d'Huez, no 6 per cent ramp to ease you in. The bottom of the climb is on the edge of Bourg d'Oisans and once through the town you are immediately onto one of its steepest sections. We flew through Bourg d'Oisans. Although the initial pitches slowed us, they didn't reduce the ferocity of the pace-making. The attack I was expecting wasn't long in coming. Once again, Herrera was the first to move and Delgado went straight after him. I countered initially, but when Herrera and Delgado went hard again I had to hold back and ride at my own tempo.

Alpe d'Huez is a bit of an odd climb, which no doubt adds to its mythical status. On the majority of climbs, the gradient is steep in between the corners, then tends to become even steeper on the corners, or perhaps gets just a little bit shallower. On Alpe d'Huez, however, the corners flatten out quite a lot, creating an unusual problem when you're trying to maintain your rhythm.

I can best explain it this way. Imagine you are in a car and you are approaching a corner on Alpe d'Huez in second gear. Normally, that would be the ideal gear in which to take a corner on a mountain, but because the road flattens out so much you get the urge to put it into third gear for a moment to avoid over-revving the engine, and you then change back down into second coming out the corner as the road ramps up again.

My physiology is the same as that car engine. I would be climbing in a 41x22 gear and doing, say, 100 revs a minute approaching the corner, then as I went round the corner I'd go up to 160 revs for 100 metres, then drop back down again to 100 revs coming out of the corner. It was that change in rhythm that used to kill me. A pure climber, on the other hand, could change from 160 to 100 to 160 to 200, and keep making changes in pace like that time and time again. It was no problem for the likes of Delgado, Herrera, Millar and Lejarreta. They were all renowned for their aggressiveness on the climbs, and that's what it stemmed from.

Consequently, I knew I was going to struggle over the first 5km on Alpe d'Huez. But after that first 5km we were in terrain that suited me. I'm a 'claw-backer'. Climbers may get a gap but once I get into a rhythm I'll claw and claw. I knew that once I got going Delgado's rhythm would not be as fast as mine on a regular gradient, and that was what I had to take advantage of.

With 5km left to the finish, Delgado had opened up a gap of two minutes, but he was unable to extend this during the last section of the climb as I'd got into a decent rhythm and maintained the gap. He may even have run out of juice a little bit. In the end, he finished 1 minute 44 up on me and took the jersey by 25 seconds.

At the finish I was spent. I'd been hoping to lose a little less time than I did because there were still two long stages in the Alps ahead of us. I had that goal of being no more than one minute down on Delgado going into the final time trial, but I wasn't far from that watershed mark already.

That evening several members of the English-speaking press came to my hotel and for once I wasn't pleased to see them. Someone told me later that I had a real go at them for bugging me at the end of such a tough stage, but I still ended up agreeing to do an interview with Des Cahill from Irish radio. By all accounts we did it in a broom cupboard, and you'd think I'd remember that. But all I had in my mind that evening was thoughts of what Delgado might have in store for me the following day at La Plagne.

I felt the advantage now lay with him. It had been hot at Alpe d'Huez and I knew that if we had the same kind of conditions again on the road to La Plagne I would struggle much more than him. His team would look after him very capably in the mountains, then, once onto the final climb, he could take care of himself. Consequently, I didn't think he'd be as worried wearing the yellow jersey as I had been. He would be more concerned with gaining as much time as he could before the time trial in Dijon.

In interviews that night he was saying that his objective was to reach Dijon with a buffer of at least two minutes on me, ideally two and a half. I knew that if he gained that much the race would be over for me before we got anywhere near Dijon. I had to keep him within a minute no matter what the conditions were like the next day.

CHAPTER 9

'BLINK IF YOU CAN HEAR ME, STEPHEN'

Riders often talk about there being days when they can't win the Tour but can easily lose it. For me, the stage that went over the Galibier, the Madeleine and then finished at La Plagne was certainly one of those days. My aim was to end the day within a minute of Delgado in the overall standings, which meant I could lose no more than 35 seconds to the Spaniard.

When Eddy Schepers and I talked the night before, we decided that the ideal tactic would be to hang on to Delgado for as long as possible and then ride to limit my losses on the final climb. However, circumstances meant that plan soon went out of the window and, ultimately, led to the spectacular finish that is so well remembered.

Right from the off, the stage didn't go as anyone had expected. Heading out of Bourg d'Oisans, the route went straight onto the Lauteret pass, which in turn led onto the Galibier, by the top of which we had gained 2,000 vertical metres over the course of about 40km. The Colombians clearly couldn't wait to get up to that kind of altitude and made a hell of a tempo going up the Lauteret. It was so frantic that there were one or two crashes near the bottom of the climb. The wiser members of the peloton knew all too well that, with the action kicking off so early, a lot of guys would be in danger of finishing outside the time limit, especially after those early crashes. We kept asking the Colombians to ease off, but it was no good. They didn't want to listen and just kept riding.

It was crazy to ride like that so far into the race. Looking around, it was not hard to see that a lot of guys were on their knees with fatigue. Everybody was tired; I know I was. You've got to remember that we were already three weeks into the race. Nowadays, the Tour would be finishing at this point, but we still had another four days to go beyond that. While the speeds may not have been as fast as they are now, the bikes were significantly heavier, so everything is relative.

In the end, I spoke to Charly Mottet and Delgado and we decided that as the Colombians had been giving us such a hard time going up we would take no prisoners on the descent on the far side, knowing that they didn't cope with the descents very well. We did this partly because we wanted to teach the Colombians a lesson, but mainly because we wanted to get rid of them before we got to the foot of the Madeleine. Otherwise, they would do the very same thing there, and perhaps again at La Plagne.

When we got to the top of the Galibier, Delgado, who was by now the eighth rider to wear the yellow jersey, had lost contact with most of his teammates because of the tempo the Colombians had set. I was on my own too, but that didn't matter to me too much as I was well used to looking after myself. We did a fabulous descent down the far side, got rid of the Colombians and found ourselves on the flat roads between the Galibier and the Madeleine.

As we rode past the factories belching smoke in the Maurienne valley, there was a group ahead of us containing Jean-René Bernaudeau and a handful of other riders, including Delgado's teammate Gert-Jan Theunisse. All of the main contenders were in our group, but the race leader had no teammates with him to set the pace or defend his interests. I saw that as an opportunity and attacked.

I've seen some footage of that stage where TV commentator Phil Liggett suggests that I must have been either extremely confident or mad to attack at that point. I don't think either description fits. My tactical know-how was one of my key attributes as a rider – I was well known for being able to read a race and see when and how to take advantage of even the smallest opportunity. I was very good at being able to adapt my tactics to any situation that developed.

I think the other factor that has to be remembered is that top riders in those days rode to win. We weren't content just to defend our interests. We were also capable of analysing the situation and modifying our ground plan at the last minute. I could have stayed with Delgado all the way to La Plagne and then ridden to limit my losses there. But when I saw the opportunity, I took it. It meant going from a long way out, but it was a chance to win the race and I didn't think twice about going for it.

You tend to see that kind of opportunism far less today. The racing has become much more formulaic. Riders radio back to their directeurs sportifs to ask what to do before attacking and often find that before they reach a decision someone else has made the move and the moment has gone. You've got to make these decisions in an instant. You don't need to ask anybody. You just get on with it – make the decision and it's done. Sometimes you might make a mistake, but after a while you do get a feel for when to move and when to stay put. I think this is all an essential part of the sport.

As fans we've got used to the top riders staying with each other until the last few kilometres of a climb and then going for it. The fact that the script changed during the 2011 Tour was what made that race so interesting. Up till the final few stages the leaders hadn't done a lot, but in consecutive days we saw Andy Schleck going for it on one stage and then Alberto Contador doing the same on the next. Hopefully, they will continue in the same vein because it would be a pity for fans to see the return of safety-first tactics. I'm sure we all want to see more of what the French describe as *exploits.*

Although I had a reputation that season for *exploits* after my stage-long attack at Paris–Nice and my offensive on the Sappada stage of the Giro, I never rode for show. I always calculated the best way to get results. Looking at the Tour as a whole, I knew there was no way I could get rid of Delgado in the last three or four kilometres of a climb. I couldn't guarantee I could gain ten minutes on him in the time trials, and I certainly couldn't guarantee that I would gain any time on him on the flat because he had a very good team around him. Consequently, I had to take him by surprise.

That day, before we reached the Madeleine, he was isolated and there was a slight chance that I might be able to get three, four or even five minutes up before his teammates regrouped. That might have enabled me to put a minute into him at La Plagne and get back into the yellow jersey. It would have been *un exploit* as well, but that wasn't my principal motivation. I saw an opportunity and thought I could take advantage. That's how riders used to think and perform back then – stay on the front foot and keep your rivals guessing.

My thought when I attacked was that if I could get across to the group in front they might ride with me. But when I caught them, they didn't help me much. To be honest, they probably weren't best pleased to have me there, as my presence in the break guaranteed that Delgado and his men would be chasing hard behind us, if, and when, they got organised. I got some relays from Jean-René Bernaudeau, who was a friend and an old teammate from my Peugeot days, but that was about it. When we hit the foot of the Madeleine nobody would help me.

I rode the whole of that climb on the front with time checks coming through saying that Delgado was a minute to 90 seconds back. But I also knew from the race radio that he had been joined by some of his teammates and they were helping him to chase me down. I realised then that I was getting into very dodgy waters, that my attack could backfire on me because my advantage hadn't stretched to the degree I had been hoping for. Of course, we still had La Plagne to come as well. So, even as I set the pace up the Madeleine, I was keeping a little bit under the pedal.

We didn't know it then, but as our breakaway headed towards the summit of the Madeleine, we were almost brought to a premature halt. At the time we didn't pause to think why there were suddenly thousands of sheep milling about on both sides of the road. It turned out the local *bergers* had been protesting about the low price they were getting for lamb and had tried to block the course to make their point. The race organisers had managed to negotiate with the shepherds so by the time we got to the planned protest point the road was clear – well, it was clear of sheep. We still had to ride through the shit they had left all over the road. They hadn't cleared that away.

Soon after negotiating that hazard we went over the top of the Madeleine and I got the news that Delgado's teammates had cut our advantage back to 40-odd seconds, so I knew my effort had been in vain. They were sure to catch me before we reached the initial slopes at La Plagne and they did so on the valley roads after the Madeleine. I'll admit I was wasted when they caught me. From that point there were about 15–20km of flat riding to the foot of the final climb, which didn't give me much time to recuperate. I was helped a bit by the fact that Laurent Fignon attacked and got away with Anselmo Fuerte and no one chased behind from our group. We all just stayed put, watching each other, with me trying to recover as best I could.

A knock-on effect of my earlier attack impacted on me as we

headed towards the final climb. When I'd attacked in the Maurienne valley I'd been close to the feeding station and hadn't been able to take on board all the food and drink I needed to see me through to the end of the stage. It wasn't a massive problem as I could get bits and pieces from the team car, but as I attempted to gather my remaining resources for the ascent to La Plagne, I took a bottle of Perform from my team car to give me a sugary hit in preparation for that final climb.

By the time we reached the foot of La Plagne I was dreading an early attack from Delgado, but I was certain this would be his intention. I knew he wouldn't want to allow me any more time to recover from my attack over the Madeleine. If he waited until the higher slopes of La Plagne before attacking there was a risk that I might have recuperated and he might not be able to shake me off at all. I also knew from previous stages to the resort, from my recce before the Tour and from reading the roadbook the previous night that the initial slopes of the climb were the toughest. In that way, it was similar to the ascent to Alpe d'Huez. But La Plagne is not as tough a climb as Alpe d'Huez by any means, although at 17.5km it is 4km longer.

What was to my advantage was the fact that, after the initial steep sections, the road climbed more steadily towards the ski station that was due to host the 1992 Winter Olympics. That meant once you'd found a rhythm you could stay in it, which suited my style of riding perfectly and perhaps suited Delgado less, as he thrived on steeper pitches where he could really make his rapid accelerations count.

The one thing you can't do in a recce, though, is to get to know a climb completely. Every climb is different in a race situation: when you're fatigued, it probably feels a lot hotter and there are thousands of fans at the roadside. Coming into this one, I'd also been on the attack for 60km, so I knew I would have to hold myself back for as long as possible and not panic when Delgado attacked, as he was almost guaranteed to do.

Sure enough, Delgado accelerated away after we'd been climbing for a couple of kilometres, just as the road pitched up steeply. I knew that if I responded immediately he would blow me out by going once, going again, then again and then again. I knew it was better to let him go because if I tried to stay with him there was no way I would see the top of the mountain, let alone be in contention for the Tour. I simply had to watch him ride off and hope he wasn't riding off to the Tour title. But I was aware that he'd slowed slightly towards the summit of Alpe d'Huez the previous day and I clung on to the hope that he might do the same again, that I might get an opportunity to strike back.

After he attacked I kept to my own tempo. His advantage was going up and up and up – 20 seconds, 30 seconds, 40, 50, a minute, 1 minute 10, 1 minute 15, 1 minute 20 . . . It got to 1 minute 20 and I thought I'd better react soon because if I didn't the Tour was done. My plan was to hold him at about that gap until between 5km and 4km to go and then give it everything I had, hoping that I could regain 30 or 40 seconds and thereby still be within a minute of him overall, as I'd been calculating on all the way along.

I had a guy from the Del Tongo team with me, Luciano Loro, and Z's Denis Roux as well. They were doing most of the riding, although they weren't working for me. Roux and Loro were riding at their own pace and that pace suited me fine. It wasn't fast enough for me to gain any ground on Delgado, but it allowed me to recuperate a little bit. I couldn't really do any turns – just the odd one now and again.

As well as being tactically adept, one of the other aspects of the sport where I was strong was on the technical side and I'm sure this came into play during the latter part of this climb. In those days we didn't have the luxury of the modern 10-speed rear cassette. We had a seven-speed block, which made the climbs very difficult to judge. You had to make vital decisions before racing. Did you opt for the 13 sprocket for the downhill or for a 22 or 23 for the climb?

I was very good at choosing my gearing. Because I was a good pedaller, a rider with a very fluid pedalling action, I always had my gearing set to suit the most difficult part of the stage, which for me would have been the climbs rather than the flat. Approaching the 5km-to-go marker I was in my lowest gear but not losing any more time. I'd reached the moment when I needed to push the chain up through the gears I'd carefully selected that morning and attempt to cut the gap to Delgado.

As I eased the gear lever forwards and the chain skipped up through the gears my legs locked for a moment, before finding the necessary force to push the bigger gear round. As my speed picked up I found energy that I never thought I had. I dug deep and got a tempo going faster and faster and faster. I reckoned I could suffer for 5km. If that wasn't enough, then so be it.

My hope was to confuse Delgado, to make him believe that he was still way ahead when in actual fact I was coming back at him very hard. I knew Delgado would be getting time checks, but in those days there were no radios linking riders to their team cars, so he would not receive those checks consistently. Consequently, he wouldn't know I was accelerating. He would, effectively, be getting time checks that were inaccurate, that were still giving him the impression that I was almost 90 seconds behind him when I was actually closing fast.

When I got to the 4km banner, he was almost at the 3km-to-go mark. I figured that if he received the news that I was now only 1 minute 10 back, he might initially think the time check was wrong. My feeling was that he would only work out for certain that I was coming back at him when he was very close to the finish. By that point he would have had a couple more time checks, realised they were correct and that I was gaining on him. However, by then it would be almost too late for him to react.

The fact there weren't as many TV motorbikes on the race then also helped me because there was no coverage of me at all until I got right up towards the line. I think there were just two TV bikes at the time and they were following Fignon, who was about to win the stage, and Delgado, who looked like he was about to win the Tour.

It definitely helped me as well that I didn't have a clue where Delgado was. Because of that I gave it 120 per cent. If I'd known I was coming right back up to him I might have managed my effort and not gone all out. I might have settled for losing 20 seconds to him on the line. But all I was focused on was the clock on the line and thinking that any time I didn't lose at the finish was time that I wouldn't have to regain in the time trial. Four hundred metres from the line I moved up into the big ring to make my final eyeballs-out effort. Once again my legs locked momentarily before I could get the gear going. I wasn't aware of what was going on around me by that point. I had tuned out everything – other riders, the fans shouting at the side of the road, shouts from my team car. The finish line was all that mattered.

I was stunned when I came round the final corner and saw Delgado up ahead. I didn't expect that at all. First of all I could just see the back of some cars, then I was able to see Delgado just in front of them. Even then I didn't know how far up he was – that didn't really interest me. All I knew was the faster I went, the closer I would get to him and the better my chance would be of winning the Tour. I think if Delgado had known I was coming back at him he would have gone a little harder as well if he'd had anything left in the tank.

As I crossed the line I didn't realise the significance of what I'd done. All I knew was that winning the Tour was still a possibility for me, but I had no idea what I'd achieved. What made it dramatic was the fact that because the journalists behind the finish line were getting the time checks from 4km or 5km to go, they assumed that the Tour was over. Everybody had their 'Delgado wins the Tour' stories written in their minds, so when I came around the corner they were all surprised, including Phil Liggett, as everyone will remember from his famous commentary as Delgado finished. I've had it played back to me a few times since.

'Once again Pedro Delgado has slipped Stephen Roche on the climb. But remember that at one point he had a minute and a half . . . and just who is that rider coming up behind? Because that looks like Roche. That looks like Stephen Roche. It's Stephen Roche who's come over the line, he almost caught Pedro Delgado – I don't believe it. What a finish by Stephen Roche, we never knew he was that close. Stephen Roche has risen to the occasion so, so well, he almost caught Pedro Delgado on the line. Surely now, Stephen Roche is going to win this Tour de France.'

The race announcer was as shocked as Phil to see me. He started yelling, '*Roche arrive! Stephen Roche arrive!*' and the journalists who had been chasing after Delgado to get his impressions on being the Tour winner did a U-turn back towards the finish to find out where Stephen Roche had come from. All I was thinking about was getting my front wheel over the line, then dragging the back wheel across behind it. I don't think everyone can push themselves as far as I went that day.

When I crossed the line, everyone wanted an answer to the same question. How had I managed to finish just four seconds down on Delgado? Nobody wanted to help me off my bike. They all wanted to be first to get the answer, but all I could do was collapse on them. Well, I didn't exactly collapse. I got across the line and was so fatigued that I couldn't get off the bike and just fell over. The journalists wanted answers to their questions; I just wanted someone to hold me up. There were loads of press and photographers there and they were eating up all the oxygen that I was desperately trying to suck in.

My collapse looked dramatic, but at the time it was frightening. After what seemed like a long time, but I now know was just a few moments, my mechanic Patrick emerged from the middle of the crowd. He got his shoulder underneath me and managed to lower me to the ground. I was lying there and I remember the race doctor, Gérard Porte, who I knew very well, saying to me: 'Stephen, keep your legs in because the cars are coming close to you.' But I couldn't move my legs or any of my limbs. I got a real fright then. I was numb. The doctor was telling me to keep calm and put the oxygen mask on my face.

That was the only time in my career that I was knocked out and couldn't feel anything. When I won Paris–Nice in 1981 and had ridden over the Ventoux in the snow and freezing cold, I finished the stage, rolled over into the car and was gone. But I went well beyond that at La Plagne. Gérard Porte saw that I couldn't move and said: 'Stephen, if you can hear me, just blink your eyes.' I couldn't talk, but I could just about manage the energy to blink. Then he gave me the oxygen and wrapped me up in a survival blanket.

All the time he was doing this, I was looking up and getting anxious as I could see the press grandstand above me rocking because photographers were doing acrobatics on it, trying to get pictures of me on the ground. I thought the whole lot might topple over on me, and I couldn't even move.

I was also worried by how deep I'd gone to finish just four seconds down on Delgado. In fact, I was to be given a ten-second penalty for what the French call *comportement irregulier* – 'irregular behaviour' – but at the time I didn't know about that, so I thought I was 29 seconds behind him. But I was more concerned about how well I would recover for the next day's stage to Morzine, which was another tough one.

Finally they picked me up and put me in the back of an ambulance. They kept me in there for about quarter of an hour or so, still breathing in the oxygen. At one point a camera crew came across and said to me: 'Stephen, can you please reassure your fans you're OK? Can you say a few words?'

I said: 'Everything's OK, *mais pas de femme ce soir.*' There'll be no woman for me tonight. That quote haunts me to this day.

While all this had been going on, somewhere nearby Delgado must have been getting the yellow jersey on the podium. Although he probably couldn't see me, he would have known where I was simply because there were so many people around me. I figured that he would be well aware of the state that I'd been in and I needed to address that in some way – to give him the impression that even though I'd been down I would be ready for more.

When I got back to my room I was still in my cycling kit. I lay down on my bed and rested. Then I chatted to Eddy for a while. At half seven my masseur, Silvano Davo, came to the room and asked what he could get me for dinner. They assumed I wasn't going down. I told him: 'No, no, no. Don't bother with that. I want to come down for dinner. I want to show them I'm OK.'

I got showered and dressed. When I came out of the room there was a choice between getting in the lift or walking down the stairs, so I decided to walk down the stairs because I wanted to see how my legs were. We were almost at the bottom when I said to Davo: 'I think my legs are OK. I think tomorrow is going to be OK.'

I walked into the restaurant trying to look sure of myself but I could hear guys saying, 'Look at Roche, he looks white, he looks very pale.' I just tried to smile as much as I could, to look relaxed. I had my dinner and tried to make it look as if nothing had really happened. But as I ate people were coming over and saying how well I'd done but commiserating with me because of how the stage had finished, saying that I was the best guy, that no matter what happened now it had been a fabulous day. They assumed I was finished. And I was just saying: 'Yeah, fine, OK. I'm OK now. Thanks very much.'

In my own mind, and having talked with Eddy, I knew that Delgado would have seen how I was when I was on the ground and felt that he could take advantage. I knew he would believe he had me on the ropes, but I also knew that the Tour had been incredibly tough for everyone and he would be struggling too. I heard later that he'd described the last 5km to La Plagne as 'a nightmare' and that he'd been so exhausted at the finish that he couldn't speak either, which underlines how much we all gave that day.

Eddy and I also knew that Delgado might be a little bit worried having seen how I had finished at La Plagne. As we talked together in our hotel room that night, we decided Delgado would have taken a bit of a psychological knock having failed to nail the coffin closed on my Tour hopes and that we needed to capitalise on that. The best way to do so would be to take some time out of him on the next stage into Morzine.

I went off to sleep thinking I wanted Delgado wondering how this guy who had been lying on the ground just the day before could now be attacking him, for him to feel that the destiny of the Tour was out of his control.

CHAPTER 10

'WELCOME HOME, OUR HERO'

My primary aim going into the Tour's final mountain stage was to undermine Delgado's confidence totally. We thought his morale might have taken a knock after he had failed to finish off my Tour hopes at La Plagne and now I wanted him thinking: 'This guy is superhuman. He can't be beaten.' Even if I only gained one second on him at the finish in Morzine, I knew it would be enough to ensure that Delgado would have a very uncomfortable night. I wanted him to go to bed asking himself whether the Tour had slipped from his grasp, sowing doubt in his mind as we got closer to the time trial in Dijon.

I talked it all through with Eddy after we'd had dinner at La Plagne. Our plan was to ride close to the front to show everyone that I was still there and still fighting, and then attack Delgado on the Joux Plane, the final brute of a climb before the descent into Morzine. Eddy was particularly determined to do all he could because he felt that he'd let me down by not being with me on the climb to La Plagne. He promised he wasn't going to let that happen again.

The odd thing about the day to Morzine is that it has become overshadowed by the mountain stages that came before it, perhaps because on the face of it not much happened until the final few kilometres. However, don't be in any doubt about the severity of this test, especially given what we'd all gone through before. It featured more climbs than any other stage, with the Cormet de Roselend, the Saisies, Aravis, Colombière and then the Joux Plane all on the agenda, before the steep descent into Morzine. Although they were not quite of the magnitude of the passes of the previous two days, they were all tough climbs.

Before we got going, I sought out Tour director Jacques Goddet to see if I could make a final appeal against the decision to impose a 10-second penalty on me, which had pushed Delgado's lead out to 39 seconds. I was furious the previous evening when I had found out what had happened. I was told that the ten-second penalty was imposed on me because I'd taken a bottle that wasn't Coca-Cola-branded – the Perform I drank before the ascent to La Plagne – from a team car. Coca-Cola was the sole provider of bottles on the Tour that year and we were obliged to use them.

Goddet told me that a commissaire had seen me take a non-Coca-Cola-branded bottle and added that someone in my team car should have emptied the contents of the Perform bottle into an empty Coca-Cola one and handed that up to me, but no one thought of it. He confirmed there was no chance of getting the penalty overturned because I was one of the most high-profile riders in the race and the commissaires had instructions to watch us all closely and come down on us if they saw anything untoward.

Goddet also explained that if he saw someone breaking the rules and the commissaire who was following them didn't report it, then that commissaire would be out of a job. Consequently, the commissaires were writing down everything they saw to cover their own backs. In the end I said I was OK with the penalty, but can you imagine how I would have felt if I'd lost the Tour by one second?

When we started towards Morzine, it quickly became clear that we were all quite happy to take it easy over the first three or four climbs. A Spanish rider did break clear on the Saisies, but it wasn't Delgado. Figuring that the overall contenders would all be happy to sit back and mark each other, Teka's Eduardo Chozas clipped off. By the time the yellow jersey group had gone over the Aravis and Colombière and were approaching the Joux Plane, Chozas was about four minutes up on us.

Eddy and I had figured that Delgado would once again wait until the final climb of the day before making his move and we were ready for him when we started up the Joux Plane. We had decided to counter any threat by launching attacks ourselves, and that's how it worked out. Eddy attacked once or twice and I'd chase after him.

The idea was to get away and make Delgado chase, rather than have him do that to us, but we soon realised that Delgado was getting lots of help from the likes of Marino Lejarreta and one or two other riders. In fact, Delgado's team had practically become the Spanish national team. That made my task even harder because I couldn't get rid of Delgado and even when I did manage to get a gap there would be some Spanish rider chasing me down. But things were still going in my favour. I was still in the group and all the time I knew that Delgado was marking this guy who had been lying on the ground just the day before and was now attacking him.

Delgado wasn't the only one getting a bit of help, though. Although I surprised myself with how well I was going on the Joux Plane, I was still more than happy to have Robert Millar giving me a bit of a dig out just as he had done at times on the Giro. Eddy was there as well. He rode shotgun for me all the way up the climb, but we weren't getting anywhere because the Spanish were too strong.

There were unwritten deals like this in every race, but especially in an event like the Tour where the stakes and the rewards were so high. Some teams would have deals that went across national lines rather than sticking to their sponsors' interests. So Italian teams helped other Italian teams, and it was the same for the Spanish teams, although perhaps not the

French. Système U certainly hadn't done much to help out Jean-François Bernard.

On the stage into Morzine, Delgado had a couple of teams giving him a hand. There's nothing written down, no money changing hands, it's just a case of offering a hand out if you can with a view to getting paid back in the future when it might be your turn for a bit of glory. One of your allies' guys might be up the road one day and you might agree not to chase behind him. If their guy was, say, six minutes down on GC, then you might agree to let his break have an advantage of two or three minutes, which was enough to give him some leeway but not enough that he could become a threat on the overall classification. Then it would be up to him to take his chances against his breakaway rivals.

Carrera had an agreement with Del Tongo to work with each other on the flat, but it didn't extend to the mountains. There has been some suggestion that it did because Del Tongo's Luciano Loro was with me on Alpe d'Huez and then again at La Plagne, but it was just coincidence. He was a good climber but not able to stay with the best. I didn't have any discussions with him at all on Alpe d'Huez. It was simply a case of him riding a tempo and that tempo suiting me. I know I couldn't have gone any faster and experience suggests he couldn't have gone any faster either, otherwise he would have been up there with the likes of Delgado and Herrera. We just happened to be on a par on the climbs; in fact, he was probably a bit better than me. But I knew that if I'd lost him, I'd have lost even more time to Delgado at both Alpe d'Huez and La Plagne, and that thought kept me with Loro.

Having given it everything going up the Joux Plane and seen all of our attacks neutralised, Eddy led me over the top and into the first couple of bends. Then I went past. My idea was to go down the mountain as quickly as I could and not worry about what was happening behind me, just as I had done at the Giro on the stage into Sappada where I dropped Visentini. I just let myself go and would then see what happened at the end. I always knew that my best chance of getting rid of Delgado would come going down the Joux Plane rather than up it.

One thing in my mind, though, was that the Joux Plane is not only a very fast descent but it's quite treacherous as well. Delgado broke his collarbone coming down it in 1984. Although I had forgotten that, he might well have had that on his mind. I was aware, though, that a former Carrera rider, Carlo Tonon, had had a very bad crash on the descent down into Morzine that same year when he hit a spectator. He was in a coma for two months and was left permanently disabled. I'd also had a bad descent down the Joux Plane in the Dauphiné with Michel Laurent a couple of years before. It was very bumpy and very dangerous, so I wasn't at all at ease with it.

As I sped down, I didn't look around to see where Delgado was. I just knew after a while that he wasn't on my wheel. I started catching some of the lead cars, which worried me a bit, but I knew that Chozas was still a little way in front of me. I was hoping that everyone realised we were on our way down and there was no one in the road.

There are days when machine and body are matched perfectly in motion on a descent, and that was one of those days. I heard later that Bernard had said that he thought that Delgado and me had been too reckless, that we were trying to destroy each other, but I didn't feel I came close to losing the bike at any point. When you're tired you can make mistakes – you over-brake into a corner or under-steer – but I was very lucid and alert. It was like the descents I'd done on the Tanneron in '81 and the Forcella on the Giro earlier in '87. Everything goes perfectly and for some reason it's your day.

When I got to the bottom of the descent I was eight seconds up on Delgado and from there it was pretty flat for 3.5km into the finish. I added another ten seconds to my advantage before the line, where I finished second behind Chozas. I didn't mind missing out on the stage win too much, although it would have been nice to take it. The key thing was taking back those 18 seconds from Delgado and driving the nail home a little bit. He now led me by just 21 seconds.

It was abundantly clear by that point that everyone was pretty spent. It's not always useful to compare the average speeds of stages, but if you look back at the mountain stages at the '87 Tour it's quite revealing. We started off in the Pyrenees covering 219km to Pau at 36km/hour. The final stage in the Alps of over 186km to Morzine was completed at an average of just under 30km/hour. Given the general state of fatigue, there was never a chance of anything much happening on the transition stage across to Dijon. A break went very late on and Régis Clère jumped away in the final kilometre to take his second stage win. I finished safely in the bunch.

When we reached Dijon, I was quickly into my preparations for the following day's time trial. Usually I'd be more than happy to speak to the press, but that night I didn't see anybody. I got into what I can perhaps best describe as a semi-coma. For the 20 hours or so leading up to the time trial I wasn't myself at all. I was in the bubble.

On the morning of the time trial, friends and family came to my hotel to see me and were outside the front door when I came down. Even now I can see all these people looking in at me. I can see my uncles, but at the same time there were no faces, no names. I couldn't take on board what they were saying to me. It's an amazing feeling, but a bit frightening as well. I was so consumed by my focus on the time trial that all my energy had to go on the bike. I couldn't even talk. Everything inside me was waiting to explode out once I got on the bike. That was the time I had to let all of my energy go.

I went out very early that morning to do a recce of the course with Patrick and Davide Boifava. The biggest discussion was about the size of chainring I should use. In the end, because of the third-category climb, I seem to remember that we opted for a 46. There was no doubt at all that I was going to ride the time-trial bike and the only question then was about the wheels. Once we'd decided on that, Patrick got to work on setting up my bike. For the previous few days, Davide had told Patrick just to focus on my bikes. I had three bikes for road stages: one that I rode, another on the first car, a third one on the second car. All three had to be set up exactly the same way. If the gear ratio on one bike had to be changed, the same change had to be made to the other two. They had the same wheels; everything was identical.

I was confident I could gain the time I needed on Delgado, but you can't be overconfident in a situation like that. If I had a bad day and Delgado had a super day, 21 seconds might have been enough of a cushion for him. I also had to bear in mind that I might puncture or even fall off. You can't be complacent. I knew this was likely to be the biggest day of my sporting life and I fully realised the importance of what I was doing. I think that was why I got into my bubble so early and was so tense. Whatever happened, I knew that the time trial was going to be a major event in my life.

Some people thought the fact there was a third-category climb on the course favoured Delgado, but I'm not so sure. I was very strong on climbs like that, as my Paris–Nice victories on the Col d'Eze prove. I would ride out of the saddle a lot on those kind of hills, especially in time trials. I could get into a bigger gear and would then get into a good rhythm, whereas Delgado, who was more of a punchy climber, would have a faster cadence but might not be going any faster than me in my bigger gear. So, the climb might have been to his advantage, but I didn't think it dis-advantaged me too much.

I stayed locked away in my bubble right until the last few moments before my start. The last person I saw before I got onto the start ramp was Darcy Kiefel, the photographer who used to be married to Ron Kiefel, who was racing with the 7-Eleven team at the Tour that year. I liked Darcy, but hadn't noticed her until she came across and put her hand on mine to shake it and wish me good luck. It was an incredible feeling, because she was the only person who'd touched me during all of the time I had been preparing for that moment. Nobody else could get near me in those last few hours before the start of the time trial, and somehow her doing that made me feel that what I was doing was real. It brought me into the moment.

With 24 days of riding behind us and 4,000km in our legs, it truly was a case of survival of the fittest that day in Dijon. I soon realised I wasn't on great form, but when Davide Boifava started giving me time checks on Delgado, who was the last rider off three minutes behind me, I got a lift as the checks confirmed I had started to eat into his lead. It wasn't long before I'd whittled his lead away and started to build one of my own. My advantage over him rose to well over a minute by the time we got onto the climb. He did pull back a handful of seconds there, but it was too little too late as far as Delgado was concerned.

I'd been almost exactly right with my estimation of being no more than one minute in arrears on Delgado heading into the Dijon test. My time was 61 seconds faster than his, putting me back in the yellow jersey with a 40-second advantage going into Paris the next day. I think I should have put more time into him and maybe I would have if I'd needed to, but I also knew I didn't have much left in the tank. I did what I had to and that's underlined by the fact that, although I finished second on the day, Bernard finished 1 minute 44 up on me over 38km. He'd given us all another Ventoux-like beating, but it was too late to make any difference.

However, when he was interviewed in Dijon he said that the result showed that if he hadn't had his puncture on the road to Villard-de-Lans he would have won the Tour. Hearing that I thought: 'Give us a break!' Almost every day the road went up, he got dropped and he only got back on again because all the big guys were together and were watching each other and not him. If he had been in yellow and had got dropped, we would have gone on without him. For the guy to come along and say that he would have won the Tour if he hadn't punctured was totally ridiculous.

Whereas I'd been a very reluctant wearer of the yellow jersey in Villard-de-Lans, on this occasion I was delighted to have it. In my post-race interview with Jacques Chancel I had Nicolas with me while Lydia was in the audience, which added to the feeling of exhilaration. As the press took photos, Nicholas was sitting on my knee saying: 'Papa, pipi!' He ended up climbing down through everyone's legs and went off with Lydia to find a quiet corner. It was still too soon for me to have a quiet moment, though.

Even though I was in yellow and the final stage of the Tour is supposed to be almost like a parade lap into Paris, I wasn't feeling cocky at all. For me, the finish line was in Paris, not in Dijon. My lead was the second narrowest in Tour history, so I still had to be careful. Anything could happen in Paris. There would be ten very fast laps on the finishing circuit on the Champs-Élysées and if it rained and the cobbles got wet, racing would become a lottery. One false move and the bike could go sideways. Back then, you were only given the same time as the stage winner if you crashed or were held up in the final kilometre. Nowadays, they have a rule that says if it is wet and slippery on the final stage, the riders' times are taken when they start the first lap on the Champs-Élysées. In other words, if they crash after that it doesn't really matter as long as they manage to finish.

The final day of the 1987 Tour was only the second I spent in the yellow jersey and, although I didn't know it then, it would also be my last. It was also Jacques Goddet's final day as the director of the Tour de France after more than 50 years in the post. Before the start of the stage I made a presentation to him and gave a small speech thanking him for his contribution to the sport on behalf of all of the riders, saying that he would be greatly missed. As I mentioned before, his departure would usher in a new era as far as the Tour was concerned.

Although not a lot of people remember this, not only did I have the yellow jersey, I was also leading the points competition going into the final stage, which not only showed how consistent I'd been, but also how few opportunities there had been for the sprinters in such a mountainous race. Lying in second place was Jean-Paul van Poppel, the sprinter on Jan Raas's Superconfex team. Raas and his former boss Peter Post were not on good terms to say the least, so Post was determined that the riders on his Panasonic team would do all they could to ensure that van Poppel didn't win the green jersey. Consequently, right from the start, Panasonic riders were attacking right, left and centre.

Although I had one of the best teams on the circuit for the flat, I was concerned that if Panasonic kept this up one of my rivals might get away in a group, which could lead to some unwanted complications. There was very little chance that a group like that would stay away to the finish in Paris, but I wasn't prepared to take the risk. So I went over to van Poppel and said: 'If you help to keep the race together, I won't take part in the final sprint, I won't finish in the first 30 and get points, so you can win the green jersey.' He agreed to that and Superconfex rode tempo on the front with my team, effectively forcing the Panasonics to stop attacking.

Coming into Paris, the weather was fine, the cobbles were dry, the crowds were massive and there were thousands of Irish flags. It was an incredible scene and one that I'll never forget. As I'd agreed, I didn't contest the final sprint, and van Poppel got the points he needed to win the green jersey. I coasted across the line surrounded by my teammates and a few other riders I was close to. I had won the Tour de France.

The strange thing looking back is that I probably feel more emotional now about what I achieved that day than I did on the day itself. At the time, it was all a whirl. I was part of this very fast train going up and down the Champs-Élysées and still focusing on keeping my wits about me, then I was whisked up onto the podium where Lydia was waiting with all manner of big-wigs. The Irish Prime Minister, the late Charles Haughey, was among them. He had been enjoying the occasion and was in great form. I really appreciated his presence because having a dignitary of his stature up there on the podium underlined the value of my achievement. Jacques Chirac, later the French president but then the mayor of Paris, was up there too.

I remember someone, I don't know whether it was Pat McQuaid, who was there working for RTÉ, or someone from French television, said to me: 'French television have put together a three-minute short of Stephen Roche riding and set it to the music of U2. What do you think?' I said I couldn't care less. So many different people were asking me so many questions that I could barely think. Later, though, when I saw what they had done, backing 'With or Without You' to some of the race action, I was hugely impressed. It was fantastic.

The first moment when what I had achieved really hit me was getting on the Aer Lingus flight to Dublin the next morning and being handed the *Irish Times*, which for the first time ever had a full-colour front page. I was on it. In fact, the first seven pages were all about sport, most of them about me winning the Tour. We were flying to Dublin for a civic reception and I remember thinking: 'There were so many Irish people in Paris, who's going to be left in Dublin?' I was on the first flight back on the Monday morning and was a bit worried there would be no one waiting at the other end. I'd have looked bloody stupid getting off the plane and finding no one on the tarmac.

But when I arrived it was incredible. There were people everywhere. They asked me to come off the plane last and when I finally made my way to the top of the steps everyone jumped over the security fence and came pouring onto the tarmac. The police had to form a human corridor for me. There were people pulling at me, wanting to shake my hand. I remember thinking that this was what the Beatles or Elvis Presley had gone through every day. It was mind-boggling.

There was a press reception in the airport, then we made our way into Dublin in a convoy of three open-top buses. The first carried the TV journalists, the second carried me and my family, and the written press were on the bus behind. It took hours to drive the half-dozen miles into the city centre to the Mansion House. There were banners and posters everywhere. 'Roche for President', 'Welcome home, our hero', incredible banners. I remember these two young lads holding up a banner saying 'Welcome home, our hero'. We'd had the reception at the Mansion House and were then heading out to Dundrum, where I lived, and I saw the same two lads again on top of a bus shelter with the same banner, but they'd added: 'It's Us Again!'

Eventually I got to my parents' house in Dundrum, where I was supposed to be staying, but it was impossible to get out of the bus because there were so many people outside. In the end, they put me into a police car and drove me off to the TV station to do an interview that evening. During that broadcast they told viewers that there was no point waiting outside my house because I wouldn't be coming home.

When I think back, it's this short spell in Ireland that stands out as the best moment for me. As was the case at the Giro, there wasn't really the time for me to appreciate my Tour victory on the day itself. It was seeing the response I got from the people of Ireland that made me realise the full significance of what had happened. I think the only time Dublin has seen anything similar since was when Ireland's football team came back from the 1990 World Cup, but that was after an heroic defeat rather than a quite unbelievable victory. I still have those images in my mind.

However, there still wasn't much time to dwell on what had happened. As Tour winner, I was already receiving lots of offers for the post-Tour criteriums. And there was still the Worlds to come as well. I knew I was in the form of my life and that if I could maintain it I could have an impact there as well.

CHAPTER 11

MORE NIGHTMARE THAN DREAM TEAM

After winning the Giro and then the Tour, as the 1987 World Championships approached I was hot property. Everyone knew that my contract with Carrera was up, although in all honesty I would have liked to have renewed with them. But the more I spoke to Carrera, the fewer direct answers I got back. I pushed and pushed, but they kept on stalling, so I had to speak to other teams as well. Finally I got a good offer from Fagor before the Worlds and went back to Davide Boifava again saying: 'Here's the contract, I'm showing you the contract. This is what they're offering me and you're offering half that. Please make an effort to move closer to what they are offering.' But he told me: 'No, we can't do it.'

In the end, I signed for Fagor just before the Worlds. I had a clause in there that would allow some renegotiation if I did well at the Worlds, but under the deal we had agreed I was already going to get good money. After I won the Worlds, I spoke with Fagor again and everything was finalised. But, just before giving them my final agreement, I went back to Carrera and said to Boifava: 'Please, please, please. I don't want to leave.' But they still refused to budge. It was only years later that Davide Boifava revealed that they had a deal with Roberto Visentini running through to the end of 1988 and the team's management felt there was no way Roberto and I could work together successfully.

Consequently, there was never a chance of me reaching an agreement with Carrera.

The advantage of doing a deal with Fagor was that they offered me the opportunity of putting together a 'dream team'. I insisted that they sign Robert Millar, Malcolm Elliott, Eddy Schepers and Laurent Biondi, who'd been with me at La Redoute. Sean Yates and lots of other good guys were already on the team, and with the new additions we looked very strong on paper.

However, things were a lot more complicated on the management side. The guy putting in the money was Agustín Mondragón, who was the president of Fagor and a cycling fanatic. He wanted things done very much his way. The team manager, Miguel Gómez, made sure that Mondragón's wishes were followed. The principal directeur sportif was Pierre Bazzo, who was a great guy but limited when it came down to embracing modern science. I was bringing Patrick Valcke with me. Patrick had been with me for years and I felt he deserved a promotion so he was going to be my directeur.

I also had suspicions about the team's organisational ability. Martin Earley had been with them for the three previous seasons and described the set-up as slightly chaotic, which in my opinion summed up how Spanish teams tended to be in those days. French and Italian teams tended to be much better organised, so I also asked Fagor to take on Philippe Crepel, who was very well known – and still is – for his logistical skills.

However, the structure I was trying to put in place started to unravel almost immediately, largely because I was distracted from focusing on the team by a recurrence of my knee problems. In between winning the Tour and the Worlds, I had taken part in three criteriums in Ireland. They had been pretty hard fought as the pros who came over from Britain weren't prepared to give us Irish guys any leeway. Rather than agreeing that I could win in front of my home-town crowd in Dublin, they wanted to make things difficult for us, perhaps because criteriums were their bread and butter at that time. They went all out to beat us, but I did manage to win, set up by the Irish lads and one or two guys we were friendly with like Paul Sherwen and Tony Doyle.

The next night we rode in Wexford and before the race the British fellas came around and asked could they ride with us. We told them: 'No, no, you wouldn't ride with us in Dublin, so you ain't riding with us today.' That evening we destroyed the whole field and Sean won in Wexford. I remember us all sitting with fish and chips in the hotel corridor in Wexford that night and joking about what was going on with the British guys, saying that the whole situation could have been different if they had agreed to let me win in Dublin.

The next evening we finished up in Cork. Once again the British fellas asked if they could share the cake with us. Once again we said: 'Sorry, but no, it's too late.' There was even more tension that evening. Our plan was for me to try to get away, then set the sprint up for Sean if I was brought back. I did get away for a few laps and in the end we wound it up for Sean. Heading into the finish there were two left-hand corners, the first one over a bridge, then left again into the final straight. I was on the front with Sean on my wheel going into the corners, and Sean came around me coming out of the first one. The second one came up so fast that no one could react as he raced into it and started to sprint away.

As the rest of us came out of the second corner, everybody behind me realised that Sean had gone and riders were making frantic attempts to get by me and chase Sean. In the panic, my handlebars got caught up with somebody else's and down we came. I hit my knee hard on the ground. People later said I actually caused the crash on purpose, which was ludicrous – impossible! Why would I want to take that risk?

I was lying on the ground and some of the British pros were diving in at me, trying to have a go at me. My brother-in-law Peter, who was standing in the crowd with my sister Carol, jumped over the barriers and was pulling everybody off me. I could see that people were very, very angry, but I would never for an instant think of trying to bring somebody down. One moment I was smiling because our tactics had worked and we were going to win again, the next I was on the ground with bodies on top of me having got a hell of a knock on my knee.

When I went to the Worlds the knee was still very sore. That was another reason why I was glad it was cold and wet that day in Villach. If it had been hot my knee might have made it more painful, but once I got going it was OK, and obviously the victory and winning the Triple Crown took my mind off it as well.

The morning after the Worlds I flew to Châteaulin in Brittany for a criterium appearance that afternoon, but my knee was so painful that I had to pull out after four or five laps. That was pretty much the end of my season. I rode the Nissan Classic in Ireland in early October then decided my normal couple of months of rest would sort my knee out. During that period I fulfilled a lot of PR duties, but when I returned to the bike again I couldn't ride because the pain was terrible. I was fine when I was off the bike, but as soon as I started to ride I'd get to the end of the road and couldn't even turn the pedals.

I had the knee looked at by lots of specialists but no one really knew what was wrong with it. Everyone was just telling me I needed more rest after what had been a hard season. I'd ride for 200 metres and the pain would come. I'd press on thinking, 'It's only a bit of pain,' but the further I rode the more pain I felt. I went to see a specialist in France and had all kinds of physio-therapy, then more rest, but the pain persisted. The doctors were giving me injections of cortisone into the knee to try to help it. It would be OK for a couple of hours, but the pain would always return. By this time we were getting close to the new season. I was the world champion, I was riding for a new team, I had a good contract – and I wasn't able to perform.

Finally, my doctor in France, Dr Jean-Baptiste Courroy, organised for me to have an examination with one of the top knee specialists in Europe. They decided that the problem was being caused by fibrosis on the tendon on the outside of the knee. They said it needed to be opened up so that the calcium that had formed on the tendon due to friction could be scraped off. Their diagnosis was that the pain had resulted in a slight change to my natural pedal stroke, resulting in a tendency for my ligaments to cross, causing friction and therefore fibrosis. So, in November 1987, I had the operation to have the tendon scraped. I allowed it time to recover, but when I got back on my bike there was still pain. Dr Courroy told me: 'It can't be anything else, Stephen. We've been in there and looked. Perhaps it's in your mind . . .'

The pain felt real enough to me and seemed to be getting worse rather than better. Complicating things still further, the atmosphere in the revamped Fagor team was degenerating as well. There were disputes between Pierre Bazzo, Miguel Gómez and Patrick. Because I wasn't on hand to lead the whole project, everyone else was trying to assert themselves and there was a lot of ill feeling developing. It got so bad that when we went on the team presentation in San Sebastián in January 1988, the riders went on strike.

What happened was Fagor's management had told me that they were letting Philippe Crepel go because they felt he wasn't valuable to the team. I had disputed this decision, arguing that Philippe was the one guy who would ensure that everything ran smoothly. I saw it as them cutting out one of my men. The other riders had known all too well about the team's previous lack of organisation and were now wondering what was going to happen with Crepel being ousted. So we went on strike. In the end, we agreed that Crepel would stay on the team as a 'consultant', but it wasn't the ideal solution. However, I couldn't say a lot because I wasn't even able to ride my bike.

I tried to ride again at the training camp but still found the pain too much to bear. During that year I was on and off the bike using the cortisone injections in the knee to quell the pain. I was also taking an awful lot of anti-inflammatory tablets. I was taking Voltaren 100s like they were Smarties. They were helping me – it was the only way I could ride the bike – but they were also destroying my insides. Fagor then decided they wanted to send me to an expert of their choosing, a Spanish knee specialist, who had operated on Maradona and the Canadian sprinter Ben Johnson.

When I arrived at the hospital in Barcelona, there were a lot of journalists waiting outside. I went in and the doctor closed the door on the journalists. He spent about 20 minutes touching my knee. When I flinched he'd say: 'You're sore.' He was the doctor; he would know. Fagor were probably paying him a fortune just to look at me. Finally, when his examination was done, he told me a little bit about his diagnosis, then stood up, opened the door and let the journalists come in. They were all pushing over the top of me, putting microphones in his face and asking him what news he had. He was sitting back in his chair telling all these journalists what was going on. I didn't think that was professional at all. I left there very, very angry.

I went back to the specialists I'd seen in France and like everyone else they were telling me I needed an operation. But when I considered the prospect of this my first thought was of losing another year. I also believed it was easy for all these experts to say that an operation was needed knowing that once they had my knee open they might find something. I'd have preferred it if they could have told me what they thought the problem was before they operated so that I could have more faith in what they were doing. However, doing so would have meant them putting their credibility on the line.

I did manage to start Liège–Bastogne–Liège but quit after getting caught up in a big crash. Understandably, Fagor were desperate to get me back on the road, but each objective we set passed. They wanted me to ride the Vuelta, then the Giro, and of course they wanted me to defend the Tour de France title. But by the end of May, having already missed the first two grand tours of the year, it was clear that I wasn't going to be fit for the Tour either.

I was doing some races but I was still in a lot of pain. Late on in the year I rode the Tour of Britain and the Nissan Classic and finished top ten in both. My problem was that I had the class to be able to hang in and get through races, but the result was no one could believe I was in that much pain. In reality, I was riding on one leg and now it was doing damage to my back.

I kept trying to return because I felt a huge responsibility for bringing guys to the team and it upset me a lot to see how things were turning out. I felt that I had to ride, but in hindsight that may not have been the best thing to do. Of course, they weren't riding for nothing. They were being paid for doing the job. But they'd come to ride for me and I'd given them the hope that this was going to be a dream team, that we were going to ride for Tour honours, for Classics honours, and everyone had a job to do.

Initially, we had the best equipment, we had Patrick as manager, Crepel for logistics, and that made it a team anyone would have loved to be part of. It was all incredibly right, then it went dramatically wrong. The whole project hinged on me and I felt guilty. I think Robert Millar was aggrieved with me because he thought I didn't give it my best shot, but I did all I could. Maybe if I'd stopped completely for six months I might not have had as many problems, but because I was the world champion I kept trying to come back again and again, because I wanted to show my jersey, to be part of the team that I'd built, to calm everyone down. In the end, because I wasn't there and wasn't performing, it all span out of control.

In May I flew to Stuttgart to do some publicity work for Opel, who gave me a car every year. Going into Stuttgart the customs officer asked how long I was planning on staying in the country. I told him I was just going to be there for the day, but he pointed out that my passport was actually out of date from that day and because of that he couldn't let me in to West Germany. I pleaded with him, mentioned the meeting I had with Opel and eventually he relented. But he said that once I was in the country I wouldn't be able to get out again until I had received a new passport from the Irish consulate in Munich. So I went in and did my thing with Opel, but then found out it was the Ascension Day holiday so the consulate in Munich was closed for a couple of days. That meant being in West Germany until the following Monday.

As I had to travel down to Munich anyway, Opel's boss invited me to a football match between Stuttgart, who were sponsored by his company, and Bayern Munich. During the match, he leaned over to me, pointed at someone sitting nearby and said: 'That gentleman there is Dr Hans-Wilhelm Müller-Wohlfahrt. Have you ever heard of him?' I hadn't.

'He's the best there is. He's got X-ray fingers. He looks after all the footballers, ice hockey players, Boris Becker, Yannick Noah, Ivan Lendl. You should see him.'

I wasn't keen. I told him I'd been to Italy, to France, to Belgium, to Spain and they'd all told me I needed an operation. 'What's he going to tell me that they don't know?' I said. 'I don't think he's seen a cyclist before, so I don't think it's worth it.' However, they persuaded me to talk to him after the match.

We were introduced and chatted, and he said: 'Here's what we'll do. Come to see me tomorrow morning first thing at eight and we'll take it from there.'

When I got to his offices he had a physio, a chiropractor, a masseur, all kinds of specialists. There were maybe five or six people there, including him. Having gone through what I had with other doctors, I was determined not to tell him what my problem was. They all did a little examination and then got together in a corner and talked in German so I couldn't understand a thing. I was lying there thinking: 'What a waste of time this is.'

Then Dr Müller-Wohlfahrt turned back to me and said in the best English he had: 'Stephen, we think you have pain here, but not here, and in this situation, but not that. We think that when you crashed in Paris in 1985 you crushed the knee cartilage. When they performed the first operation on you to shave the cartilage, we think that too much was taken off the left-hand side. When you rested it, you lost some of the muscle bulk in your quadriceps, particularly on the external side, because you weren't riding your bike. When you did return to the bike, because of the pain you had you weren't able to push hard enough to build that muscle up again. As a result of that your kneecap was moving slightly from side to side. Consequently, you ended up with bone rubbing against bone. So, yes, the cortisone injections will help you and so might another operation. But the ideal solution is to build up that muscle again so that it can hold your kneecap in place.'

I was impressed by their insight into how my problem had developed, but the key, of course, was whether they could do anything for me. Dr Müller-Wohlfahrt was certain they could. 'First of all,' he said, 'I want you to stay here for ten days.' I told him I couldn't do that. I had to get back to my family in France, as they had only been expecting me to be away for a day. But he insisted. 'I can't say I can cure you, but before you go away and say Dr Müller-Wohlfahrt can't cure you I want you to give me my chance. I reckon in ten days I can guarantee you an improvement.' I thought he was putting his neck on the line so I said OK. I called Lydia, explained why I was staying and settled down for my ten days.

First thing each morning I would go to his offices and he would inspect my knee. He'd even check its temperature. After that he would work out a schedule for me for the day. I might go for a massage, then have a special salty bath, then go to the chiropractor, then for laser treatment, then to the weight training room. Finally, I'd go back to him last thing at night. Some days I would be waiting to see him for an hour or so in his VIP suite, with the likes of Boris Becker and Franz Beckenbauer in there waiting to see him as well.

He explained that his plan was to build up the muscle around the knee so that it would stabilise the kneecap. At the same time he would inject some kind of glycerine gel under my kneecap to create a false cartilage, which meant that I could actually power train without doing any damage. He would check the temperature of my knee at the end of the day because the work I was doing was making the knee warm, but he didn't want it to get too warm. Once he had done that, he would get his assistants to pack loads of this very smelly, paste-like anti-inflammatory cream on my knee and bandage it up mummy-style. Then the next morning, he'd remove the bandage and we'd be off again.

After ten days he told me to go home for a week, spend 10–15 minutes each day on my bike, then return to Munich. I felt a little bit of pain that week, then spent another week with him, but this time I had my bike with me and he had me doing half an hour most days. One of the most interesting aspects of my time there was realising that he was building up a balance sheet of how my knee was responding to treatment. If I told him the pain had come back, he would tweak things a little bit. He was very sensitive about the way his athletes felt. I could see that it pained him if I told him my knee was sore again. He absorbed everything you said, analysed it and then reacted. We quickly developed a good relationship.

The only time that we almost fell out was because I wanted to know what exactly he was injecting into my knee. After he gave me an injection he used to put the empty ampoule in the bin. One day, after he'd completed his treatment on me and gone through to see another patient, I took the ampoule out of the bin, put it in my pocket and took it home. I gave it to a doctor in Paris to analyse and it turned out it was extracted from calves' livers. I was intrigued, so a couple of weeks into my treatment with him I asked him about it and told him I'd had one of the ampoules analysed. He froze and stood back.

'Stephen, I'm very disappointed,' he said. 'I've been a doctor for 25 years and no athlete I've with ever worked with has been involved with doping or even suspected of doping. My office has never had a hint of scandal. Everything we use is a natural product. I don't know how you could have thought that we might have used anything suspicious. No one has ever questioned me before. No one has ever taken anything from my office.'

I felt bad about what I'd done, but there was good reason for it. 'The thing is I have to be very careful,' I told him. 'I'm responsible for what goes into my body. I'm the one who does all the dope controls and I don't ever want to have a problem so I like to know about everything that's going into my body. I'm very sorry to have doubted you.'

Other doctors I'd seen had suggested that it was normal to have a problem with my knees given the amount of stuff they believed I must have taken to have been so successful in 1987. But it wasn't that way at all. My knee problems all stemmed from that accident on the track in Paris.

Over the course of the 1988/89 winter, I would spend a week with him in Munich then head back home for two weeks, then have another week with him, then go home for three weeks.

Finally, in early 1989 I was able to start competing again. With no pain and some good training behind me, I finished second in Paris–Nice behind Miguel Indurain, but beat him in the time trial up the Col d'Eze. Then I finished third in the Criterium International behind Indurain again. I was still under treatment, though. I'd do a race, then fly in to Munich the day after for a consultation with Dr Müller-Wohlfahrt, who was steadily allowing me to increase my workload.

In the end, I didn't need another operation and haven't had one since. Over the subsequent years I've met some of the doctors I had consultations with and they can't believe that Dr Müller-Wohlfahrt didn't operate on me. But when I've shown them my knee they can see that there's no sign of an op. The scar from the tendon ops are there, the hole from the meniscus op is there. But Dr Müller-Wohlfahrt got me through to the end of my career without the need for a fourth surgical investigation of my suspect knee.

Unfortunately, as things started to go right for me from a physical perspective, everything at Fagor was changing. Robert Millar and just about everyone else had left the team at the end of 1988. There were only 6 riders remaining of the 16 the previous year and the organisation was all over the place. I was left with a reasonable team, but not a patch on what it had been the year before. What seemed like a dream scenario little more than a year earlier had turned into a nightmare.

The split between the riders and the team management had become more pronounced. I felt that Pierre Bazzo devoted more energy to his relationship with Mondragón and Gómez than to the riders. They loved the prestige associated with having a bike team, but didn't provide us with the leadership we needed. Patrick Valcke was well respected by the guys that came on board with me, but his problem was that the other managers on the team kept pulling the carpet from under his feet all the time. It made it very complicated and frustrating. When things were going wrong I had no voice at all because I had been out of action for so long and had lost a good deal of my influence.

On the road, however, I steadily edged back towards my best. I won the Tour of the Basque Country, which was a great result for Fagor as the company was based in the region. Then I decided that rather than opt for a debut appearance at the Vuelta I would stick with my programme from 1987 and ride the Giro in order to build towards that year's Tour. For the first couple of weeks in Italy I was going pretty well and thought a podium finish was well within my reach. Going into a stage to the Tre Cime di Lavaredo after two weeks I was lying second overall just behind Erik Breukink. But the weather started to turn bad that day and from then on I struggled with back problems. This was a new issue, but one that increasingly affected my performances for the rest of my career.

During the Giro's final week the only real impact I had on the race was to give Laurent Fignon a bit of a dig out when he was halted by a puncture on a very tough stage through the Dolomites to Corvara. We were coming down this long, long descent when Fignon punctured. Flavio Giupponi and one of the other Italians took off like crazy men, which wasn't the done thing at all. I could have gone with them but instead I drifted off the back of the group and waited for Fignon, then I drove hard on the descent ahead of him. We worked together on the few kilometres of flat road leading to the final climb and caught Giupponi's group on the early slopes of the climb, where I blew apart. Fignon, though, managed to stick with them. Giupponi did win the stage, but Laurent took the *maglia rosa* that day and held it to the finish, where I finished ninth overall. Not great, but not bad considering where I was coming from with my injury.

As I waited for my flight home from Milan Airport, Fignon walked in with his team manager, Cyrille Guimard. He came over and shook my hand and said: 'Thanks, Steph.' That was a nice touch, but for me it wasn't reasonable to attack a guy when he'd punctured, especially on a descent because it was dangerous as well.

I was disappointed to have faded during the final week at the Giro, but was optimistic because I felt it set me up well for the Tour. Unfortunately, it didn't work out like that. Once there, I was never in contention at all and was forced to abandon after a stupid incident on the stage to Cauterets. I was out of the saddle climbing when a gear slipped and my left knee banged into the end of the bar. I felt it right away. I bruised the tendon and very quickly it became near impossible to turn my legs. I finished the stage – not for the first time Eddy Schepers coached me through to the end – but I was in a really, really bad way. I thought a night's rest might sort it out, but when I got up the next morning to go down to breakfast I couldn't walk. The Tour was over for me and by that point I knew that my stay at Fagor was all but over as well.

CHAPTER 12

'WHAT DO YOU MEAN MY TEAMMATES HAVE GONE?'

In 1987 I had had any number of big-line teams battling for my signature, but two years on the situation couldn't have been more different. My relationship with Fagor had been unworkable, but I didn't really have much of a choice between other teams with my knee injury still very fresh in everyone's minds. I had been hoping that a good performance at the '89 Tour would stoke some interest, but it hadn't been a great experience, once again because of problems with my knee. I guess that everyone had a lot of doubts about where I was coming from and where I was going to go next.

I was being linked with the Colombian Postobón team because Raphaël Géminiani was there and he wanted to work with me again. Bernard Tapie was interested in teaming me up with Jean-François Bernard at Toshiba. Carrera were also interested, but the best offer came from the Belgian Histor-Sigma team. Patrick had some contacts with them and they showed a really genuine interest in taking me on board, perhaps thinking that I might return to my best and raise their profile in the same way that Greg LeMond raised ADR's in 1989. ADR were similarly a small Belgian sponsor and had taken a chance on LeMond after his comeback from that shooting accident. LeMond had repaid them with an incredible victory at the Tour. In my case, Histor were also happy to make Patrick the directeur of the team, so it looked pretty good all-round.

One of the key motivations for me in negotiations at that time was signing for a sane team. The situation had been completely mad at Fagor and I wanted to get back to a normal set-up. Initial talks with Histor went well and I was encouraged to hear that they wanted me to be their figurehead and to build the team slowly. In the end, I met with Histor's team boss, Willy Teirlinck, on the Tuesday and signed on the Saturday. Willy was a good guy and I got on very well with him. He was serious and had a good business mind. The offer was financially attractive as well. It all fell into place nicely for me.

I know some people thought that I'd been hasty in making the commitment to Histor, and that I tended to act too quickly. However, I always felt that the decisions I made were the right ones for me at the time. I don't believe in having regrets. Of course, I look back and know that I made mistakes in certain situations, but life is about learning from those experiences and using them to your advantage in the future. Perhaps I didn't see the Histor deal in its true light, but the human side of it appealed to me. I didn't have a manager to advise me, so perhaps I wasn't able to stand back and be more objective. However, I preferred to negotiate my own deals throughout most of my career, getting feedback from people whose opinion I trusted, like Sean Kelly. So I'm prepared to stand by my mistakes.

Going into that season with Histor, my winter preparation was back on track for the first time since 1986/87. When I was injury-free, I would end the previous season at the Tour of Lombardy, then ride one or two six-day events to wind down because I knew that halting completely one or two days after racing wasn't good for me. Then I would stop for between six weeks and two months and do no work on the bike at all. I wouldn't abandon exercise completely, though. I'd go walking for hours in the mountains, go running, work with weights or do circuit training in the gym. I needed to recharge both mentally and physically, and I'd only get back on the bike when I was happy about doing so.

That way I knew I'd be good for another year. Generally that happened around Christmas, but up to then I'd be eating and putting on weight, often a lot of weight. On Christmas Day I would have my big feed – Christmas pudding, Christmas cake, mince pies, lemonade and everything else – and that would be my last treat. From there through to New Year's Day I'd back off a bit, eating just a bit of cake, starting to get to bed at regular hours and occasionally going out on my fixed-wheel bike. On New Year's Eve there'd be a party, then on New Year's Day, no matter what time I'd gone to bed, I'd be up bright and early and out on the bike. That was the start of my year. From that day until the end of the Criterium International I would cut out all cakes, ice creams and other foodstuffs that are good for the soul but bad for the body.

I'd have training camps in January and February, followed by the early-season races on the Med. There would be a bit of a gap after that and I'd fill it by doing a training camp with Sean Kelly based at a hotel in Villeneuve-Loubet, near Nice. Then he'd go off to do Het Volk and we'd both see each other again at the start of Paris–Nice, after which it would be Milan–San Remo and the Criterium International. From there I would fly back to Paris. Lydia would collect me from the airport and we'd go to an Italian restaurant near the Champs-Élysées and have a huge pizza and the biggest ice cream on the menu.

Back at home, Lydia would have made a lovely strawberry tart or something similar. I'd have one, maybe two, perhaps three pieces and go to bed. During the night I would usually wake up knowing there was still half a cake in the fridge and go down for another piece or two. Then the next morning at eight I'd be out on the bike for two to three hours riding all the shit out of my system. And then it would be back to the normal routine until the end of Liège–Bastogne–Liège. After that the next treat day would be after the Tour. On the Tour I wasn't completely abstemious, but I was fairly. I did lead a normal athlete's life, not being as careful as Sean, for example, who might get a slice of apple tart and cut it in half. I'd definitely have the full slice.

I think people used to look at my round face, my cherubic cheeks and think that I overindulged a bit. But that was all down to genetics. When I won the Giro, Tour and the Worlds in 1987, my body fat was down to 9 per cent. My son Nicolas's body fat is often around 5 per cent, largely due to diet but partly because he's inherited Lydia's slighter physique. If I'd have lost another 3 or 4 per cent of body fat, I'd have lost another three or four kilos. But would I have ridden any better? Perhaps, but we'll never know.

From a psychological point of view, having a slightly more relaxed attitude suited me. I wasn't someone who could live like Sean and be extremely careful about everything I ate and did. For me, life was too short. Even though I was completely focused once I got on my bike, it wouldn't stop me having an ice cream. I just did things differently from Sean and from some of the other guys too. I could have been a bit stricter, but would I have got the same amount of enjoyment and had as much success? My success came not only from my talent but from the way that I lived. I did what worked for me at the time.

Over the winter of 1989/90, I also did a lot of work to build up the muscle around my knee. It had wasted away when I was laid up and I needed to restore the muscle circumference and, consequently, the power in it. My aim was not only to strengthen the area around my kneecap but also to recuperate some of the power lost over two years of being in and out of operations. Even in late 1989 I had still, to some extent, been riding the bike on one leg, afraid to push with the other.

I felt the benefit of that preparation very quickly in the 1990 season, which, in turn, boosted my motivation. I was also helped by the fact that it quickly became apparent we had some good riders at Histor, who were also going well. Francis Moreau won the prologue at Paris–Nice and led the race for a couple of days, which provided us with a huge lift going into the mid-race team time trial at St-Étienne. That day we absolutely steamrollered everyone. Over 44km, only three teams finished within a minute of us. It was enough to put me in the leader's white jersey.

I held it as far as Mont Faron, where our weakness on the climbs was evident as Miguel Indurain won the stage and took the lead. We had lots of good *rouleurs*, guys like Moreau, Brian Holm and Etienne De Wilde, who were incredibly strong on the flat, but once we got to the mountains I couldn't count on much support. The team did keep me in contention through the rest of the race, and I finished just eight seconds down on Indurain overall, having beaten him in the Col d'Eze time trial, which was won by Toshiba's Jean-François Bernard.

Later on in that season there was some talk about me joining Toshiba in order to take some pressure off Bernard, who hadn't emerged as the Tour de France contender everyone had expected him to be after he finished third in 1987. Patrick Valcke had some connections with Look, who were Toshiba's main sub-sponsor, while I had been having on-and-off conversations – going all the way back to 1983 – with team owner Bernard Tapie.

As it turned out, the talks in 1983 were probably the closest we came to agreeing a deal. A couple of years later, on the day I won the Tour stage up the Aubisque, I was coming back down the mountain and Tapie waved me to a halt. He had this fabulous camping car, basically a very souped-up Ford Transit with cush-ioned seats and fridges filled with champagne. The door swooshed open and there was Tapie, waving at me and telling me to get in. I said to him: 'I can't get in there now,' because I was still fighting for the title with LeMond and Hinault, the leaders of his team. Despite that, he wanted to drive me back down the mountain.

Tapie was obviously controversial as shown by his later run-ins with the law, but he had a very flamboyant personality and I kind of liked the guy. He once invited me to a football match with him in Lille when he owned Olympique de Marseille. I picked him up at Lille Airport in the big Opel Omega I had at the time. He got in and asked me to put the air-con on, so I rolled the window down.

After the match he said: 'You aren't going back to Paris in that old car of yours without the air-conditioning, are you? I'll take you home. Give your keys to my friend and he'll drive your car back to Le Bourget and we'll meet him there.' Then, he took me to his private plane. I thought I'd be sitting with him, but he got into the pilot's seat and started flicking switches.

I said to him: 'Do you know how to fly this thing?'

'Yeah, yeah.'

'Do you have a licence?' I asked him.

'Not yet, but he has,' he said, pointing at the co-pilot in the seat next to him. And, with that, he flew us back to Le Bourget.

In the end, nothing came of the deal, despite the papers saying that an agreement had been reached and that I'd be taking a number of French riders with me to join Bernard. It's true Patrick had been talking to them, but for some reason it just never came off.

Through all that talk, I continued my build-up to the Tour, which was going well although wins were proving elusive. I had top tens in the Criterium International, Tour of the Basque Country and Flèche Wallonne. Finally, I did manage to top the podium at the Four Days of Dunkirk, which went down well with the team as they had sponsors based in that region. It was a real battle winning the race as well. Often the smaller races were much harder to win than major tours or the biggest Classics because so many riders felt they were in with a chance. When you lined up in a major tour you knew that there were probably only six to ten riders who were likely to contend and that everyone else was looking to finish and maybe have a sniff of glory on the way. But at a race like Dunkirk, dozens of guys knew they could win if things went their way.

I took the lead in the time trial on the second day, but my chances almost completely disappeared later on. Although called the Four Days of Dunkirk, it actually takes place over six. On the fourth day we were riding onto a cobbled section. Positioning is everything on roads of that nature. You're going to get a very bumpy ride whichever line you choose, but the key is to keep your momentum going. I was second in line, figuring that was the best place to stay out of trouble. As we went onto the cobbles, the rear tyre of the guy on the front blew out and he slid down. I tried to bunnyhop over him at about 60kms an hour, but when I was in the air above him his front wheel flipped up and hit my pedal and brought me down heavily on my hip, elbow and shoulder.

By the time I got to the finish there was blood everywhere. It had been pissing out of my elbow and down onto my front wheel. They cleaned me up and took me to the hospital, where they picked the gravel out of my wounds and stitched me up. The doctors told me I needed a week off. I said to them: 'I'm very sorry, but I have to race tomorrow. It's the final couple of days of Dunkirk and I'm the race leader.' So they made me sign a discharge form saying I was leaving the hospital of my own free will.

The next day there were two stages on Mont Cassel, the cobbled climb that is one of the race's main features. The first was a 4km time trial. I knew everyone had seen the extent of my injuries the day before and knew that I'd been in hospital. They would be on the look-out for any sign of vulnerability. They could also see I had my arm wrapped up in quite a large bandage. I thought if I could ride a good time trial I might get a bit of peace in the afternoon. But I knew if I didn't go well in the morning the pace would be hot right from the start in the afternoon as riders would be figuring: 'Roche must be down, so I'm going to go for it.'

It wasn't an easy time trial either. The course went down one side of Mont Cassel, then around and back up the other. Thankfully, though, I went pretty well, finishing third behind Jelle Nijdam and Thierry Marie, who were both specialists over that kind of short distance. The route for the afternoon's stage passed over Mont Cassel maybe 10 or 12 times, climbing its tarmacked side and descending its cobbled side. Patrick had put some foam on my handlebars to provide some cushioning, but every time we came down the cobbles I had to have my arm off the bars because of the pain caused by the vibrations.

My teammates managed to keep it together until the last lap, and it was only then that there were some attacks as my rivals realised that I was in a lot of pain. But I came through OK, bluffing it to some extent, and kept hold of the lead going into the final day, which was a straightforward stage that ended with a bunch sprint.

I went home that evening still feeling sore. That night I was asleep in bed and woke up covered in sweat. Lydia didn't know what was happening, but she was aware of an awful smell – the wounds in my elbow had become infected. She took one look at them and fainted, then once she'd come round, went to get her parents up from the apartment downstairs where they lived. Her mother saw the wounds and fainted as well. Her dad ended up treating my elbow with disinfectant.

When I woke up on the Monday morning my elbow had locked up and my hip was massively swollen with a huge haematoma, so I rang up Dr Müller-Wohlfahrt in Munich for advice. He told me to get an MRI and an ultrasound scan done and to send him the results. I went to the doctor at my local hospital in Paris and they said it would take ten days to book these appointments. I called the Tour's doctor, Gérard Porte, to see if he could pull some strings. Gérard came back to me and said it would still take a few days, so I called Dr Müller-Wohlfahrt to update him and he said: 'No, no, that's not soon enough. Leave it with me.'

He rang me back mid-Monday morning and said: 'Stephen, you've got a flight leaving for Munich at 1 p.m. Your MRI is at this time and place, the ultrasound scan is at this time and place. Once they are done, you will come to my offices, we will look at the results and we will discuss what has to be done. Then you have a flight back home at 9.30 this evening.'

I remember driving to the airport with my arm in a sling as I went off to see him. I had the scans and when I got to his office he took out a huge syringe and pulled all the blood out from under the skin in my hip. He treated all around my elbow with acupuncture, or mesotherapy, in fact – little injections which helped get the joint mobile again. Incredibly, everything was done in a day. He believed athletes shouldn't be kept waiting. For him time was money, and he felt that it was the same for an athlete. He had me back on the plane home that evening. That was the genius and the commitment of the man.

I wasn't laid up for very long at all after Dunkirk. I finished in the top ten at the Dauphiné Libéré in early June, but struggled in the mountains there. It wasn't a good sign with the Tour just a few weeks away, but it proved an accurate one. I finished 44th in the 1990 Tour, an hour down on the winner, Greg LeMond. There was talk of a viral problem, but I think that at that time when people weren't getting results there was always talk of a virus. There could have been any number of reasons for my poor showing, but I simply wasn't going well.

Histor already knew that I was getting some interest from other teams and told me they would not object to me leaving as they wouldn't be able to raise my salary for the following season. Once again, Patrick had been working on a deal that included Look. With Look on board, that September we agreed to move to another Belgian team, Tonton Tapis, where I would share leadership with

Dirk De Wolf and Patrick would be a team director alongside Roger De Vlaeminck. However, this deal was starting to come apart even before we got to the end of the 1990 season, leading in turn to the breakdown in my ten-year association with Patrick.

Patrick is actually an accountant by training, but he is a genius as a mechanic. We met in 1981 when I was a new pro at Peugeot and he was a new addition to the back-room staff. As new guys, we often found ourselves shunted off to the sides together, which made for a natural bond between us. Over that year our relationship got closer and he started looking after my bike.

We left Peugeot together and went to La Redoute, then moved on to Carrera. By that time, though, he was more than just a mechanic. He'd help me in all kinds of other ways. For instance, he used to be my driver for the post-Tour criteriums. This sounds straightforward enough, but he'd do all the planning for the trips, sorting out the hotels, where we would stop for meals, everything. When we got to an event, he'd set up my bike while I signed autographs. While I was racing, he'd be planning the trip to the next criterium – the food, the road, the hotel. When I had finished, I would go off and shower, and he'd clean my bike and my clothes. I'd pick up my contract money, then we'd be back in the car and gone.

My goal during this quite intense period was to recover after the Tour and not let the relentlessness of the criteriums get me down because riding every day is very hard when you're travelling, not eating properly and living out of a car and a suitcase. I was also keen to maintain the good condition I had coming out of the Tour for the Worlds, with the idea that one day I might have a chance of winning the title. I felt the form I'd got during the Tour was something that shouldn't be abused and having Patrick as a driver for the criteriums was one way of staying fresh.

He also had very good tactical knowledge and understood what support I needed in time trials. He knew exactly when to shout and when not to. He was excellent when it came to equipment, helping me make my choice on bikes, tyres and every other piece of kit. I'd ask him: 'What do you think?' and he'd give me his opinion. We didn't debate it. I'd listen, take what I wanted and then make my decision, which was final and never questioned.

It was nice to have someone there who did everything for you and fought for you, sometimes literally. After one particular race in Italy we got into an altercation with a policeman, and Patrick turned round and planted one on him. He ended up in jail for a few hours that day and once we had got him out he couldn't go back to Italy for three years. But that's just the way he was. He was always there, fending people off me. At the same time, he knew when and how to give me my space, to let me be on my own in my bubble. He would still be there in the background, making sure I had everything I needed to perform.

His desire to support me in any way that he could also revealed itself in other ways. When I needed to train behind a motorbike, for instance, he'd drive down from his home in Lille to Paris, we'd do a session behind the motorbike of up to 100km perhaps, then he'd drive the two hours home again. Or I might go to his place and stay the night. His house was my second home. He had a genuine track moped and he'd take me out riding behind that. When we went out motor-pacing, he knew when to ease off and when to press because he was so aware of my strengths and weaknesses on the bike.

As time went on, Patrick felt that he should step up to a more powerful role and I was happy to push for his promotion to a role as a team director. That couldn't happen at Carrera because Davide Boifava had his own team in place there, but Patrick got the chance to step up at Fagor. But it was when Patrick stepped up that another side of his personality became more evident, a side that was less helpful to me, even though it took me some time to realise it.

Despite the many qualities he had, in my opinion Patrick didn't turn out to be the best of team directeurs. I know that some of the riders he worked with thought that he was out of his depth, but I think that's unfair. He was extremely good when it came to tactics and team logistics. He was also great at recruiting young riders. He'd go and watch young kids and be able to detect those who had quality, guys like Francis Moreau, for example. Later on, when Patrick was a journalist working on the Tour, he'd always do well in the competition to guess who would win each day because he knew the riders and racing so well. Everyone would go to him for tips.

But I felt he could be a bit headstrong, quite intense, and I felt he was often too pernickety. He looked for problems even when there weren't any. In my opinion, he wasn't the right man to hold the reins of a big team. He was tutored in the old methods by Maurice De Muer and Raphaël Géminiani and had heard stories about working with the likes of Anquetil and guys from that era. And when he talked to other riders he'd be saying: 'Stephen does this and Stephen does that . . .' But not everyone could relate to what I was doing. Everyone is different, everyone has their own way of doing things, and to get the best out of them you have to focus on each individual's qualities rather than trying to make individuals fit into a template.

At the end of 1989 when Fagor folded, things began to change between us. We moved on to Histor, but it wasn't a great year for me and we quickly moved on to Tonton Tapis. The set-up was completely new and had been put together by Noël Demeulenaere, the 'Mr Fixit' of Flemish cycling, who was behind the establishment of any number of teams and regularly brought new sponsors into the sport. It was well backed by a carpet retail chain owned by André Debor, who was Tonton Tapis – literally 'Uncle Carpet'. It sounded extremely promising, but it was where it all fell apart between Patrick and me.

In common with many cycling pros, I've always been a bit of a petrolhead. I not only liked tinkering with cars, but loved driving them quickly as well. Patrick was also keen and this shared passion led to us doing some car rallies together in France and Ireland from 1988 onwards. It was mostly second-division rallying, but we received invites to bigger events as well.

Patrick was my co-driver and used to look after the budget and all of the other logistical aspects. During 1990, we were negotiating with Tonton Tapis and were also looking to bring some two million francs to the table that we'd negotiated from Look, which was owned by Bernard Tapie at the time. It looked like we had the makings of a good team. I had agreed a good contract, so had Patrick. But the deal with Look suddenly fell apart and with it went the two million francs, which was where our salaries were supposed to come from.

At about the same time, Patrick and I were supposed to be competing in a rally in the south of France, the Rallye des Vars, which was part of the second-division championship that we were involved in. Patrick said to me: 'Look, we're contracted to do this rally in the Vars, we've got to do it.'

But I told him: 'Patrick, our careers are at stake and they're more important than driving a car. The car is not our career, it's just a pastime. Our real job is the bike and we have to find a way of getting this money back for Tonton because we're going in with two million francs less than we said we would have.' But Patrick insisted on taking part in the rally. I said I wouldn't drive, that we had to work on getting this team together, that it was ridiculous to be thinking of doing anything else.

But he told me that if I wasn't going to drive then he would. He was normally my co-driver, but he went off and drove the rally and things got really complicated between us then. I told him that we couldn't work together when we had such different priorities. And that was the end of it between us. Our working relationship basically stopped there. We did patch things up a few years later, but it's never been the same.

I went back to Tonton Tapis, told them I was very sorry that the Look money had gone and worked at finding some new money from somewhere. Ultimately, we didn't find any, but they were happy that I had rolled in with them and we negotiated a new deal.

As well as marking my break with Patrick, the season I spent with Tonton Tapis was the turning point in my career in other ways too, principally because that was the year I missed the start of the team time trial at the Tour de France. Securing a place at the Tour was the team's main objective in its first season. With that in mind I went well during the early part of 1991, taking back-to-back wins at Semana Catalana and the Criterium International. But as the Tour got nearer I was struggling badly with tendonitis in my arm, which was making it extremely painful for me even to change gear. That injury forced me to quit the Dauphiné Libéré, although by that point we'd earned enough ranking points to gain selection on the Tour.

I won't hide the fact that I wasn't very fond of our team manager, Roger De Vlaeminck. I didn't find him much help at all. I needed a certain amount of interaction with my team directeur. I preferred them to be involved and supportive like Raphaël Géminiani and Davide Boifava had been. But I felt Roger wasn't interested in knowing me, what I was doing or how I worked. I doubt I was the only one who found him difficult to work with. I remember before the Dauphiné that I'd said to Roger that he should come along and see what we were doing on the training camps. I reckoned they were useful for team directeurs as well as the riders because it meant that when it came to race day they would know where we were and what was going on. But he would never come on a training camps with me.

I wasn't happy with the situation, but I was being paid to ride a bike and I knew I had to get on with it. In fact, I was really looking forward to that year's Tour because my brother Laurence was on the team with me and was about to make his Tour debut. My parents were coming across from Ireland to watch us race. They'd rented a camping car and were taking Nicolas and Christel away for a week to watch the Tour around Normandy and Brittany, where half a dozen stages were taking place. Consequently, there was no reason whatsoever for me to be thinking about not finishing the Tour, although many people were soon insisting the opposite.

I didn't have a great start to the race, finishing well down in the prologue, but came home safely in the bunch on day two. When we got to the team time trial the next day, Tonton Tapis' management were out in force. Demeulenaere was there, De Vlaeminck was there, there were assistant directeurs everywhere, which made what happened next even harder to explain.

The team time trial started in Bron, in Lyons' eastern suburbs. We started our preparation by going out for a short ride on our time-trial bikes on neighbouring roads. Coming back from a warm-up like that, I never used to stop because if I did I would end up with people all around me. At that point I just needed to be in my bubble, focusing on the test ahead and not wanting to talk or see anybody. I'd got my wheels changed, my skinsuit on and gone off to the warm-up circuit that had been created for the riders. Located about 100 metres from the start, it was approximately 500 metres around.

Back at the team cars, meanwhile, someone realised we'd all been told the wrong start time. I think it was Francis Moreau who went to the podium to sign on and spotted the error – we were due on ten minutes earlier than we had been told. He came back and told the other guys. There was panic. However, as I was still warming up on the circuit, I wasn't aware of this. At no point did anyone come to find me and tell me what was going on. The riders didn't because they were all frantically getting themselves

In the yellow jersey at the Tour de France on the morning of the final stage into Paris.

Heading for victory in the '87 Tour's long time trial to Futuroscope on a day when several of my rivals wilted in the heat.

Slumped at the foot of the press gallery, I'm given oxygen having pushed myself right to my very limits finishing at La Plagne.

The 1987 Tour all came down to the final time trial in Dijon, where I am slowly building a lead on Pedro Delgado heading up a climb.

Not long to go now… Having taken the race lead from Delgado the day before, Paris and victory is not far away.

'I've done it!' On the final podium with second-placed Delgado (*left*) and third-placed Jean-François Bernard.

(*Right*) Victory in Villach. Adding the world title to the Tour and Giro crowns to emulate Eddy Merckx's achievement of 1974.

Sadly, a recurrence of my knee injury meant that I didn't get to wear the rainbow jersey (*left*) as often as I would have liked.

Later in 1987 I received the rare honour of a private interview with the Pope. I am pictured here with Lydia, my daughter Christel, in the white shoes, and my son, Nicolas, who is clutching a framed yellow jersey.

I had hoped that Fagor would be an outstanding team, but my knee problems meant I was sidelined for much of my time there.

I rode pretty well at the 1989 Giro and I
was happy to help out Laurent Fignon,
here in the pink jersey, when the Italians attacked after
he had punctured.

I was never on the pace when I rode the Tour
with Histor in 1990, by which time my back
was troubling me as well as my knee.

On the attack in the 1992 Tour de France. You can see race leader Miguel Indurain among those trying to chase behind me.

With my eldest son, Nicolas, who I am very proud to say is making
his own mark in professional cycling.

ready, while the management all appeared to leave it to each other.

As I was riding around I met my former Carrera teammate Davide Cassani and asked him what time his Ariostea team were off. He told me his time, which he had written down on a piece of paper that was stuck on his stem. I told him his time couldn't be right given the time I had been told, but he assured me it was. I was equally sure my time was right, but I thought I'd better go back and see what was going on. When I returned to where our cars had been parked there was no sign of them or anyone from the team at all. By now I was panicking too. I asked someone: 'Where's the team?' and was told: 'They've gone, they're gone, you'd better go.'

'What do you mean? Where have they gone?' I said.

'They've gone, go, go, go.'

I rushed down to the start ramp, where somebody tried to drag me off my bike because I was late and the Ryalcao-Postobón team were about to start. There was very briefly some frantic talk as the commissaires tried to decide what to do with me, but just I pushed them away and sprinted off down the course. I still didn't know what was happening. I just rode and rode and rode. I was caught and passed by a couple of teams and finished 14 minutes down on the fastest team and well outside the limit for elimination. If the delay before I'd even started riding had been taken into consideration, it would have been a good individual time-trial effort. But when I got to the finish all anyone was saying was that I had been eliminated and that I was going to be sacked. It was crazy.

Someone asked me: 'What happened, Stephen?' I told them I'd been on the warm-up circuit, had stopped for a piss in one of the toilets nearby and didn't hear that there was any problem. That explanation spiralled into a story about me having diarrhoea and being locked in a toilet when I should have been racing, but what I actually said was that the only time I left the circuit was to go for a pee, but that I'd always been in the warm-up area. Anyone could easily have found me.

I got in a car and was being driven back to the hotel when I heard on the radio that I was expected at Demeulenaere's HQ in Belgium the next day, where I would be sacked. I was sat there wondering: 'What the hell is this?'

When I arrived back at the hotel, the mechanic said he'd been told to take my bike off me. I told him I needed it and he let me keep it, but asked me not to tell anyone that he had. That evening I went to see the Tour director, Jean-Marie Leblanc, to apologise for what had happened and to give him my side of the story. He was glad I'd come but confirmed that the race's rules had to be followed and there was no way back for me. I also tried contacting De Vlaeminck that evening, but he was suddenly very difficult to get hold of.

So I flew back to Paris that night, then drove to Flanders the next morning to see Demeulenaere at his office in his carpet factory in Flanders. The press were all waiting outside, expecting me to be sacked. I went in to see Demeulenaere and we talked it all over for quite a time. He told me that I had acted very badly, that it was my fault, that as a professional cyclist I should have known when my start time was, that it was nothing at all to do with the team manager, even if the team manager had made a mistake. Ultimately, he said, it was down to me and said that if I hadn't wanted to race I should have told them. I insisted that there was absolutely no way I hadn't wanted to race. We argued about all this for a while and ended up in polarised positions. Demeulenaere wanted me to leave the team, but I said I didn't see why I should.

Demeulenaere said I had two choices. The first was for me to leave, for me to accept being sacked. The second was that I could insist on staying with the team, in which case they would take me to court, which meant I wouldn't be able to race or change teams. We talked some more about this and finally we agreed that the team would pay up a small part of my contract and in return I would agree to leave peacefully. It wasn't the ideal agreement for me, but it was better to have a good solution than an unwanted court case. I was out and that was all that really mattered.

By that stage I was totally wiped out in terms of morale. All kinds of stuff were being said about me, none of it very pleasant. Journalists were writing that I'd been capricious, that I was sulking because the team wouldn't do what I wanted, and because of that I had decided to pull the plug on the Tour de France. But I would never do something like that. It was being said that my head had been turned by my successes in 1987 and that I'd got lazy. But I totally refute that. I was very cut up, particularly as some people who I would have expected to take my side were writing this kind of stuff. That really got to me. It was even being reported that my career was over, that no one would want to take me on again. I felt demoralised. All I wanted was to be left alone. Ultimately, the only good thing I can say about the Tonton Tapis experience is that it got me pointed in the right direction once again.

CHAPTER 13

COMPLETING THE CIRCLE

In the wake of my difficulties with Tonton Tapis, I wasn't really sure whether I wanted to continue with my racing career at all. I was so low I was seriously thinking of stopping. Sitting at home one day in early November, I got a call from Carrera boss Davide Boifava to ask what my plans were for the 1992 season. I admitted to him that I felt wasted and was contemplating retirement. Always a good man when it came to lifting morale, Davide tried to raise my spirits and made me an offer. 'Come and join us,' he said. 'You can't leave the sport by the back door. I've got confidence in you.'

We had a few conversations over the following days and, finally, I agreed that I would re-sign with Carrera dependent on a couple of conditions. I gave him my price and said that for superstitious reasons I wanted to sign the contract on my birthday, 28 November. I also asked him to give me a complete break between that date and the team presentation. I wanted to have no contact with anyone at all at the team so that I could rest. Finally, I told him that if I was to decide during the 1992 season that I wanted to retire I didn't want him trying to hold me to the terms of a contract. I didn't know if I could get myself together to compete at the top level for another year and didn't want to be obliged to do so. I didn't want any pressure whatsoever. I wanted it to be an open agreement.

He was happy with that. 'OK, done,' he told me and went about sorting out the details. In the end, Davide couldn't physically get a contract to me on my birthday because there was fog at Linate Airport in Milan. Instead, he faxed it to me, I signed it and sent it back immediately. That same day I started training for the 1992 season.

One of the best things about the time I spent with Carrera was that there had always been mutual respect between myself and Boifava. Going back was like going home. Even though we'd split up in difficult circumstances, Boifava and I had always stayed in contact. I also knew most of the staff and a lot of the riders very well, including Claudio Chiappucci, who had established himself as team leader since I had moved on and Roberto Visentini had slipped into retirement. The idea was for me to help Chiappucci calm down a little bit and also assist him with his time trialling.

Trying to manage Chiappucci was not as easy as I thought it would be. He'd change his handlebars one day, his stem the next. One day he'd have an 11cm stem, the next it would be a 10cm, then a 12cm. Someone would look at him and say: 'Claudio, you look very stretched on that bike. Do you feel like you're too stretched out?' And he'd go and put a shorter stem on just because I'd said he looked stretched. Then a couple of days on someone else would look at him and say: 'You look a bit tight there.' And he'd go off and put a longer stem on. He was always changing his bike around and never really settled on what was the ideal set-up for him.

Boifava thought that in helping Chiappucci I might also be able to help myself and the team. I didn't really see myself as a domestique as I believe that labels of that kind limit what you can achieve. That's why I always say to Nicolas today: 'Don't lock yourself completely into a team role. Don't believe you're just a team rider. You have to be selfish, but in being selfish also be a nice guy. Above all, though, don't forget that you have to look after yourself.'

Riders today can hide behind labels such as 'leader' and 'domestique'. They try to make the public think that cycling is very complicated, that every rider slots into a different category, but the sport is quite simple really. You race, you see opportunities and you try to take them. Or you see opportunities that your teammates have and you try to do what you can to help them take advantage.

After what was a very stress-free winter compared to the previous few, I felt revitalised when the new season started and that showed in my performances on the road. I had top ten finishes at Tirreno–Adriatico, the Criterium International and Tour of the Basque Country. I did OK in the Ardennes Classics and then made my debut at the Vuelta a España. My overriding memory of that race is of the appalling weather. The biggest stage was actually in France to Luz-Ardiden. It was so misty that you could barely see the road on the descents and so cold that it was difficult to pull the brakes firmly enough to stop yourself heading into the snow banks on the corners. I didn't really feature, but climbed well in the latter part of the race to finish 14th overall. Not outstanding by any means, but it was my first grand tour finish for two years and boosted my morale going into the Tour de France.

I started the Tour quietly enough. That changed with the team time trial halfway through the first week. One of the achievements I am most proud of during the years I spent with Carrera is that I never finished lower than second in a team time trial with them. That day in Libourne, Panasonic pipped us by just seven seconds, which pushed Chiappucci and me right into contention. Boifava was so pleased with our performance that he bought us all champagne that night. He said it was the best time trial the team had ridden since I'd left.

The safe strategy then would have been to hold back until the Alps and challenge defending champion Miguel Indurain on what most people would regard as the most testing terrain. But I never viewed the major tours quite like that. Opportunities could come on any day, and you had to be ready to take them.

At the end of the first week there was a stage into Valkenburg finishing just beyond the Cauberg climb where the Amstel Gold Classic is decided each year. I'd said at the Tour presentation the previous autumn that Indurain could lose the Tour on that stage. My feeling was that it was hard enough for one team to defend over the course of a day in the high mountains, but on a stage like that over rolling terrain featuring numerous little ramps it was almost impossible. Just think how tough it is for one team to defend a leader during Classics like Amstel. Those races are so relentlessly difficult that teams have to make alliances if they want to keep the bunch together. I suppose I might have been giving Indurain's Banesto team a warning, but no one took me seriously and I couldn't blame them, given the state I was in at the end of 1991. But I was determined to show everyone what I meant.

With about 50km to go I got across to a break with seven other riders in it and from there into the finish I rode like a man possessed, all the time thinking: 'I told yer! I told yer!' About 30km out, the pace I was setting saw four riders fall back on a climb, including my old Histor teammate Brian Holm, and all the time our advantage over the main peloton was increasing.

By now I was with Gilles Delion, Rolf Jaermann and Valerio Tebaldi, all strong guys and all of them focused on the stage win while I just wanted to gain as much time as I could and make things as tough for Chiappucci's rivals as possible. The other three riders were happy to let me do most of the pace-setting and ultimately that did work against me in terms of the win. Delion in particular wasn't contributing much and he profited in the end. I attacked from a kilometre out, but he overhauled me in the final 50 metres. He was delighted with himself, although I wouldn't have been shouting about it if I'd been sitting on for so long. I was disappointed that I hadn't won it because I'd worked so hard for it, but I was pleased that I had followed through on my warning to Banesto.

To a degree, I paid for that effort in the Luxembourg time trial a couple of days later. Indurain's win that day has gone down as one of the great time-trial performances in racing history, but I don't agree with that assessment. Yes, his average speed of 49km/h over a 65km course was incredible, but the course was as flat as a billiard table and extremely fast. Indurain got an awful lot of credit for his fabulous performance that day. But who was second? Armand de la Cuevas, who was three minutes down. Who was third? Gianni Bugno, who was almost four. No disrespect intended, but they weren't exactly great time triallists.

Guys like Fignon, Mottet, LeMond, Bernard and me, who had been the top time triallists in the previous few years, were all past our best and no one apart from Indurain had come through to replace us. He performed just as he should have done given his power and strength. The same goes for riders like Bugno and Chiappucci. However, there was no longer anyone filling the gap in between Indurain at the top of the time-trialling hierarchy and riders who were likely to be his main challengers in the mountains. So it was a great performance in terms of the time differences and speed averaged, but I think the time-trialling weakness of his rivals made it look better than it was.

A few days later I was in another break with Jaermann. This time my old sparring partner Pedro Delgado was with us as we headed for St-Gervais. I was riding for Chiappucci and Delgado was riding for Indurain, and this time Jaermann took advantage by sitting on. Delgado and I were hoping that we could get rival teams riding behind, enabling our leaders to stay fresh for the big stage to Sestriere that followed. Consequently, after we'd pushed hard going onto the final hill, Jaermann rode away from us to take the stage. But I loved being in the situation I found myself in on that stage – at the front and riding hard, knowing that people are chasing just behind you and that, from a tactical point of view, I was making things tough for them by pressing here, backing off there, then going again.

The work that I put in that day may have helped Chiappucci a bit with his staggering performance on the stage to Sestriere the day after, although others have suggested that there may have been other reasons behind his incredible ride over five climbs. All I can say is that Chiappucci always had a mark against that stage because it finished in Italy. He himself would never have dreamed of doing the ride that he did. He attacked on the first climb of the day, the Col de Saisies, with little more than 20 of that day's 254km covered. First over the Saisies in a small group, he led over the Cormet de Roselend and dropped his final breakaway companion on Col d'Iséran. He climbed Mont Cenis on his own and even when he reached Sestriere I think his time for that climb was just about the fastest ever. I do know that he rode it a good deal quicker than me as I rolled in more than ten minutes down.

The next stage was to Alpe d'Huez, never a happy hunting ground for me, and I lost another chunk of time that dropped me out of the top ten. But after finishing second at Valkenburg and third at St-Gervais, I still felt that I had good form and was happy to save it for a day when I was more likely to make it count. The stage through the Massif Central to La Bourboule looked the pick of those that remained. In fact, it was the final mountain stage of that Tour so it was the last opportunity for me to come out of the race with something.

On the face of it, it wasn't an ideal day for me because it was so hot. But the conditions started to change when we reached the Col de la Croix-Morand with about 30km to go. There were three breakaway riders still ahead of the bunch when I attacked early on the climb. I passed two of them fairly quickly, then moved again and caught Peter de Clercq. Once up to him, I just kept going. I wasn't going to take any prisoners after what had happened in Valkenburg and St-Gervais. I didn't want to do all the riding and be caught out at the end.

My plan was to go full blast up the Croix-Morand, then, as I was a good descender, take the descent handily enough and recuperate a little bit up to the foot of the climb to La Bourboule, where I wanted to give it everything I'd got and hopefully hold off the bunch. But as I climbed the Croix-Morand, the weather changed. The sky came down, it got misty and started raining. It rapidly went from 30+ degrees down to about 8. As I got higher the rain turned to hail. I didn't mind the conditions, but going down the far side, where I'd hoped to recuperate, I was on a wide-open road into a headwind so I wasn't able to recuperate at all. I had to pedal down the damn hill.

At the bottom it was straight up to La Bourboule. I always remember hearing from the race radios as the motorbikes were going past: 'Peloton at 35 seconds.' I also knew that attacks were going and being brought back all the time. I was hanging out there on my own thinking: 'They're not going to catch me, they're not going to catch me.' I gave it everything and I think by the finish I'd only lost about five seconds to the bunch on the final climb.

I'd won my stage and when I crossed the line, the journalists crowded in around me. I remember saying: 'This one is for me, my wife, my family, everyone who has supported me over the last couple of years because things haven't been easy. Now that I've come back, it's over. I'm going to retire next year. I know at 33 years of age I'm not going to win another Tour. Next year will be my final year and that will be my career finished.'

Philippe Sudres, who was the Tour's press liaison officer at that time, always reminds me that the press conference that day was the only occasion he'd seen a roomful of journalists give the day's winner a standing ovation both before and after their press conference. Everyone was so pleased that I'd come back after my injury and everything else I'd gone through. I look back on that victory now and see it as one of my really big days. It was super.

But something broke inside me that day. I hadn't really been thinking about retirement before, but that day I knew I was finished, that I would just do one more year. I had no reason to go on.

It turned out that the early '90s was not a bad time to quit racing because of the increasing influence doping was having on the sport. At the time, I could see that the sport was changing, but as I was getting towards the end of a long career I thought that my impression that speeds were increasing was down to my advancing years. When you're a pro cyclist, you live in your own world and, although you can see things happening, you may not be able to see a reason for that immediately. In hindsight, that reason may become clear, but when I was racing I never used the thought that other riders might be doping as an excuse, to suggest that's why I had been beaten, because you simply don't know. You hear all these things about different riders, but who's to know what's true? I hear things about myself as well and I know they're not true.

In those years leading up to my retirement, there wasn't much talk about EPO. Doping was something that I'd always been aware of, but doping then meant steroids, cortisone and hormones, products that might make a little bit of difference. The difference with EPO was that it could have a huge impact on performance, like turning boys into men. However, it was almost impossible to know what anyone else was up to. Riders had their own relationship with their team doctor. I don't think I was ever – or only very rarely – in the doctor's room when somebody else was there. Everyone did their own thing and no one really spoke about it.

My own philosophy on cheating was to avoid it in any and

every form. I didn't want question marks raised against my achievements because I had, for instance, hung on to a bottle from a team car, sat in behind a motorbike or taken dope. I still say to Nicolas now, 'Whatever you do, stay clean because the guys who are cheating have to live with it. If you cheat, where are you going to end up? If you're caught then you're destroyed for life. Everything you have ever done will have a question mark hanging over it, whether it's exam results at school, victories you took as a young kid or success you've had at the top level. You've got to stay straight and believe that the testing procedures will enable clean athletes to shine eventually.'

As my career entered its final season, physical issues continued to be my primary concern. My knee was almost 100 per cent by then, but I had a growing problem with my back. I was still seeing Dr Müller-Wohlfahrt regularly and he diagnosed it as two slipped discs between L5 and L7, two of the vertebrae in my lower back. He realised the injury stemmed from overexerting my back when I'd had my knee problems, but it only became evident when I got to 80 per cent fitness. Once I was at that point I found it difficult to get up to 100 per cent. In time trials, particularly, my left leg would go dead because the herniated discs were rubbing on the sciatic nerve.

Dr Müller-Wohlfahrt described the injury as being 'big enough to hurt, but too small to operate on'. He said the injury wasn't going to go away and had to be dealt with, but there was a question over how invasive the treatment needed to be. He said an operation was possible, but explained that there was no guarantee of success and that I'd be off the bike for six months. I didn't fancy any more time out, so he gave me a series of exercises and stretches to do to alleviate the pain, backed up by regular manipulation. That did ease the problem to a significant extent, but it is fair to say that from 1987 onwards I never really had both legs working perfectly at the same time. Even with his treatment I probably only got back to perhaps 85 per cent of the power in my left leg.

When I rode the major tours I would talk to him regularly. He'd also visit me on the race, usually before the second batch of mountain stages. I remember him coming with a physio to see me during the 1993 Tour at Isola 2000. I think he'd already been once during that Tour because my back would tighten up after five or six days of racing, leading to a loss of power in my left leg. But I hadn't been expecting to see him at Isola 2000. I'd been on the phone to his secretary, Betty, saying my back was a bit tight, but that everything would be OK. I explained that I was well down on GC, so it didn't matter that I wasn't at my best.

When I arrived at my hotel after the stage to Isola 2000 I found him in the lobby. He said that Betty had given him the message, but he thought he'd come down anyway. A friend, Rudi, who had a private jet, had flown him and a physio down from Munich to Nice, where he had picked up a helicopter to Isola to treat me for 90 minutes. I wanted him to stay for dinner, but he had to get back to Munich because Boris Becker was flying in that evening for treatment. That was the kind of guy he was, totally committed to the athletes he worked with.

By that point, I had no doubts that retirement was the best option for me. I'd ridden the Giro one final time, finishing ninth largely thanks to an attack on a descent on the penultimate stage that boosted me a couple of places up the GC. Even then, though, I was well aware that I'd lost some of my nerve. That year I really had to think when I was on the descents, which I'd never had to do before. It was a clear sign that I was getting too old for racing.

I wanted to produce something special at the Tour that year, even if it was a moment that only I remembered. In the first week I instigated a break on the stage into Verdun, attacking on a descent about 5km from the finish and hoping that I might get clear on my own. But five other riders joined me and a young American called Lance Armstrong won the sprint. I didn't really know anything about him before then, but at the end of that season I was heavily indebted to him because he beat Miguel Indurain to the gold medal at the Worlds in Oslo, preventing Indurain from becoming the third man in history to complete the Triple Crown.

The Worlds was just about my last race as a pro and I didn't finish because the circuit was incredibly dangerous in the heavy rain that fell just about all day. I hadn't fallen, but I'd seen bodies going off everywhere, particularly on the descents. I remember one rider – I think it was Canada's Steve Bauer – ended up in the middle of a railway line after crashing over a fence.

My last really good moment that year was at Pla d'Adet in the Tour, when I came fourth behind Zenon Jaskula, Tony Rominger and Indurain. They'd told us there was a very steep part near the end of the climb and I held a bit back hoping to catch the three riders ahead of me on the steep section and attack them straight away. But there was no steep rise. I was coming back at them, but afraid to give it everything in case I hit this ramp, which never appeared. I ended up just 25 seconds down on them and feeling pretty frustrated.

With that went just about my last chance of signing off with a final Tour success, but I was still keen to mark the race in some small way. I was very nostalgic starting the last day but had little time to dwell on that as there were attacks right from the start. As the stage calmed down a bit, I decided it would be nice to be the first rider across the finish line at the start of the first lap on the Champs-Élysées in Paris.

So, coming off the corner by the Place de la Concorde, I accelerated, crossed the line, then backed off. The Banesto train came by me, leading Indurain, and as they passed Gérard Rué, Jean-François Bernard and a few others gave me a real bollocking.

They said I should know that the race leader's team always leads the race onto the Champs-Élysées. I told them to point out where it said that in any rulebook. Guys had been attacking right from the start and if they'd stayed clear they could easily have ended up leading the race into Paris. But they hadn't got a bollocking for that. Plus, I had eased off after I'd gone through the line and hadn't made them chase. I was very upset, very emotional. Here I was finishing my Tour career and I felt these guys should show me a little bit of respect.

The next time around, I was riding up near the front, just behind the Banesto train, and going around the Concorde I had Indurain himself leaning on me. I put my hand on his bars and told him there was no need for him to push me off the wheels. But he was pissed off with me because he'd seen his teammates giving out to me. I said to him: 'Miguel, you're only *un petit champion*. If you were *un grand champion* you'd have more respect for me.' Then I pushed his bars away.

Maybe I should have gone to them earlier in the stage and said I'd love to cross the line first, but for me it was a race. Did I have to get on my knees and say: 'Please, guys, can I cross the line first?' There was no written or even unwritten rule that said that the team with the yellow jersey should cross the line first. Looking back, though, that was the one run-in I had with Miguel. He was a very nice guy and a real gentleman.

I do wonder, though, how people can describe him as one of the sport's greatest champions. He was a great champion at the Tour de France, but take the time trials out and Miguel wouldn't have won. He was a great climber, but I didn't think he had the best tactical sense. Or, perhaps it would be better to say that he never had to put his tactical nous into action. Tactically, he wasn't in the same league as Eddy Merckx or Bernard Hinault, for example, and he didn't win as many races away from the Tour as them either. He was one of the best Tour riders of all time, yes.

Was he the best time triallist the race has ever seen? I'd say he was. Away from the Tour, though, he didn't win many time trials. He was a super nice guy, but in my view a little bit overestimated.

I also felt that he didn't do a good enough job for cycling at the time. I think he could have made more of an effort to interact with the public and the press. One day I said to him: 'Miguel, you should try to learn a bit of French.' He smiled and replied: 'Stephen, you speak three languages and you're always with the press. I just speak one language and things are *tranquilo* . . .' That was very true and that's the way he was. He wasn't a very public man.

As it turned out, I took a better memory away from the Champs-Élysées on that final day of the '93 Tour as Carrera took the prize as the best team for the second year in a row, ensuring I ended up on the podium in Paris. That was a fabulous way to finish. A couple of small coincidences also seemed to indicate it was the right time for me to leave. Throughout my life the number 13 has had a lot of significance, not least because I finished 13th in my first Tour. Fittingly, I finished 13th in my last. A full circle. In addition, the last climb on that race was the Aubisque, where I'd taken my first Tour stage win eight years previously.

There's never a right time to stop racing. The time simply comes when you're physically and mentally prepared to say: 'This is it!' My biggest concern over the last couple of years was fear. I didn't even ride the last few races on my programme in 1993 because I was afraid I'd do myself some damage. Having got through my career with just the one serious, crash-related injury, it would have been terrible to have had one then. The incident in the '87 Giro when my forks broke on a descent was always in my mind and still is whenever I go downhill even now. Another particular fear was the bunch sprints, as they were becoming chaotic. Finishes got really scary and I'd find myself riding at the back with Tony Rominger and a few other guys who felt the same way as me, hoping there wouldn't be a crash.

Other things were getting to me too. Early on in my career, I used to be able to ride right through the middle of the peloton to the front rather than go up the outside because I was very supple and very straight on my bike. If there was even the smallest of gaps I'd be in there. But at the end of my career guys would be yelling: 'Get out of here, take your brake lever out of my arse.' I started to make enemies in the peloton because the new riders coming in were a bit hot-blooded and more inclined to put their hand out and push you off, which was even more dangerous because if you're riding with your hands on the bars and someone pushes you, you can't control yourself too well and can easily go over. It made my blood boil.

You also have to bear in mind that riders tended to retire relatively early in those days. I was not even 34 when I retired. Hinault was 32 and Fignon a similar age. It wasn't as if I was particularly old and Carrera did want me to continue on and work with Marco Pantani. But I refused, and I don't regret the decision. I never regret. It won't change anything and will only give you more hardship if you do.

Factor in also that I was a stage race rider and that meant being away from home for up to four weeks or even more at a stretch. I never really rode one-day races except for Liège, and even then I'd do Flèche Wallonne as well and would still be away for a week. I was always away from home and it had been like that for 13 years. Consequently, the weight on my family life also led me to believe that it was the ideal time to stop. I always said that if there was a 50.1 per cent chance of me winning I'd keep on racing, but when it dropped to 49.9 per cent I would stop.

Like a lot of other athletes at retirement age, I was soon to realise how hard it is to earn a living in the outside world and that at 33 years of age you still have a very long life ahead of you.

Nobody left cycling a millionaire in those days and I certainly wasn't one. I'd earned some good money, bought a property, but I knew that I was going to have to work at something. I was offered something like two million francs to continue and had nothing concrete waiting for me in retirement. Consequently, if I had the choice again I perhaps would have done another year or two – but only because of what I know today.

But I have no regrets about taking the decision. In many ways, it's made me stronger and, ultimately, I wasn't in the sport just to be a number in the peloton. I was there to win. And when I felt that I couldn't win any more, it was the right time to stop.

CHAPTER 14

'BEING THIS DRIVEN CAN BE A PROBLEM'

While I was certain that I had made the right decision to quit racing at the end of 1993, I didn't have a clear idea of what I was going to do next. I knew I was going into a different life, but I had never worked out beforehand exactly where I expected that life to take me. I was 33, I'd had a great career in cycling, made a name for myself, and everyone had told me that it was going to be easy for me to get a job. They told me I was totally cut out for marketing and that some multinational company was sure to pick me up, especially as I spoke three languages. So retiring from racing didn't seem like a big deal.

Thinking that everything would simply fall into place, I initially distracted myself by driving a few rallies. I had an offer to drive a car for a year or two and, foolishly, thought I was going to make some money out of it. The problem with rallying is that you always want to go faster and always want a better car. But the only people who earn money in rallying are mechanics and repair shops. You're always servicing that kind of car and spending money on it. You convince yourself you're earning money, but when you add it up at the end of the year you've spent more money on the car than you've put in your pocket.

Although I think I did surprise people with the standard of my driving, I knew what my limit was. I did get some good results in Ireland and France – qualifying for the 'Turini' night stages of the

Monte Carlo Rally being one of my best. But any money I earned always went back into the car, so I quickly realised that rallying was only going to be a short-lived career and that I was never going to be a champion driver at 33 years of age. It did help me stay straight for a while, but I had two houses, two young children and, for the first time in my whole adult life, no guarantee of any salary. By the end of 1993, I knew I had to find something else – and soon.

I started by digging out all of the business cards I'd been given over the previous months and years by those people who had insisted I had a guaranteed future in marketing or PR. I made calls, went to dinner, had lunches, but every time they ended the same way. My host would talk me up, get me thinking I was close to something good, then when it came to the crucial question of what they could offer me they would let me down. After a while I could predict what they were going to say. It was always along the lines of: 'Stephen, you're a great guy, you'd be an asset to any company, but we haven't really got a place for you as yet. I promise you that if any job comes up you'll be the first one I'll call. In the meantime, my son is a great fan of yours, so would you sign the menu for him?'

The only solid lead I had was doing events with a friend of mine, Gérard Picq. We formed a company that organised VIP days at rallies, then I started to organise VIP days at races like Paris–Nice, the Dauphiné, the Tour of the Med and the Midi Libre. I would do perhaps eight events over a year and was paid a small monthly salary. It wasn't a lot compared to what I had been earning before, but it was something. However, it wasn't enough to lift me out of the depression I felt.

After a while, though, I started to wonder: 'Why am I doing this to myself?' I had never waited for anyone to help me before, so why was I waiting for someone to give me a leg-up now? Why was I sitting around moping because nobody was giving me a job?

I realised that the solution was not to wait for someone else to emerge with a job for me but to develop something myself. I decided it was best to start with what I knew. I also thought I could put something back into cycling, share my passion, and this led to my decision to set up a company running training camps.

Initially I was looking at doing something with kids in the Paris area. I wanted to share my passion with them and show them the good side of cycling, show them that rather being a struggle the sport can be very enjoyable. But there were all kinds of obstacles when it came to dealing with parents, insurance, liability and federations. I wanted to set up something that was fun, not a bureaucratic nightmare. My next idea was to try to establish a company offering cycling holidays in Majorca, as it was clear there was a growing demand for bike-based breaks and training camps in warm-weather destinations.

I got together with Claude Escalon, who had been my team directeur at the ACBB more than a decade before and had remained a good friend. Claude was still with the ACBB, but the team was no longer what it once was and he was looking for new opportunities as well. He was doing a bit of freelance work with Michelin that took him to Majorca and while he was there he started looking at hotels we could use as a base for guided rides of varying difficulty on the island. He found a few options for us to consider. I flew over to join Claude and look at them, and we settled on one in Palmanova. It was close to the airport, it wasn't as windy as other parts of the island and, although it was near the mountains, there were plenty of flat roads. The other big plus point is that Palmanova is a year-round resort so there is plenty of life there even out of season.

We started to approach potential sponsors such as Peugeot to ask if they'd be interested in lending some bikes. They liked the concept of a company run by renowned figures in the sport offering training camps and fully supported rides to bike enthusiasts, but came back after a few months with one major concern. We had told them that our initial target markets were cyclists in France, the UK, Ireland and the USA. If that's the case, said Peugeot, what language are all these cyclists going to speak? I said they're all going to talk cycling, that cyclists aren't English, French or Italian, they're just men and women in Lycra. It wasn't a question I'd asked myself. I was simply thinking I was creating a cyclist's paradise and it didn't matter where the clients came from. In the end, Peugeot turned us down, which upset me as I'd banked on getting their backing.

Once again, though, Carrera came to my rescue. I asked Davide Boifava for a favour. Davide said that Carrera's 1994 team bikes had all been pre-sold to journalists, but he stopped the sale of those bikes and gave me 25 Carrera bikes for my first year. With the hotel and the bikes in place, we set up the company – Fitness, Vélo, Evasion (FVE). We brought in Philippe Lauraire, an ex-pro who had been a very good sprinter. Claude managed the set-up, Philippe assisted him and looked after everything concerning the bikes, the guides, the roads and the routes. I looked after the promotion and advertising and went out every weekend or so to spend time with the clients.

Philippe eventually moved on to set up his own business, but the structure has remained essentially the same for the last 18 years. We've always had a high rate of return visits from our clients, so we've never really had to advertise all that much. It's been a great success, but I think we could have done even better if we had applied more of a business focus to it. We've run it more for fun than as a moneymaking enterprise. Our main concern has always been that the clients are happy, so we didn't want it to become so big that the clients would suffer.

The company got a bit of an overhaul in the winter of 2011. That stemmed partly from Claude wanting to step away from the business because he was having treatment for cancer and partly from me having more time to commit to the business having sold my hotel in the south of France. We used to joke that the company was professionally run by amateurs, but I've now brought in a professional management team to run the show with me. They have got long experience of working in this type of company, and the aim is to reinvigorate the business and set it on the road for another 20 years. Claude will, however, always be part of the business. After all, we've been friends for more than 30 years and partners for 18.

While I was working to get the holiday company off the ground, Eurosport approached me with an offer to work as their co-commentator on their bike racing coverage with David Duffield. Initially we worked in their London studio, but as time went on we went to an increasing number of races.

I know that David tended to polarise opinion among fans, but no one can deny that he has done an enormous amount of good for the sport in English-speaking countries. When I came on board, Eurosport weren't that bothered about cycling, but David brought it to a new audience, to people who weren't necessarily that interested in cycling but wanted to know about the cultural side of France and other countries – the wine, architecture, cheese and all kinds of colourful stuff. Of course, some cyclists thought he was crazy for going on more about the cheese and wine he had consumed the night before than about Johan Museeuw winning the stage, but what they didn't realise was that if David hadn't been talking about the wine and the vineyards, Eurosport wouldn't have had the same number of viewers and the sport might not have been on television at all.

David used to put an awful lot of work into his live show. The homework he did was unimaginable. When we were on the Tour together he'd drive, commentate, then go off to his room at night-time, often with a bottle of wine, so that he could do all his homework. He'd have all kinds of tourist guides with yellow Post-it notes stuck in them all over the place. He was a pleasure to work with because he had an incredible knowledge of cycling and was a great one for the culture of the sport. He would try to get that culture and passion across to the occasional viewer, who was just as interested in what was going on outside the race as in the action taking place within it.

I felt that my role when I was working with David was to provide insight that viewers wouldn't have themselves. I think that when you are commentating you should give your honest opinion and it needn't be mainstream. You may not always be right in what you say, but I believe that being perceptive, critical and controversial gives you credibility. When you've got an opinion that goes against the flow, people listen to you, and when you can demonstrate that opinion is right people have more respect for you the next time you stick your neck out.

When we were at races I used to work just a seat or two away from my old rival Laurent Fignon, who was commentating for French Eurosport. He felt it was a privilege to be in such a position and to be able to tell people how he saw it. He was very outspoken at times, but his sense of humour, his feel for tactics and his expert analysis meant that fans responded to him. I felt that I was in the same privileged position, watching the racing from an expert's perspective and offering viewers that perspective, even if it meant telling them that someone had got their tactics all wrong.

When I'm watching races I can still feel things happening, see them before they happen and can pinpoint when riders have missed an opportunity. It's easy to say when you're watching television, of course, but on the bike I was an opportunist and was always ready to react. For example, one of the strategies that I've been very critical of in recent seasons is riders making their teammates ride on the front on the climbs to set a tempo. For me, all they are doing is telegraphing the fact that they are going to do something later in the stage.

When I was racing I always had my team hiding. When the time came for them to ride on the front, I'd click my fingers and they were there. They would always come up right away because they appreciated that I was tactically astute. They knew that if I asked them to ride on the front, it wasn't just so that they could set a tempo or to guarantee we didn't lose any time. We did it for a reason and only came to the front when we had to.

When I see riders like the Swiss time-trial specialist Fabian Cancellara riding on the front of the peloton on a climb nowadays it frustrates me. I realise that he's working for his team leaders, but he's not a climber and he's being asked to set the tempo on terrain that doesn't suit him. I think that means his huge ability is often wasted. There's another side to that as well, because other riders end up letting Cancellara set the tempo on the front, while they just sit in behind him. But what other teams should be doing is disrupting that tempo, making things much more difficult for any team that is trying to dictate the pace. Any team will find it hard to maintain control when the speed at the front of the bunch is fluctuating.

The same goes when the sprinters' trains get going. Often their riders are right on the limit, just dying for someone to come past them so that they can drop back. I say this to young guys today and they come back at me saying: 'Yeah, but they're doing 65km an hour, so if I jump off the front I'm only going to get 100 yards away, then get caught in the wind and get blown back again.' That's true and everyone else is thinking the same thing, but nevertheless if you can go off the front, and especially on a climb, you can disrupt any pace-making.

After a few years with Eurosport, it became increasingly difficult for me to fulfil my commitment to them. I was also working with Coeur de Lion, who sponsored the awards for the most aggressive rider at each stage of the Tour de France. My commitment to them meant I had to be in the start village every morning to present the award. I would then tear off to the finish in order to go live with David. As Eurosport started showing even more live action from stages, some of them from start to finish, I simply couldn't be with David at the finish because of my role with Coeur de Lion, so David would end up doing the first three hours on his own.

It was very complicated for everybody and very dangerous for me because I was driving fast to get to the finish. If I got held up, I'd only arrive just an hour or so before the end, which meant David would be commentating on his own for four or five hours. It was unfair on him and embarrassing for me. In the end, as Coeur de Lion were my main payers, I stuck with them and reluctantly stepped away from Eurosport.

Later on, when I was going through my divorce and had stayed away from going on the road for a couple of years, Eurosport asked me if I'd do a programme from their London studios in Feltham. It was a pre- and post-stage show in which we could preview what might happen and later debate what had happened. It got me involved in TV work again and I really enjoyed it because once again it allowed me to use my knowledge to set out what I thought was going to take place each day and then reflect on what had gone on.

One incident that I remember well – and I honestly don't want it to seem that I am picking on Fabian Cancellara – was the 2010 Tour stage into Liège when he effectively stopped the stage after half the field had crashed on a descent. Everyone was saying conditions had been terrible, but I came out and said that situations like that revolt me because legends have been created riding in treacherous conditions and removing those conditions from races makes them less attractive. If you want to follow that line and make races safer, why not take the cobbles out of Paris–Roubaix because they're dangerous too?

I felt that we were allowing one man to change the pattern of the race and that the Tour organisation were effectively condoning that. I think that if Jean-François Pescheux, the Tour's route director, had told them all to get on with it instead of neutralising the stage we would have had a much better race because of it. But Jean-François seemed to be thinking that if Frank and Andy Schleck, the brothers from Luxembourg who were the main challengers to defending champion Alberto Contador, were to lose four minutes that day, the Tour would be over, and Contador would saunter to victory.

But I don't think it would have been like that at all. If Andy Schleck had been four minutes down he'd have been forced to attack 20, 30, 40km out on mountain stages, rather than just on the last 2km of climbs. The other side to the decision to stop the stage is that, while Schleck arguably gained from it, other riders lost out, principally Norwegian sprinter Thor Hushovd. He could well have won the stage that day and even if he had missed out he would almost certainly have taken enough points to ensure victory in the green jersey competition, which he ended up narrowly missing in Paris.

Later on, people agreed with me, saying that it had been monotonous the way riders had paraded up the climbs and the Schlecks had waited for the final kilometres to attack. It was a similar thing when Contador attacked after Schleck's chain jumped. People were saying Contador didn't show fair play and shouldn't have done that. I said: 'Bullshit, we're in a bike race here. If you're in a war, shooting at each other and one guy gets a blocked barrel, the other guy doesn't say: "Don't worry, I'll wait for you." You just keep going.' I don't think Contador should have apologised for attacking in those circumstances. In fact, I think when he apologised for attacking he made a fool of himself.

I see these things and voice my opinion. I'm not always right, but I was never one to play to the crowd or to say what I thought people wanted to hear. I describe what I see, say what I feel and try to be honest about it. I think viewers want to know things that they can't pick out themselves and they also want a bit of controversy.

In more recent times, I've also had the opportunity to have a more hands-on impact on the sport as a member of the UCI's Professional Cycling Council, which advises the governing body on all aspects of racing. With me on the PCC are guys like Charly Mottet, Jonathan Vaughters, Gianni Bugno, Erik Zabel and Christian Prudhomme. Between us we represent the UCI, the race organisers, the teams and the riders. UCI president Pat McQuaid attends most of the meetings, which take place every three months or so.

Recently, we've talked a lot about race radios. That's a very hot debate. My opinion is that Radio Tour, which provides vital information and instructions to the team cars during races, should be transmitted to the riders, but I don't think riders should have contact with their teams' cars – or perhaps one rider should have that contact. At the moment, Radio Tour gets transmitted to every vehicle on a race and the team directors relay any instructions to the riders. That means that every rider is getting instructions telling them, for instance: 'Guys, in 5km the road turns sharp left, be careful.' That results in everybody fighting to get to the front, potentially creating a bottleneck where big crashes can take place. I'd like to see a situation where riders have to think more about the tactics of racing, not only depending on race radios but also using the roadbook, as we used to years ago. But that debate has got a good way to run yet.

One of the UCI's other main concerns is improving the image of the sport and helping sponsors increase the value of their investment in cycling. When you're considering how to improve cycling's image, you have to wonder where cheating starts and ends. A couple of issues came up as part of that discussion. One was the 'sticky' bottle, the practice of hanging on to a bottle being passed out of a team car for a free tow. Even though it is now more likely than ever to attract a penalty, I think that directors and riders should be severely penalised for this.

If you're a spectator at the roadside watching the bunch going past and then see a guy hanging on to a bottle or the side of a car or sitting on the back bumper of a race vehicle to get back up to the bunch, you don't know what's happened to him back down the road. You don't know if that guy is trying to get back on after a puncture or a pee break, you just see someone cheating. It damages the image of cycling. Nowadays you see riders stopping for a pee and their director stopping for a pee with them. They all know he's going to pace them back up to the bunch again, and I don't think that's correct. I think there's another important safety aspect to this issue as well. Why wait for someone to go through the rear windscreen of a car and be totally disfigured before we do something about it? Let's do something before this happens.

One other topic for discussion is jerseys with a full zip that end up flapping in the wind. Clothing manufacturers spend a fortune on clothing and material research, but we still see riders going up climbs with their jerseys wide open. The manufacturers aren't getting a lot of benefit from that and, to be honest, there's no point in them spending millions developing fabrics if riders have their jerseys open all the time.

The other aspect to this issue is that if the jersey has, say, the Ag2r logo across the front but it's been opened right down the middle, then all you can see is the guy's medallion. You can't see the team sponsor's name. You could end up with a situation where the whole bunch is riding along and no one knows who is riding for who because all you can see is medallions and white chests. I'm not saying that jerseys should just unzip to the chest, as that makes it complicated to get them off, but I am saying that zips should only go down to stomach level so that the logos can be seen. I can guarantee that having your jersey completely open doesn't do anything for you in terms of keeping cool.

Naturally, we've discussed doping laws as well. For example, we've looked into the possibility of imposing life bans to prevent riders not only putting their own future in jeopardy, but also the future of dozens of fellow riders, managers and other team staff. We discovered that European labour laws don't allow employees to be permanently blocked from working in their chosen profession, so we set up a working committee to evaluate what other steps might be taken to bolster the impact of doping bans. That led to a new regulation that stipulates that points won by any rider found guilty of doping will not count towards the ranking of any prospective new team. That came out of a long debate to decide how we could make a guy who's been involved in doping less interesting to a new sponsor.

I'll confess that the subject of doping never impacted on me much when I was racing. However, since I retired I have thought much more about it, particularly on a couple of occasions when the issue has loomed very large in my own life. I learned a lot when I read Paul Kimmage's book *Rough Ride* about his time in the sport, although when I first read it a lot of what he said seemed ridiculous. Later on, when I wasn't competing and had time to listen to what other people were saying I realised that a lot of what Paul was saying was true. I admit I was very naive.

At no point during my career did I ever look at anybody who beat me and think they may be taking something, even though you did hear rumours about certain riders. In my later years, however, there were a lot of strange-looking results that made you wonder if something was going on, although we never knew exactly what that might be as riders weren't testing positive. Was it steroids? Was it EPO? I didn't know. For me, doping was always out of bounds. It wasn't something that I was going to get into, not even in a criterium. Let's face it, there was no point in a criterium because the racing's all organised anyway.

That is not to say that I wasn't involved in practices that would seem dubious now. Most evenings when I was racing I'd go to the doctor's room and have my vitamins. Nowadays, needles are banned, but in my era they weren't, so the fact that we used them doesn't mean we were doping. Some of the products we used in those days that were regarded as natural vitamins might also be regarded as doubtful nowadays. But I simply went with the times and stuck to the rule that whatever was on the banned list was out of bounds.

I was always very careful about whatever medication I was taking because I felt that if I was ever caught taking something by mistake then everything I'd ever done in my life – my schooling, my apprenticeship, everything – all the credibility I'd built up, would be gone. That's why when I look at myself in the mirror, I can say that I never cheated and why nothing I've achieved can be taken away from me.

That's also why I was so determined to defend myself when David Walsh came out with his revelations in 2004 saying he had proof that I had taken EPO. He rang me before publishing the article in *The Times* and asked for a comment. All I said to him was: 'David, be very, very sure of what you're writing because it's not something that can be proven, there's no evidence there. I'd go back to any proof you think you have and make sure it's dead on.'

When the article came out I was extremely upset. It said something like 'proof that Roche has taken drugs' and featured a document that allegedly showed blood values of various riders, whose identities were protected by codenames. I blew the article up so that I could see the blood values more clearly and they didn't seem to prove anything at all. In fact, the values seemed quite random, changing significantly from one day to the next.

Of course, all this created a huge stir in Ireland. I was invited

onto *The Late Late Show* to discuss Walsh's allegations. I agreed
to appear, then got a call from the programme's researcher the
night beforehand asking if I would mind if David Walsh came on
the show as well. I said I had no problem with him being there,
I would be happy to answer any questions at all. I think they were
shocked that I'd agreed to that, but I had nothing to hide. As it
turned out, they reckoned it was one of the most intense editions
of the show ever. Initially, I was to get 10 minutes or so, then
spend 20 minutes debating with David, but we went on for 45
minutes and people like Uri Geller who were supposed to come
on after us never appeared.

Even before the show, though, I wondered how all this could
have happened and rang Dr Giovanni Grazzi, who was the doctor
at Carrera during my second spell with the team. 'Giovanni,
what's going on here?' I asked him.

He told me: 'This is what happened. Every two or three months
we'd carry out a blood test. The samples would be sent back to
the University of Ferrara. The next day we'd get the results back,
and we'd be able to tell that, for instance, you were low in iron,
this was your vitamin B reading, this was your vitamin E, and so
on. And that was it.'

'How come these values are all coming out?' I asked him.

'It's quite simple,' he told me. 'Once we'd given you your
results, the blood was stored. We knew it was from Stephen
Roche, we knew when the sample had been taken, we knew how
many kilometres you'd done. Then we carried out experiments
on it as part of the university research programme.' He told me
those values could not be my values. For a start, they were all
codenamed and, more importantly, they were not valid because
you could see that the blood had been manipulated. 'It's not your
blood,' he confirmed.

'I know that, you know that, but how do I explain that to these
journalists?' I asked him. I hadn't been giving blood every day,

but these allegations suggested that I had, making it extremely hard to maintain my credibility.

Over the course of my career I have made some mistakes and perhaps the biggest one was not going after the newspaper and the journalist for defamation at that point. I felt that the job had been done on *The Late Late Show* and there was no need to go after them. However, I didn't have the money to pursue them either because I was in the process of getting divorced and I didn't want any more negative publicity. I did contact a lawyer in London and he said it would cost me £50,000 just to get through the initial stages and a lot more beyond that.

I didn't have £50,000 to hand then, but even if I'd had that kind of cash available and had ended up clearing my name, who'd remember it? You always get pages and pages when a scandal blows up, but when everything's all sewn up at the end you get a small correction at the bottom of a page saying: 'Stephen Roche has been cleared . . .'

In Italy there was a five-year investigation into the case that centred on Dr Francesco Conconi, head of the sports medicine research team at the University of Ferrara. Eventually, Conconi and Grazzi were acquitted of charges of sporting fraud. The magistrate said there was insufficient evidence to show that any deliberate drug use had taken place, but described Conconi and Grazzi as being 'morally guilty' of promoting drug use. The magistrates can do that in Italy even if there is no firm proof that an offence has taken place, and it was very damaging because it gave David Walsh the chance to say: 'Here's the proof, the magistrate has said all the athletes involved were all doping.'

The magistrate said she got no cooperation from anyone involved, so she had to conclude that the doctors were doing it and the riders were doing it as well. Strangely, despite the fact I was supposed to be one of the seven or eight people on the list who was blood doping, I never ever got a call from anybody involved in the investigation asking me to come in and be interviewed. So, if I'm one of the prime suspects, why wasn't I called? If I had been, I would definitely have cooperated.

In the end, I was labelled as guilty by assumed association. Grazzi was the doctor at Carrera. He was also working under Professor Conconi at the University of Ferrara. But I think I only ever met Conconi once. Giovanni Grazzi was the guy I worked with. He was a really nice guy whose goal was to use his research at Ferrara to help old people with muscular problems. He had his sights set on a clinical career.

The other aspect to this is that by that point in my career, I knew myself extremely well physically and had worked out how to look after myself during every part of the season. I knew, for example, that from Christmas through to Paris–Nice I didn't need any vitamins. I'd fatten myself up over the winter and I would naturally lose weight by racing and training. I knew that from that time on I might be low in iron, for example, which could affect me in the Classics, so I'd start taking some iron supplements. Before a big race like Liège I'd always take some B vitamins.

I also felt that if I had an injection of B12 the night before a big race I might have heavy legs and struggle if the race went hard from the gun. I don't know how accurate it was, but I had that in my head. So if I was going to have a B12 injection I always preferred to have it on the morning of the race so that it would get into my system as we were going along and would hopefully be acting coming towards the end, giving me a little bit more power. So I did have a fair idea what I needed to be taking. In fact, we all knew what we needed from the blood tests we took.

You also have to remember that sports science was a relatively new field at that time and everyone tended to do things on feel. You'd talk to the doctor and tell him that your legs felt a bit heavy, and he might suggest a B6 multivitamin because it would help free up the muscles the next day. Some people might look at that and say it's doping, and it may be in a way because you were injecting foreign elements into your body. But you have to remember that, although it is prohibited now, it wasn't prohibited then.

I think just about every rider had a little case that you could open anywhere – in any airport or police station – and in it there'd be your vitamins, your extract of calves' liver, some syringes. We used to call some riders 'rolling pharmacies' because of how much they had in their cases. But I didn't like to take too much, just what I needed when I knew it could help me. Vitamin C if I had a bit of a cold, B12 if I had heavy legs, and the doctor would be there to advise you.

One thing that the doctors could always tell when I underwent tests like the Conconi Test was that I had natural class. I had a very highly tuned engine, which meant that I could be at the front right through the season. I climbed well, I time trialled well, but I didn't sprint well – although there's no product anywhere that can change that. The doctors knew I had my vitamin programme and that I stuck to it. They also knew my philosophy on doping. I simply would not consider it.

In addition, if you look at my results throughout my career, I was always consistent. I was always a talented rider. I won the Rás at 19 and I'm still the youngest rider to have won it. I was doing a full-time job when I won it as well. When I left my job and went to France in 1980 I had loads of room for improvement and that quickly showed when I won my third or fourth race, the GP de Les Issambres. I won Paris–Roubaix, Paris–Reims, 19 races in total during my first year in France. Then I turned pro and finished second in GP de Monaco, won the Tour of Corsica and then Paris–Nice, the only first-year pro ever to win it. At different periods when I was injured I always came back. Was all that down to doping right from the very start? You can't just look at things in isolation and say that results suggest I was doped. You've got to look at my results as a whole and anyone would agree that I was a very talented rider. And the more I raced the better I got.

It's difficult for me to defend myself because I don't have any records from those days. It wasn't like today when they can store a rider's blood samples for ten years and will be able to look back to see what he might have been doing as the testing procedures advance. The only thing I did have was a diary that Carrera gave us for 1987. That year I wrote everything in there – absolutely everything. There'd be a cross on a day to mark when I had vitamin D, vitamin E, when I had sex. Everything was marked down.

That book was precious to me, but when I started moving around I lost it. I know that that year I did around 37,000km because it was in that book. I've no idea how many kilometres I did in any other year. If I could find it I think it would be a great resource for young riders today.

It did come in very useful to me one day after I joined Histor-Sigma. I wasn't going very well and they took me to the University of Ghent to do some tests. I told them that I could bring something with me that would show them everything that I took in '87. I gave them the diary and said: 'It's all in there.' About a week later the doctor contacted me and asked: 'Where's the other book? The book with all the other stuff.'

'What other stuff? That's the only book and that's everything that happened,' I told him.

He dug deeper into the difficulties I was having and it turned out that when I had all my knee problems in 1988 and '89, the anti-inflammatories I'd been given had damaged the walls of my stomach. Consequently I wasn't absorbing all the nutrients I should have been from food and was also getting bad stomach problems. So they put me on a course of amino acids and that started to turn things around for me again.

That book is testimony to how I was and everything I did during the greatest season of my career. It would have been something to give to Paul Kimmage and David Walsh to let them see for themselves that, yes, I was taking injections of C vitamins and B vitamins and whatever. It would underline that natural class counted for an awful lot.

It is very frustrating that all that stuff was laid out on the table. During the latter years of my career I did start asking myself questions about what certain riders might be up to. Initially, I put their improvement down to power and heart monitor training, which were relatively new to the sport in the early '90s. As I'd tried them myself, I realised they could make a difference. It became clear doping was taking place and I can understand why a lot of people became cynical about the sport.

However, it depresses me when I see and hear that cynicism now. Most of the young guys are doing everything right, doing their utmost to get results, and it's part of their education to learn that it's not good to dope, that doping is cheating, that it doesn't get you anywhere. Clearly some riders still resort to doping, but there are lots of them out there who are sticking to the straight road and, unfortunately, end up being lumped into the same basket as those who are doped.

The other occasion when the issue of doping loomed large over events in which I was involved was when the Tour de France went to Ireland in 1998. Although Ireland gave the race a fantastic few days, to some extent that success was overshadowed by the initial phase of the Festina Affair. I have to admit, though, that at the time my mind was very much on other difficulties much closer to home.

I had moved back to Ireland in 1996 and had been working for the Irish tourist board and the Tour in Ireland's organising committee, which was headed by Pat McQuaid and Allan Rushton. When foreign journalists came to Ireland I used to go around the Tour itinerary with them, showing them the country's best sights. I put a lot of time and effort into it, hoping that the tourist board might realise people like Sean Kelly and me could be a real asset to them on the world stage.

But my relationship with them went sour when, just a few days before the Tour was due to start in Dublin, they realised I was working for a French cheese company. They weren't at all happy with that given the importance of the dairy industry in Ireland. I told them I was happy to step away from my deal with Coeur de Lion if an Irish company would pay me the same money. But they weren't prepared to look at that at all and the issue put me in their bad books. Within a few days, a lot more people had me in their bad books. Regrettably, Sean was among them.

To a large extent, the fall-out was not my own doing. It stemmed from the fact that Irish Television, RTÉ, were broadcasting the Tour's team presentation but their sports department had no budget to pay for it. Consequently, they had to take everything from the news department's budget. Sean and I had both done lengthy one-to-one interviews for an RTÉ news programme and when they were producing the footage to go with the official team presentation they went back into their archives, pulled out those interviews, then edited them down.

I'd been asked about all sorts of things – my career, my training camps, my family and also my plans after the Tour left Ireland. I explained that my kids were finishing French school in Dublin, that they couldn't go any further, so we were moving back to France so that they could continue their education. I'd also been asked for my opinion on Ireland's youth and had said that much more should be done for them, that the government and the sports council weren't putting enough money into sport, with the result that kids were turning to drugs and drink. But, during the editing process, those two answers were edited together so that it looked like I had said: 'My kids are going to get a better education in France because the kids in Ireland are taking drugs and drinking.'

Going out in the middle of the Tour de France presentation all over the world, that interview made me look like shit. Screening the original in its correct context would have been OK, but cutting it up made me look terrible, especially as I seemed to be saying there was no future in Ireland for our kids. You can imagine how popular I was. The tourist board and organising committee asked me to retract what I'd said and I ended up going on a chat show to defend myself, which I did with mixed results. Not everyone wanted to shoot me down. But any prospect of a working relationship with the government or the tourist board was dead.

That wasn't the end of it for me, though. At that time I was working for Eurosport and was fairly familiar with all the riders, so I was asked to co-present the Tour riders on the presentation podium. Each team would come up, the riders would be intro-duced and I'd pick out one rider and ask him some questions. It seemed to go OK, but after the show I met Sean and his wife, Linda, and both of them went berserk, saying: 'How could you do this? All we can see is you on the television and in the paper. Sean's been left out of it.'

I was devastated. I'd never had an argument with Sean and Linda. We'd been very close, and Sean is Nicolas's godfather. I tried getting my argument across, explaining it wasn't my fault, I'd just done what RTÉ had asked me to do, but they felt Sean wasn't getting a look-in. However, I felt I'd explained myself and that everything was OK between us. Sadly, I was wrong.

The next evening there was an official dinner in the govern-ment buildings, with all kinds of government and cycling dignitaries including Tour organiser Jean-Marie Leblanc. He was going to present Sean and me with an award called the Wild Geese in recognition of how our achievements had cemented links between France and Ireland. Leblanc delivered his speech and then said: 'And now I'd like to ask two great Irish cyclists, Sean Kelly and Stephen Roche, to come up and receive their awards.' I started walking over towards Sean so we could go up onto the podium together. But when I got to him, Sean stayed in his seat.

Linda started having a go at me again and said that Sean wasn't going to accept the award, that he hadn't been treated appropriately. Very intelligently, Jean-Marie Leblanc came down off the podium, took myself and Sean by the arm and led us across to the podium to present the awards. But from that evening on it was nearly ten years before Linda and I spoke again, which I regretted terribly. I'd still meet Sean from time to time and he'd say a bit jokily: 'The wife says hello.' Finally, in 2008 I think it was, I was asked to go to the Murphy and Gunn team launch in Ireland. Sean was part of the set-up and Linda was there as well. I saw her walk in and thought: 'What can I do?' I just went over and hugged her and that was it. Since then, and especially when my son Florian was sick, we've spoken regularly and Linda has provided a great deal of comfort during one of the most difficult periods of my life.

I still look back at that Dublin Tour launch and shake my head at what went on. Everything had been going so well, then over the two days right before the start everything went sour. I'd been hoping I'd get a job with the Irish tourist board, but that was totally washed out and I ended up with no work in Ireland at all. Lydia and I already knew that our kids' education was going to suffer if we didn't move back to France, so our decision was made.

Unfortunately, just as things were taking a turn for the worse for me, the Tour also ended up in a dismal situation. The 1998 Tour will always be remembered more for the Festina Affair than as the one Tour Marco Pantani won. Sadly, I think Irish cycling suffered immensely because of that as it was hoping to piggyback on the race coming to Ireland. Thousands of people got on bikes, which was absolutely incredible, but because of Festina all of the funding was lost and all credibility went with it.

One of the last things that I did before I left Ireland that year was to meet up with Paul Kimmage. We'd been friends for a long time, teammates and roommates as pros, but had had little to do with each other since he'd written his book. During the time I'd been back living in Ireland, Paul had continued writing articles that were very critical of cycling. I didn't think that was right coming from Paul Kimmage, who's got so much from the sport.

Before I left Ireland I wanted to apologise to Paul for criticising his book when it had been published, to say that I honestly didn't know what was going on and to admit that I'd been naive. But I also wanted to say that it wasn't cycling's fault that he had doped for a post-Tour criterium, that it was his problem he'd accepted an invitation to ride knowing that he was out of condition. I felt he shouldn't be generalising on the issue.

I said that the only big hang-up I had about it was his appearance on *The Late Late Show* to promote the book. When Gay Byrne had asked him: 'Well, if all these guys were taking it, were Stephen and Sean taking it?' Kimmage had told Gay Byrne: 'I can't answer that.' I told him that he should have said either yes or no, otherwise the suggestion was that Sean and I had been doping. He should have clarified the issue, rather than leaving this big cloud hanging over us. I said I held that against him because he knew me. He had shared the same room as me for a year and a half, so he could have answered that question one way or the other.

I had known Paul since we had cycled together as kids. We went hostelling together, had some fabulous weekends with the likes of Noel O'Neill and Peter Crinnion. He'd gone on to represent his country at the Olympics, become a professional, ridden the Tour de France and had achieved all of his childhood dreams, apart from winning the Tour de France. I told him he should not be saying to people not to put their kids into cycling because it's drug-riddled. I said as a journalist he should be capable of looking at a situation, analysing it and giving his opinion and that I wouldn't fall out with him because of that. That was his job. But I asked him to provide some balance, to talk about the bad side as he saw it, but not to forget to tell people how good cycling had been to him and to his family.

His parents met riding bikes, his dad was an Irish international, his brothers represented Ireland, and they all did really well out of cycling. Cycling also opened the door to another career for Paul. While we were sharing a room at the Tour, he was writing a column for the *Sunday Tribune* and every night he'd be typing away in our room. It didn't bother me because that was his thing. One day Paul said to me that the *Tribune* liked what he was doing and wanted to give him a full-time job. I said: 'Paul, cycling ain't for you. If I was in your shoes I'd take up the offer.' And Paul did take it. I felt that cycling had provided him with a lot to get to that point, but I told him that I had a problem with the way he had turned the whole thing around, tending to focus on the negative aspects of the sport.

I said that not everyone in cycling was taking drugs, that there were people who were clean and that it was his job as a journalist to highlight that, to give them credit for what they were doing rather than just spotlighting the bad guys. At the end of it all, I stood up and went to shake his hand. But he wouldn't offer me his hand. He said goodbye, but didn't look at me. He just kept looking down at his paper.

In hindsight I realise he was brave enough to talk about things that he'd seen, so I've since given him more credit than criticism. If I'd realised the way things were going at that time, maybe I would have dealt with the situation a little bit differently.

Since that day I've only seen him at a distance once or twice. We've not spoken at all. I was at a function one day and he'd given a speech before me. I listened to him, and as I went on one side of the stage he went off the other side, but that's as close as we've ever been to each other.

We moved back to France after that. We'd lived in Paris before and I knew the south of France quite well from the races and training camps I'd done down there, so we decided to give it a go in the south. We renovated a house and while we were doing that a friend found a restaurant in Villeneuve-Loubet. He didn't have enough money to buy it by himself, so he asked me if I would come in on the deal with him. I looked at the property, saw it had huge potential and agreed to go in on the deal to buy it.

The idea was to refit it completely. He would manage the restaurant and I'd take care of the marketing and manage the renovation. Thanks to the time I spent tinkering on cars with my dad and granddad, to my apprenticeship in the dairy where I maintained all kinds of machines, and to the fact that I'd already renovated three houses and built two more, I was very handy at work like that and it's something I really enjoy doing. We had a three-year plan and would see where we were then. So we got a loan, which I was the guarantor for, and bought it in June 1999, which meant I was renovating my house, renovating the hotel and restaurant, working for Eurosport and Coeur de Lion, and still doing my training camps all at the same time.

We got the plans finalised and closed the restaurant up that October with a view to reopening the following May after the work had been completed. But then my friend dropped a bombshell. He had no money left and he couldn't get a loan to help finance the renovation. But he said he had a Portuguese friend who was a builder and would do the work for cash. I wasn't happy with that. I wanted it all to be above board as my name would be on the hotel and it was my reputation that was at stake.

So, I stepped away from the project and said that he could pay me for my share when he got the money.

He invited Laurent Fignon, a good friend of his, to invest. Fignon looked at it and said: 'I've got to find money to buy Roche's share, then pay for the renovations, so what are you putting in?' This guy said he had nothing. So Fignon stepped away as well.

One day the bank rang me and said: 'Mr Roche, very sorry to bother you, but you are the guarantor for the loan on this property. Do you know that the loan has not been paid for the last six months?' I called my friend, who said he had no money and couldn't pay the loan, and told me to do what I wanted with the hotel. But before I did that I had to pay him off. So I negotiated with the bank, sold a property I had in Dublin to pay for the refit and oversaw the work myself. Dad came over from Ireland to help. He played gaffer and kept the French builders in line and we worked around the clock, managing to complete it in record time. We reopened the place the following June. We had clients arriving on the doorstep, and while they were being checked in downstairs, Dad, Mum, Christel, Nicolas and Lydia were upstairs getting their rooms clean. It was very tight. The effort was worth it, though, as we had a really good season.

At the end of it I put the place up for sale and almost had it sold when a big storm demolished half of it. I hadn't put up any storm protection barriers because you wouldn't usually see a storm of that ferocity coming in October. It was a fluke event. Understandably, I lost my buyer, but I had some money left and was able to sell another property I had in Ireland to finance the repairs. The insurance paid out about 18 months later.

I ran the business with Lydia for a bit then, but over time it became more and more difficult for us to work together. We had problems in our relationship and when we eventually separated she got the house and I took over the hotel and brought in a management company to run it. I moved back to Paris and spent most of my time there with my new girlfriend, only dealing with the hotel from a distance.

That changed when Florian fell ill in 2007 and I returned to Nice. Once back at the hotel I found lots of letters that made it clear that bills weren't being paid. At the end of every year we had to pay the local council for the right to use the seafront terrace at the front of the hotel, but the council hadn't been paid for the previous three years, which meant they were threatening to cut off access. Without that outside space, the business was worthless. I ended up taking the hotel over myself.

Still determined to make a go of it, I spoke to a friend, Salvador, who came in and took over the restaurant, while I looked after the hotel. I closed it for a couple of days and totally repainted both the hotel and the restaurant over two days and two nights with some friends. It cost me €1,500 in materials, plus the price of a few pizzas and some trips to McDonald's. Two days later, we were open again. We then built it up from 37 per cent occupancy to 57 per cent when I sold it. It was hard work but I really enjoyed it. It got me close to my kids and it took my mind off the break-up with my girlfriend in Paris, which couldn't be repaired when I returned to the south of France.

One of the other good things about going back to the hotel is that it brought me into contact with Sophie, a childhood friend of Salvador's who used to come in and see him from time to time. We became friends and went to dinner once or twice, and our relationship developed from there. We've been together for three years now and live in the south of France with her two daughters, Juliette and Caroline.

Sophie used to see me working at the hotel and started calling me Ken, like the doll, because all I did all day was go, go, go. She said to me one day, and I understand where she's coming from: 'I'm glad I wasn't with you when you were cycling because I can imagine you running your career the same way you do your hotel.

You don't look left, you don't look right. Your ambition is to make this hotel a success and that's all that matters.' I'd go in at six in the morning and I'd still be there at midnight some days and wouldn't even be tired.

That's the kind of energy I have. Sometimes being that driven can be a problem because I don't analyse how best to get where I want to go. I just want to get there, to succeed.

CHAPTER 15

THE PLEASURE AND PAIN OF PARENTHOOD

The relationship between every professional cyclist and their family is bound to be complicated. That doesn't mean to say that it's difficult, simply that due to the nature of the sport and the commitment required by it, riders are always going to spend a lot of time away from their families. Even when you are back at home, the pressure to train, to eat the right way and to rest is often of paramount importance. It is a job, after all, and to do it well, to earn promotion through the ranks, you have to give it all you can.

I was lucky during my career that my wife Lydia understood the commitment required of me and did all she could to accommodate my needs. I've mentioned before that we were a team, in as much as I was out working and looking after the financial side of things and she had the house and the kids to look after. When I retired, I guess we both thought that I'd be around a lot more, that I'd have more time for her, Nicolas and Christel. I know Nicolas has said that he thought Lydia and I weren't used to spending a lot of time together and that my retirement quickly made this apparent and pushed us apart, but I don't see it like that.

Although Lydia and I were together a lot more than we were used to in the first months after my retirement, that soon changed and before too long I was spending as much or even more time away from home than I had when racing. That created great tension between us. Lydia had thought that when I retired she was going to see more of me, but I was still running around a lot. I felt that I had to do it. I had to earn money. I had to succeed and to do that I had to work hard. I was almost possessed by that thought. My new commitments soon led to some difficulties in our relationship. We ended up separating for almost two years. I was in Ireland trying to get a business off the ground, while Lydia was in Paris with the kids.

In 1996, Lydia and I got back together. By that point, the venture in Ireland had folded because it wasn't making any money and my business commitments were mostly in France. However, I'd not been back at home for long when it was announced that the 1998 Tour would start in Dublin. It was odd really. A few months before I'd been living in Ireland and travelling regularly back to France. Then, having returned to France, I suddenly found myself spending a lot of time in Ireland. Life wasn't any less complicated and in the end we decided that it would be good for us to be in Ireland. Lydia loves the place, we felt the kids would benefit from living in a new country, albeit one that they already knew well, and I had work there.

Life was very good for all of us during those years in Ireland. Lydia bought a boutique on Grafton Street, which allowed her to make the most of her eye for design and fashion. The location is a good one nowadays, but it wasn't so good back then. Although it wasn't a great success, it did give Lydia the chance to have some independence away from the family until our third child Alexis was born in 1998. However, once the Tour had come and gone, my work dried up. I was commuting back and forth to France again, and the kids really needed to be there for the sake of their education, so we decided to return to France but to try somewhere new. We both liked the south of France, so we flew down and started looking at different areas.

We'd been thinking of Aix-en-Provence or Montpellier, but a

series of coincidences led us to Antibes, where we ended up buying a house with an international school next door. Everything we needed was there and we settled in well. In 1999, I bought the hotel on the seafront at Villeneuve-Loubet and started on that new venture. The following year, we had our fourth child, Florian, who was born in the L'Archet hospital in Nice.

Lydia is a fantastically hard-working mum. I knew that when we had more children she would want to fulfil her role as a mother as she saw it, which was by doing absolutely everything she could for the kids. She was tireless. The kids were always spotless, there was always washing in the machine, everything was ironed to perfection and the house was immaculate. That was Lydia. She is the very same today. However, selfishly per-haps, I wouldn't have minded us having more time to do our own thing, but running a hotel and having four kids made it very complicated. I know I may have been too demanding and made things difficult for her, but I wanted us to do more together. I imagined we would travel, but instead life became increasingly complicated for both of us, largely because of the issues we were having with the hotel. We had had to work flat out to get the business up and running again and were looking after separate parts of it. There was always lots of pressure.

Lydia is a lovely person, but I think she is too soft in a business situation and some of our staff took advantage of that. She was running the business like it was a family, trying to keep everyone on good terms with each other, but you can't run a hotel like that. At times they abused her good nature. I'd walk in and find Lydia cleaning the floors with the cleaning lady looking on, saying she'd got a sore back, or waiting on tables because the waiter had to go and pick his sick kid up from school. I kept telling her she needed to be harder with people.

Things finally came to a head when I returned from working at the 2002 Tour and we started to talk about divorce. We were both drifting apart and she thought that by talking about divorce we might be jolted back together. But talking about a permanent split came as a bit of a shock to me. We separated for a few months, then thought we would give it another go, but after a few more months it wasn't working out and we split once and for all in 2003.

It was a very difficult split because I soon met someone else and Lydia did not like my new girlfriend, which was quite normal. But my girlfriend didn't help the situation because she was very hard on Lydia. I also didn't have the balls to say to my girlfriend: 'Lydia is the mother of my children, she deserves respect. It's no surprise that she doesn't like you because she feels that I'm running off with you. Seeing another woman come in and take her young kids away for the weekend has to hurt, so please show some compassion.' But I didn't say that and it resulted in there being a lot of tension between all three of us. I think part of the problem was that I didn't know anybody who was divorced, so I didn't know how to handle the situation very well. In the end, our relationship with Lydia was terrible. I said a lot of things that I regret and I know I would do things very differently if I were in the same situation today.

I went off to live with my girlfriend in Paris and really only communicated with Lydia at a distance. I had the kids every other weekend and things with Lydia went up and down until life changed for all of us in the late summer of 2007. It started that September when I took Alexis and Florian over to see Nicolas competing in the Tour of Ireland. One evening Florian got sick and threw up his dinner. He didn't have a temperature and there were no after-effects, so we thought everything was OK and went back to France the next day.

A few days later he was with his mum, who had just bought a new apartment and was decorating it. Florian was outside on the terrace and was sick again. This time we thought it was sunstroke or perhaps appendicitis because I'd had that and knew that the symptoms don't include fever. A day or two later he was ill again and this time he was complaining about having a sore head. Lydia took him to the hospital and asked for a scan and a blood test to be done. The doctors said his blood was pale and sensed that something was seriously wrong. They asked Lydia to sit in the waiting room while they got a more expert opinion.

That day I was out on my boat with Nicolas and some friends and the first I knew about it was when I got a call from Christel telling me: 'Daddy, something's wrong with Florian. He's in the hospital. Can you get here quickly?' I couldn't believe what I was hearing. We tore into the harbour, jumped into the car and dashed into the hospital. By then the specialist had arrived and he took us all into a room and said that it had been confirmed that Florian had acute leukaemia – his blood cells were 600,000 for 10,000. You should have 10,000–15,000 white blood cells, but he had 600,000. In layman's terms, his system was completely mal-functioning. Having that many white blood cells meant there was a chance he could die within hours. While they were telling us this, they were arranging for Florian to be transferred to the Nice L'Archet hospital. It was where he had been born, but it also has one of the best paediatric leukaemia centres in France.

When we got there, Florian was taken straight down to the operating theatre while the specialists told us what would happen and how dangerous it was. I felt even then they weren't telling us everything we needed to know, but I'm sure they were right in doing this. Laying out what was likely to be ahead could have overwhelmed us. This was the start of nine months of intense treatment for Florian.

His blood count started coming down, but after a few days it went back up again, despite the treatment. The doctors were baffled. They called us in, told us what was happening and explained that there was a new protocol that they thought would work on Florian. It hadn't been made available at that point, but had been tested. However, before they could go ahead with it they needed our approval as well as authorisation from the research centre in Brussels. We all gave the OK and Florian started with the new treatment. Straight away his white blood cell count began to come down and he went into an isolation unit for the first time. He was in and out of there three times. When his blood cell count went up, they'd restart treatment and isolate him again. Thankfully, though, he would recover very quickly.

They were also looking for a bone marrow donor as they reckoned he needed a transplant. Tests revealed that Alexis was 100 per cent compatible with his brother. Apparently it's very rare for a family member to be 100 per cent compatible, but if they are the chances of a successful transplant increase.

Florian's treatment continued as they built up towards the transplant. There was a lot of red tape to get through, though. For example, we had to go to Marseilles to meet up with more than a dozen professionals – doctors, psychiatrists, health-care specialists, people from the government – plus myself, Lydia and Alexis. They explained to Alexis, who was only nine at this point, what was going to happen. They even had Lydia and me leave the room so that they could ask Alexis if we were coercing him into being a donor.

One of the doctors then explained to Alexis how the treatment works. The way he described it was incredible. He told him: 'Your body is like a factory. Florian's body is like a factory too. For the factory to produce good blood, good vitamins and good platelets, everything has to be perfect in that factory. Your body's factory is working perfectly. However, for some unknown reason, Florian's factory is not functioning properly and is producing too many white blood cells. If that continues, those white blood cells will eventually kill everything, the factory will close down and Florian will die. To prevent this and to make Florian better, we are going to close down his factory, bring it down to zero. Then we will take some bone marrow from you, which will regenerate. You won't feel a thing, but you will have a sore butt for a couple of days. We will put your bone marrow into Florian and it will restart his factory, helping it get better, better and better until it's functioning properly again.'

At the same time, though, they were preparing him psychologically so that he wouldn't feel any guilt if the treatment didn't work. The doctors and psychologists told him if Florian's factory didn't work properly, it wouldn't be Alexis' fault, that it wouldn't be because he had given Florian bad bone marrow. They stressed there was no 100 per cent guarantee that the treatment would work.

The whole experience of having a child who is severely ill in hospital is very emotional and all around you there are other parents and their children going through the same thing. You get friendly with each other and you all speak the same language because you are fighting for the same cause. Some of the parents that lived a long way from Nice had been forced to quit their jobs to be close to their children, because this is the only thing that matters. Everyone knows that treatment can go wrong for anyone in the unit. The statistics say that 80 per cent of the kids will be saved, but that obviously means that two in ten won't make it.

Ten days before Florian's transplant operation they allowed him to go home in order to boost his morale because they knew that he wasn't going to be well for many weeks and feeling so ill was going to be extremely hard on him. Lydia had to keep the house sterile and everyone had to take the utmost precautions to prevent germs getting in. We had to wear masks, green swabs and sterilise our hands. His body had a bit of resistance, but we couldn't take any risks.

The procedure started when they took some of Alexis' bone marrow, sterilised it and put it into a drip that went into Florian. It normally takes 21 or 22 days for the bone marrow to start producing white blood cells, but Florian was producing them after 16. For those 16 days he was totally wasted. By this point his system was very low, he had blisters all over his mouth and his nose, and was on morphine. It was awful to see. He was kept in a sterile room for four weeks and Lydia and I used to take turns spending time with him.

The stress took a toll on us all. Nicolas's anxiety resulted in him getting stomach ulcers, while I got so worried about bringing some kind of germ in that I ended up contracting a virus. That meant I couldn't go into the sterile room for two weeks. I had to make do with speaking to him on the intercom phone, or by writing messages on a blackboard when he was in too much pain to talk.

During that time Florian flitted in and out of consciousness, but sometimes his strength and character shone through. Our friend Salvador, who ran the restaurant in my hotel, used to go and see him. One day he was chatting away to Flo on the phone that connected into the sterile room, joking around with him. Salvador told him that if he saw any nice nurses he had to ask them for their number. The pair of them were having a laugh about it, but Florian was only semi-conscious. He came round for a bit, opened his eyes, turned to Salvador and said: 'I don't know if the nurses are nice or not, because they're all wearing masks. But I haven't forgotten you.' It was only a little thing but it showed how resilient and courageous he was.

The month he was in the isolation unit after the transplant was a nightmare as we waited to see if his system was responding. After those 16 days they started taking blood again and it seemed like it was, that his factory was starting to work once more. I can't describe how relieved we all felt knowing that he was reacting to the treatment. It's only when it's over and you think back that you realise how close the situation came to being tragic.

All the time either Lydia or I would be with him. When I was there I would try to play with him, try to keep his mind off what was going on. On more than one occasion he said he loved me being there because we would have fun. Often I'd be in there all night and it would be a very emotional experience, but I felt I had to keep a lid on that. When I left in the morning, I'd get back on my scooter and would end up crying into my helmet as I rode home, wondering how all this could be happening. It's something you would not want anyone to go through, especially someone as small as Florian. You simply have to have confidence in medicine and science, and hope that it just goes right for you. You can't do a thing yourself.

At the same time, Lydia really came into her own during his treatment. She was very strong and positive, and very protective of Florian, perhaps overprotective sometimes. She analysed absolutely everything that happened. If the doctor told her something and a nurse came in and was a millimetre off the protocol, Lydia would tell them to go away. She left nothing to chance. She would inspect the nurses before they went into his sterile room, making sure they had their masks on, their gloves on, that they were washed, cleaned and sterile.

She had a strong vision of how things should be done. She would listen to the doctors and specialists, but she had her own opinion. No one was going to pull the wool over her eyes. I think they used to dread her when they saw her coming. However, because she was extremely protective, it kept things straight. She was almost like a bodyguard. It was her way of looking after Flo and making sure he got the best of what was needed.

The doctors were surprised how quickly Florian responded to the treatment and were confident that his recovery would be boosted even more if he could spend some time at home. They admitted that, having seen how protective Lydia had been of him in hospital, they didn't have any concerns about him going home; they were confident it would be even cleaner at home than in the hospital. They told us that as long as we respected the rules, there should be no problems.

Although Florian was better off at home than in the hospital, he was still so wasted he couldn't even walk. We had to carry him everywhere. That was in March 2008, but it would still be another two years before he could go back to school and begin to have something like a normal kid's life. In the meantime, Lydia gave him classes at home on the blackboard in his bedroom. She would go to school in the afternoon to get Alexis and pick up Florian's homework, then do the homework with Florian in the evening and take it into school the next morning when she dropped Alexis off again. The teacher would then correct it during the day.

When he did go back to school in April 2010, he had missed almost three years of classes. He was put in a class a year below where he should have been. After a while, though, he told his teacher that he was a little bit bored and that he wanted to go back into his original class. The teacher told him that if he could catch up with the work he had missed while he was ill, he could move back up again. So he worked right through the summer holidays and managed to catch up. Now he has one of the best averages in his class and totally understands the value of working hard at school. In fact, Lydia says when Florian talks it is like listening to me 20 years on. He knows the value of things. He knows he won't get anywhere without working hard. He knows he has to get a good education.

He's back at school full-time now and if all goes well up to September 2012 it will be five years since he was ill and he'll be given the full all-clear. The doctors have said that he won't be able to play any sport, but we're not sure whether that means he won't be able to ride the Tour de France but can still ride a bike. He has certainly got no fear. He's very active and very competitive as well.

In fact, I think all my kids have got innate athleticism. Christel certainly has the physical attributes to be an athlete. When she rode a bike she had a lovely turn of the pedals and she was a fabulous swimmer. That ability comes as much from Lydia as it does from me. Lydia was a champion runner in the Ile de France as an under-16. She comes from a very sporting family and was very dynamic. Christel liked doing a bit of sport but she was more into the academic side and came through her schooling very well.

She went off to Canada as part of her degree in business, marketing and communications and then had to do an interim job and was lucky enough to get the offer to go to Ireland. When she was finishing off the job there that would enable her to complete her degree, she was headhunted by the French Commission, which has an office in Dublin. She has a job with them now helping to promote French brands in Ireland.

She did run the hotel with me for a while and we worked well together, but I think going off to work with somebody else will be of greater benefit to her in the long run. She loves her life in Dublin. It's a lively city, she's got lots of friends, a big part of her family is close by, and she certainly has more choices there than she had working in the hotel. I think she misses the sunshine, but she always reminds me that by the time she finished work in the hotel the sun would have long gone.

Alexis has had a rollercoaster ride during Florian's treatment. He's incredible really, lacking in maturity in some ways, but hugely mature in others. He was very courageous in the way that he took on Florian's illness and was always very supportive of him. They used to play quite roughly before Florian got ill. Florian would try to grapple with Alexis, who would bat him away like a piece of dust, only to find Florian would keep coming back. When Florian got sick, he would get very emotional and agitated at times and would start boxing Alexis, and Alexis would take everything, absolutely everything. I felt sorry for Alexis at times because here he was at nine, ten, eleven years of age and his little brother was walking all over him. But he had the maturity to accept that his brother was sick.

When Florian was back at home, Alexis would fix you with an X-ray stare when you went into the house – shoes off, hands clean, mask on . . . He didn't say anything but he was X-raying you. He'd put his hand out and stop you going in if you had your shoes on or hadn't done something properly. He was very mature in that respect and it was proof that he understood the challenge that was there, the importance of being clean and of good hygiene. But in some respects Florian is more mature than Alexis. They've gone through two different stages in life. It's sad in one sense for Florian because there are certain things that a young boy should experience that he didn't and won't. He's like a little man in a kid's body. He's been pushed into an adult world and you can see that in his vocabulary.

Alexis is now starting to show that he's got a bit of talent on the bike. Last year when we were with Carrera, Davide Boifava showed him a carbon-fibre bike and said to him: 'Alexis, when you win your first race that bike is yours.' He hasn't won his first race yet, but he's got a nice aluminium bike to keep him going till then. He's also got Lydia's old Gios connected up to a home trainer. That's the same bike that Nicolas started on.

In one remarkable way, Alexis reminds me of me when he's on the bike. Raphaël Géminiani always used to say: 'With Roche you can put a glass of water on his head, send him down the road and it will never spill because he's so smooth.' I never really paid much attention to that at the time, but the first time I took Alexis out on his bike he just blew me away because I realised what Gem had meant. He was out of the saddle and his head wasn't even moving. Nicolas isn't like that. He moves about and looks very powerful when he's pedalling. But Alexis' head doesn't move, whether he's in the saddle or out of it. He looks like a natural and pedals extremely well too.

Alex is 13 now, but the good thing about him is that he's not all bike. When he's racing he wants to do well, but most importantly he's having fun. I'd prefer him to see things that way rather than being like some kids who are completely focused on cycling. He's got a very good attitude and I hope that it will pay off for him later on, but I wouldn't like to see him focusing all his energies on sport. I'd like him to be strong academically as well. He's very intelligent, very much like Nicolas, and I think he could go a long way. If the talent is there it will always be there, so if he concentrates on his studies I think it will be an advantage later on because he'll be able to balance the two.

Then there is my eldest, Nicolas. I always tell him: 'No matter what you do, I'll always be the proudest father under the sun because you chose the same sport as me, and it's any father's dream to see their kids following in their footsteps. I can only be proud of you.'

His racing career began in 1996 at an event run by Joe Daly Cycles in Dundrum. Every year Joe used to organise a charity run from Dundrum to Enniskerry, which seemed like a long way when I first did it in the early 1970s, but it's only about four miles. I used to do it every now and again as a favour to Joe for the help he'd given me and that year I had agreed to hand out the prizes. Joe asked me to bring Nicolas, who was just 12 then. Lydia had an old bike, that same Gios that Alexis uses now, and we got it together for him.

He finished second that day and started doing a few more races. He was into football at the same time, but got interested in cycling a bit more after he twisted his knee playing football, damaging the ligaments. By the time we left Ireland in 1998, he'd been racing with my old club, Orwell Wheelers, and having some success.

When we moved to Antibes he rode with the local club. Then one of his friends was riding for Draguignan, so he joined them for a while. He moved on again to what seemed like a reasonably good position with the Nice Sprinter club, but it wasn't what he had been hoping for. They rode a lot of local races, but he wanted to compete in bigger and harder races, national events. So from there he went to VC La Pomme in Marseilles.

Nicolas had got his school certificate before he joined the Pomme and by that stage it was clear that he wanted to see how far he could go in cycling. I said I'd finance him for one year while he worked in the hotel. 'If you're doing things right and you want to go on I'll pay you for a second year,' I told him. 'But there'll never be a third. So it's up to you to concentrate on your cycling, do the work on the hotel over the wintertime and I'll support you for a year.'

I felt it was a way of taking his mind off cycling and getting him dealing with the real world – washing up at midnight in the restaurant, cleaning the rooms in the afternoon, dealing with the clients' complaints. He didn't surprise me at all in the way that he took on the role. He was very committed. When he replaced me as manager of the hotel he'd go in there with a shirt and tie on. The staff were more afraid of him than they were of me. He'd kick arse. People knew where they stood with him. He did a very good job. That was the real world and I wanted to give him a taste of it. It also kept his mind off cycling, so that when he did turn back to it in January it was all go.

That will be the way it is with Alexis if he decides to go down the same route, especially as it's getting increasingly difficult to achieve results in cycling. You have to give priority to schooling, but giving kids a feel for the sport gets them out of the house, allows them to meet good people and teaches them good values for both sport and life.

During that first year I supported him, Nicolas got the

opportunity to race as a *stagiaire* with Cofidis. It's effectively like work experience for potential professionals, giving them the chance to see whether they can cut it as a pro and letting them see what racing at the very top level is all about. He did OK in the first few races he had with them, well enough to attract an offer from the Belgian MrBookmaker team – a very good offer in fact.

I think it was Mickey Wiegant at the ACBB who told me: 'If you think about the money, you won't win races. If you win races, you win money.' That was something that stuck with me throughout my whole career. For me, the most important thing was to negotiate my contract, put it in a drawer and only take it out when it was about to expire. If you think about the money and contracts, it takes energy away that you need for racing.

So I said to Nicolas: 'You can see quite obviously MrBookmaker are taking you on for your name. If you were at the end of your career I'd say to do it. But you don't know where you're going to go. You don't know how long MrBookmaker will be around. The set-up isn't as good as Cofidis. I don't think it's a hard choice to make, even though Cofidis aren't offering the same kind of money. You should go with Cofidis because it's a world-class team.'

Nicolas then had a really good ride for Cofidis at the GP d'Isbergues. He nearly won it and ended up taking the prize as the most aggressive rider. He was called to the podium, but before he got there the Cofidis soigneur met him at the finish and gave him a wash down. He gave him a dry jersey, a bottle of water, took his bike, had his suitcase waiting for him at the showers.

The MrBookmaker team was there, and when Nicolas came down off the podium I pointed them out to Nicolas and said to him: 'Take a look around. There you have Cofidis with the bus, the camping car, the big truck and the small truck. All of the suitcases – not bags but suitcases – are in the shower area where the riders are. You've got a soigneur looking after you all the time. But look at the guys from Bookmaker. They're on their own and their bags are by the back of the truck. The riders are coming in and taking their own bags to the showers. You might get better money with them, but the comfort you'll have with someone like Cofidis is fantastic.' He saw that I was right and accepted their offer to turn pro in 2005.

I didn't have any qualms about him turning pro at all, but I made it clear to him that it wasn't going to be easy, that he'd be compared to me until he made a name for himself. If he'd been a footballer that wouldn't have happened, but because he'd chosen the same sport as me, one where I'd made a name for myself, it was automatically going to be hard and he had to be prepared to accept that. At the same time, I've always told him that cycling has given me everything that I have. I've seen the world, I speak three languages, I've made a name for myself and I got some good results. Consequently, I can't see any reason why my son shouldn't go into bike racing if he's got the quality to do it and he's got a good education behind him.

Another thing I said to Nicolas is that because he is a Roche, he always needs to be careful what impression he gives, that to some extent he's a target because of his name. I told him early on that if he does even the slightest thing wrong, everyone will know about it because people will be expecting more of him.

I've also been asked if I had any fears about him going into the sport because of doping, but I've had none at all. I think making it clear to a child that doping is cheating is part of the education you give them, just as you would tell them not to spit in the street or steal from shops. You have to make it clear that there is no shortcut to winning races or being successful. You've got to stick on the straight and narrow because cheating always backfires some day. If you say that, then there's a good chance your child won't cheat.

I honestly don't think there's any limit to what Nicolas can do. He's got a huge amount of talent, enough to finish on the podium of a major tour if all goes well for him. But I think he wants to advance too quickly, which has led to problems with his focus. He doesn't concentrate completely and is always burning up energy thinking about what could be, what might be, what will never be. I always try to calm him down because, although he always looks very calm on the outside, the fire is always burning on the inside.

I also feel that sometimes he doesn't listen closely enough to the advice I offer him. But, let's face it, none of us listen to our parents all of the time, do we? I'm not saying that if he listened to me he would be better, but I don't think he realises what an asset I could be to him. He does listen to a lot of people but in some instances I'm not sure they are necessarily the right ones.

One incident at last year's Critérium du Dauphiné sums it up. I was sitting down with Nicolas and his team boss at Ag2r, Vincent Lavenu, who was a teammate of mine at Fagor. Lavenu was telling him what a great time triallist I was, that I never left anything to chance – my gear was always calculated, my tyres, my bike, the wind, my race line, my recce – everything was programmed and planned in advance. You would have thought that having said all this Lavenu or Nicolas might have asked me for advice about the time trial he was about to ride in Grenoble, but they didn't.

Later on, I went out with Nicolas on his recce of the course. At one point I suggested: 'Maybe you should try this hill out of the saddle because you'll get a lot more power and leverage, and it might also be good for your legs.' He told me he didn't plan to do that because some testing he'd done in a wind tunnel had shown that he puts out so many more watts when he is down on his tri-bars than he does when standing on the pedals.

I understood his point, but asked him: 'Does the wind tunnel take into consideration you've been five days on the road, you've got a headwind, you've got a 45km time trial that constantly goes up and down to deal with? Does it take into consideration the fact that for 3km you're going to be under pressure, that you're going to have to go down a gear at the top of the climb to ride fast again on the flat? The wind tunnel doesn't take all this into consideration. It's OK for giving guidelines, but you've got to rely on your own knowledge and feelings as well.'

In fact, I've regularly said to him that time trialling is one area where being fully focused could make a big difference to his performance. I always used to get on to him about the importance of a recce and of getting into your own bubble. You've got to cut yourself off from the outside world, but that day Nicolas spent the three hours before his start sitting in the team bus. I told him that I'd have been in a hotel room and would only have come down to the bus an hour or so before the start. Instead, he had his seven teammates coming in after doing their own race and shouting their mouths off about how it had gone. If you've done a recce in the morning, you know in your own mind which gear you're going to ride, you know where you're probably going to gain time and lose time. But if you've got guys coming on the bus and giving their version of the stage, you cannot help but listen to what they're saying, which will certainly disrupt what you're thinking.

To an extent, he hasn't had the people around him to take him to the next level. If he was working with Bjarne Riis or Johan Bruyneel – and I mean no disrespect to Vincent Lavenu, Julien Jurdie and the rest, who are great guys – I'm sure he'd realise how important the small details are. Nicolas needs a team manager who can tell it to him straight, who can say to him: 'This is not good enough, end of story.'

Having said all this, I also realise that a lot of people tell me that I'm very hard on Nicolas. I know that a lot of them pat him on the back and tell him they're proud of what he's done because he is still a young kid in their eyes. They think he's still learning and that his time will come. But if I were to be like that as well would I be doing him a favour? So, yes, I am hard sometimes, but I'm just trying to pull him back down to earth. I don't want him to have regrets when it's all over.

Consequently, when I talk to him I give it exactly as I see it, although it's never simply a case of me wanting him to do things as I used to. It'll never be: 'I this and I that . . .' What I want to give him is food for thought. In the end, whether he listens or not is not a problem because, ultimately, he's the one who's pedalling and I can't express how much pleasure I get from seeing him do that. I'd like to be at more races to see how he's getting on. I don't need to be associated with Nicolas's success, but what I'd like most of all is to help him take shortcuts towards that success.

One of the main reasons I haven't been able to see Nicolas racing more often is because my girlfriend Sophie has been battling against serious illness for the past two years. In April 2010, the same month Florian returned to school, Sophie was diagnosed with breast cancer, which was another huge shock. She underwent chemotherapy initially and later had radiotherapy and an operation. She had every side-effect to the treatment that it was possible to get, but she fought incredibly hard to get through it. In November 2011, Sophie's treatment finally came to an end and a few months on she's back at work part-time and we're both fully involved in completing the renovations to our house.

CHAPTER 16

NO BACKING OFF

I've always looked at cycling as a big wheel full of spokes. One spoke was myself, one was my family, one was my team, another was my mechanics, then there were my soigneurs, the public, the press, the television, the radio. Just like a bike wheel, each of those spokes needed to be finely tuned. If they stayed that way, if everyone kept interacting, then that wheel would run dead straight. However, if one of those spokes was removed or even slightly neglected, the wheel would start to wobble.

When I look back on my career, I think my wheel always ran fairly straight. In fact, it has kept on running pretty straight since I retired. I am aware that some people don't view my career in the same way, seeing it as a bit of a rollercoaster ride where incredible highs were quickly followed by terrible lows. I can understand that viewpoint, but I don't agree with it. In fact, I totally disagree with it because, over the last 40 years, cycling has given me so much.

I don't want this to sound as if I am glossing over the bad times. I'm not. There have been plenty of them, but I believe they have helped to make me the man I am. I can perhaps best explain what I mean by outlining my attitude towards the so-called 'curse of the rainbow jersey', which is believed to condemn the winner of the World Championship to a year of bad luck. I can understand why many people have pointed to my year as world champion as evidence that there is something to that phenomenon, but it's not something that I really think about. I recognise that my season as the world champion was almost a total write-off and that if luck had been with me I could perhaps have won another Tour. However, if I hadn't had my knee problems that year, I might have suffered some other setback, perhaps something even more serious. In other words, whatever happens I believe you have to see the good within the bad.

I am convinced that the key to success in sport, business and any other part of life is not to dwell on setbacks, but to regard them as unavoidable obstacles in life. The obstacles are there for you to get over. The more obstacles you cross, the more interesting your career and your life is. They may be annoying, but you learn from them. There's no point in saying, 'What if . . .?' or 'It could have been . . .' That's the way it was – end of story.

Consequently, when I reflect on my career, I put every aspect of it – all of the victories, defeats, injuries and mistakes – into one big basket. Seeing my career from that perspective, I cannot help but be happy.

It is now 40 years since I made my racing debut and my passion for the sport is as strong as it's ever been. It's where I get my kicks. I could not not ride my bike. It once provided me with a career and it's still my way of releasing pressure, of giving myself time to think and reflect. I've lost count of the number of deals and problems I've resolved just by taking the time to go out for a ride. I can be in a mental cul-de-sac, desperately trying to find a solution to a problem, then I go out on the bike and suddenly things click into place. I end up thinking: 'That was so easy. Why didn't I think of it before?'

The only time I've really disconnected from the bike was immediately after I retired from racing when I was looking for something else to do because I'd ridden the bike for so long. I tried swimming, running, a bit of tennis, and one day I asked myself: 'Why the hell am I doing this?' I was doing it because everyone says that after riding for so long and with such commitment, you're bound to end up saturated with cycling. But I reflected on all the enjoyment I'd got out of cycling both before I turned pro and during 13 years of top-level competition and thought: 'Why not just ride the bike rather than look for something else?'

In fact, there was actually a moment when I realised that cycling meant much more to me than racing, than it being my profession. In 1994, I was building a house in Ireland and renovating another. I was separated from Lydia and living on my own for the first time. Sitting at home one night, I thought: 'Why am I bothering with all this other stuff when I got so much from riding my bike?' The only bike I had was one on which I'd won the Giro or the Tour, I forget which. It was stored in the attic and when I brought it down, the tubulars had no air in them and the Look pedals had no shoes to go with them. I didn't even have a pump or any kit.

I rang up my old friend Peter Crinnion, who lived a few miles away, and asked him: 'Peter, have you got a pump? I have a bike here and I want to pump up the tyres.' He said he could help me out, so I put on some football shorts and tennis shoes, got on the bike and rode straight down to Peter's house. He saw me coming and went: 'Aaargghhh, get off that bike. That's crazy! Scandalous! You shouldn't be riding that bike with flat tyres.'

Once we had sorted the bike out, I went off and did 30 miles or so. My ride ended with a climb back up to my house. Before tackling it, I stopped at the shop at the bottom and bought about five or six Mars bars and a bottle of Lucozade, sat down and went through most of them, thinking how nice it felt because I was so, so hungry and absolutely knackered. I had a real feeling of exhilaration.

That was the only time in 40 years I've really backed off from cycling and I realised immediately how much I had missed it. Since then there have been periods when I've spent five or six months away from the bike due to business or other distractions, but I am always keen to get going again, knowing all too well that it will hurt. After a few weeks, a minimum amount of condition comes and the spark is there again.

That spark also brings out my love of competition. Although I always insist that I will never ever race again, I still love to participate. For me, cycling's no longer a matter of putting a number on my back and racing, but I love going out with Nicolas and Alexis or with the local lads on a Sunday, having fun and, now and again when I feel the form is good, turning it on a bit. The guys I ride with always say that you've got to be careful when you go out with Stephen. They know that if any of them crosses a certain line, there will always be payback. When things come together and I'm feeling strong again, I love having that one day when I can go out and give back some of the pain they've been dishing out to me.

That same feeling provided a good deal of my motivation when I was racing. It could come in absolutely any event. A race was never too small not to want to win it. And, once I'd won a race, I'd immediately be looking to win my next. I never felt like sitting back. I always wanted to go forwards even when I was injured. Motivation was never and is never my problem. I might lose a bit for 24 hours, but even then I'd say to myself: 'What are you up to, Stephen? You can't be doing this. Get out and do something.'

I also felt that winning a race was compensation for all the hard work I'd done. I'd think to myself: 'I've worked hard for this and I've won. Isn't it a great feeling? But let's get back to work now for the next one.' That meant I never went over the moon about winning races. I was training to win, and when I won I would train for the next. I think a lot of the guys I competed with were like that. They wanted to win wherever they raced. Sean Kelly, for example, was extremely strong in the Classics, but when he went off to the Tour of Switzerland or the Tour of Romandy he didn't just go for training. If he could win, he would try to.

One major benefit of racing in this way is that I know from my own experience that you can win a race when you're at 80 per cent of your best, but can miss out when you're at 100 per cent. Racing is about seeing and trying to take opportunities. I felt the more opportunities I saw or created, the greater my chances of winning. Consequently, I don't think it ever really came into my mind to say: 'Today I'm only training. It doesn't matter about the win.' When you race, you race, and when you train, you train. There are no trophies for training in races.

Wins give you confidence as well, which means winning is a good habit to have. I couldn't go long without getting a result. They nourished me, they helped me get better, they helped me get out training and to train harder. But even on those days when I missed out, I still thought it was important to come away with the feeling that I had been capable of winning. That helped keep my confidence and motivation high.

I don't think most riders today view racing in the same way. Their seasons are more programmed, focusing on a few specific events. I understand why that is, that the rewards for one or two key wins are huge, but I don't think that perspective does the sport any favours. However, that is not to say that I don't admire many of the current generation of riders.

It's impossible not to be impressed by someone like Philippe Gilbert, who's competitive throughout the season as riders always used to be. I also like to watch Cadel Evans and Alberto Contador. Both of them are very clever tactically and have made the most of their strengths. Evans showed that in winning the 2011 Tour, while Contador's achievement in winning the 2009 Tour was incredible, given the way that most of his Astana team, including Lance Armstrong, took sides against him. Having experienced the same thing at Carrera during the 1987 Giro, I understood completely what he was up against and how tough it was to come through and win in those circumstances.

I think the characteristic that stands out in all three of those riders is that they almost always give their all. I imagine that each of them will have some regrets when they retire, but I don't believe that any of them will feel that they didn't try hard enough. I certainly have at least one regret about my own career, and those of you who remember the 1987 edition of Liège-Bastogne-Liège will know exactly what I'm talking about. I never won a Classic and that race was the one that suited me best. I could and perhaps should have won it that year, but I can't really complain about anything that happened to me during that season. It was the year that made me, the season that changed my life.

I realise that some people feel that 1987 didn't change me for the better, that my head was turned by what happened to me, that I got soft and lazy. Unfortunately, that was a label that I had to carry for a long time. But I don't think those people who stuck that label on me knew exactly what I was going through, about the work I did with Dr Müller-Wohlfahrt to get my knee right and the time I spent going to different physicians and specialists. Psychologically, it was very traumatic for me to be world champion but not be able to ride my bike. If I rode 100 yards, I had to turn back because of the severity of the pain in my knee.

Anyone who's ridden a bike knows that when you've had several months off, it takes a long while to get back to your former level. I was playing catch-up all the time. I was world champion but couldn't ride a bike. I was being paid to provide returns, but I couldn't give anything back. A lot of people thought the problem was in my head, because it took so long for anyone to establish what it was exactly. But I kept working and believing that it would come right, and in the end it did, although my form never again reached the level I achieved in 1987.

During the period that Dr Müller-Wohlfahrt was treating me,

he said he thought I had an extraordinary ability to see the positive side of things. That has always been one of my main attributes and still is today now that I'm in business. A lot of that comes from my parents. My mum is a very positive person, while my dad is very calm. But it also came from people like my team boss at La Redoute, Raphaël Géminiani. I remember him convincing me that I could win at the summit of Guzet-Neige on the 1985 Tour of the Midi-Pyrénées after I lost all chances of contending at the 1984 Tour on that very same climb. He was great for motivation and I think his positive approach chimed with mine. It provided a feeling of confirmation, that I was doing the right thing.

I got a similar feeling from Carrera boss Davide Boifava. He helped me out during one of the lowest points in my racing career in 1991, giving me the chance to return to Carrera. When I went back there I took the opportunities when they came, which is something I believe very strongly that all riders should do.

One other slight regret I have about my career is that in my day no one left the sport a millionaire. I know I didn't. However, I feel very fortunate to have competed in the era I did. I believe my generation stood out because of the quality and depth of the star performers. I'm not knocking the current generation by saying that either. If you look back to the Merckx era or to Hinault's early years, there were perhaps just a handful of names that stood out, riders who were recognised as strong stage-race performers such as Bernard Thévenet, Raymond Poulidor, Joop Zoetemelk and Luis Ocaña. But I think in my era there were two handfuls who stood out. Most of them were riders capable of winning both Classics and major tours, and most were competitive right through the season.

I think that made our generation much more interesting for the fans and is one of the reasons why riders from that period are still so highly revered. Any time a fan put on the TV to watch a race, no matter what time of year it was, they would see a lot of very familiar faces in contention. Of course, we didn't wear helmets or glasses either, which made it even easier for fans to recognise and identify with us. Nowadays, the riders are a lot harder to pick out with their identikit shades and helmets. I know they are well rewarded for wearing them, but I think it impacts on their image and personality. I don't know whether today's riders will be as well recognised in 20 years as the riders from my generation are now.

My generation also had a closer relationship with the fans because there were no team buses where we could hide ourselves away. That ensured that the public were able to relate to the riders more and were more aware of us as personalities. Nowadays, there is a lot of talk about results, but not so much about personalities, and I don't think that helps in any sport because personalities draw people in. Back in my day, guys like Delgado, Hinault, Fignon and Kelly were personalities the fans knew all about, men they could relate to. Now the fans might know who won Paris–Roubaix or the Tour de France, but they are less connected to the man and I think that's very unfortunate. Put a guy in front of me in his helmet and glasses and I might recognise the cyclist, but I wouldn't recognise the man.

Even now, despite the fact that 25 years have passed and I'm carrying an extra 15 kilos, that bond with fans remains. I can be in a restaurant and people will come over, congratulate me on my career and ask for an autograph. That never annoys me. You've got to take a step back and ask why it's happening. During my career I gladly gave a lot to the public and to the press. With that in mind, wouldn't it be disappointing if I were totally forgotten?

The recognition is not something I need, but it is nice. It's a reward for the hours that I put in quite voluntarily throughout my career. Everyone likes to be remembered, whether we admit it or not. It's easy for me to say that I could do without it, but I'd only be saying that because I'm getting it. If tomorrow I became totally anonymous, would I be sitting here saying it doesn't bother me? I think deep down it would hurt a little.

The principles that served me well in racing – being positive, hard-working, determined, focused and approachable – have continued to benefit me during my business life. I know that I sometimes go into deals too quickly, just as I did during my racing career. I take things at face value and give my word, and being like that has rebounded on me sometimes. On occasions, it would have been easier to have a manager looking after my interests in order to prevent me getting so involved.

However, the other side to that is that I love wheeling and dealing. When deals come up now I still feel it's like Christmas. I get such a buzz from it. I often think that I should back off with some of my business dealings, but I doubt I ever will because I love doing what I'm doing. I don't ever sit back for long. At the moment I'm working on renovating my house here in Antibes, which is a big project. It has taken a long time to get the plans in order. I'm working on some special cycling projects for 2012 and beyond with a good friend of mine, Sven Thiele from HotChillee, including London–Paris and the Alpine Challenge. They're the kind of events that I love as they are all about sharing passion for the sport. I've also taken over my camp in Majorca and am revamping that.

Florian's illness has also led me in another direction. Once he was on the road to recovery, I started to do a few charity events and realised how much good these events were doing, not only for the different charities involved but also for those taking part. I decided I only wanted to be part of events where I knew where the money was going and spoke to a friend of mine in Cork, Aiden Crowley, who felt the same way. Aiden does something every year for his sister, who has learning disabilities.

We decided we wanted to know exactly where the proceeds for

our event went and that led to the idea of the Stephen Roche Tour de Cure. We approach four or five hospitals or associations in the Cork area and say: 'We've got the budget to buy you something, what do you need?' We've bought specialised beds for the school that Aiden's sister attends, defibrillators for the local 24-hour response unit, and we're contributing towards the purchase of a scanner that will help to detect cancer. As our admin costs are covered by a variety of sponsors, every penny that comes in goes to the different associations that we select each year.

I really enjoy doing it. In 2011 we raised €49,000 and had 1,700 people taking part. Having gone through all I have with Florian and met all kinds of people during that time, I can see how much the 10 or 20 grand that we've given to these people means. However, although I'm hoping that the Tour de Cure will continue to expand, I certainly don't see myself as some kind of budding Lance Armstrong figure in that area.

More than anything, I simply don't have the time to be able to do that. Juggling all these different balls at the same time does mean that my life tends to be pretty frenetic. However, I love going to bed at night feeling like I've put another brick in the wall, that I've achieved something during the day. Even though in three years' time the house will be done and the business in Majorca will hopefully have taken off, I always believe there will be something else out there. I'm not going to fool myself by saying: 'In three years' time I will be OK, so I can back off.' In fact, I don't know whether I would enjoy backing off. I get such a buzz out of doing things, and that still includes riding my bike.

INDEX

ACKNOWLEDGEMENTS

I would like to give special thanks to my children, Nicolas, Christel, Alexis and Florian. I am immensely proud of all four of you. It's been a hard road for all of you at times, and it makes me extremely happy to see what you have already achieved in your lives. My thanks also to Lydia, I know things have not always been easy between us, but you have never wavered in your love and support for our children. I also appreciate hugely the assistance you have given me during this project.

To Mam and Dad, I would like to express my gratitude for setting me on the right path and always being there when I have needed you. So much of what I have achieved is the result of the principles you instilled in all of the Roche children and the happy upbringing you gave us. My gratitude also goes to my brothers and sisters and the rest of the Roche clan for all of the encouragement and support you have given me over the years.

I owe a great debt to a great many people who assisted me during the course of my racing career, including everyone at the Orwell Wheelers, particularly Noel O'Neill, Paddy Doran, the late Noel Hammond and Steve Flynn, who sadly passed away before this book was published, to Peter Crinnion, to the late Joe Daly in Dundrum, to Pat McQuaid, Mickey Weigant and Claude Escalon at the ACBB, to Patrick Valcke, to Maurice de Muer, who died just before this book was published, to Raphaël Géminiani, to Hans-Wilhelm Müller-Wohlfahrt for his vital assistance with my knee problem and for prolonging my racing career, to Davide Boifava and his staff at Carrera, to Eddy Schepers, Sean and Linda Kelly, Martin Earley, Paul Kimmage and David Walsh. In addition I would like to thank so many others who know themselves as my friends and colleagues. I can't mention you all individually, but you know who you are.

Special thanks is due to my partner Sophie and her two girls, Juliette and Caroline.

I would also like to thank all those who provided their assistance and insight during the course of this project, including Frank Quinn, Graham Watson, Erik Breukink, Tony Doyle, Brian Holm and Daniel Friebe.

I would like to express my gratitude to my literary agent David Luxton and everyone at Yellow Jersey for their help with this book, particularly my editor Matt Phillips, Justine Taylor, Stephen Parker, Fiona Murphy and Claire Williamson.

I would also like to express my particular appreciation to Peter Cossins for his commitment at every stage of this project.

Thanks too to my good friend and business partner Sven Thiele, who has been a driving force behind this book and has provided extensive feedback.